M000105720

Alphabet Fun

For Little Ones

Activities For Preschoolers

Published by HighReach Learning®, Inc.

HighReach Learning® Inc. is committed to creating high-quality, developmentally appropriate learning materials that facilitate a creative, integrated, hands-on learning experience for the whole child. Our goal is to enhance the development of readiness skills and encourage a love for learning in every young child.

Project Director: Heather Muench-Williams
Editors: Paige Russo, Angela Reese
Copy Editors: Pamela R. Jarrell, Lane Standefer
Cover Design: Wes Whalen
Design: Kerry Meier
Illustrations: Lisa Gillen, Kerry Meier, Knox Crowell
Layout: Gayle Graham

© 2006, HighReach Learning® Inc., Charlotte, North Carolina. The purchase of this material entitles the buyer to copy activities and reproducibles for classroom use only—not for commercial resale. Reproduction of these materials for an entire school or district is prohibited. No part of this book may be reproduced (except as noted above), stored in a retrieval system, or transmitted in any form or by any means (mechanically, electronically, recording, etc.) without the prior written consent of HighReach Learning® Inc.

Printed in the USA. All rights reserved.   ISBN 1-57332-379-9

Table of Contents

© HighReach Learning® Inc.

Introduction

Alphabet Fun for Little Ones provides hundreds of activity ideas that cover every letter of the alphabet. The purpose of this book is to provide activities that will enhance and enrich your learning environment. This book can be used to inspire ideas or as a supplement to other teaching materials that you may be using.

There is a chapter for each letter. Each chapter contains a variety of activities that reinforce that letter. Children and classrooms are unique; teach the letters in the order that makes sense for your particular situation. There is no suggested length of time that should be spent on each letter. Introduction of new letters depends on the needs and interests of the child or the class. Activities are included for both short and long vowel sounds. If you prefer to focus on only one sound for each letter, choose the activities for either the long or short sound consistently for all the vowels.

Various patterns, reproducible pages, and displays are included in each chapter. Feel free to use these materials in any way you like to meet the needs of your child or class. For instance, you may wish to use the letter patterns to create bulletin boards when you introduce new letters. You may also wish to display the entire alphabet in one area of the classroom. Make sure to display the materials at the children's eye level.

Maintain a safe environment at all times. Consider the maturity of the children as you select activities and offer only those that the children can carry out safely. Provide supervision to be sure that materials are used appropriately. Be aware of choking hazards. Always check with the children's families before serving any food. Any food can be dangerous to a child who is allergic to it! Raw eggs often contain salmonella, which can be especially dangerous to young children. Do not allow children to handle raw eggs or taste mixtures that contain raw eggs. If you would like for children to help prepare a recipe that calls for using raw eggs, substitute pasteurized eggs or a pasteurized egg product. Pasteurization destroys salmonella. Cooking also eliminates salmonella, so once foods are cooked, eggs do not present a problem. All recipes refer to degrees Fahrenheit.

© HighReach Learning® Inc.

© HighReach Learning® Inc.

The Letter A

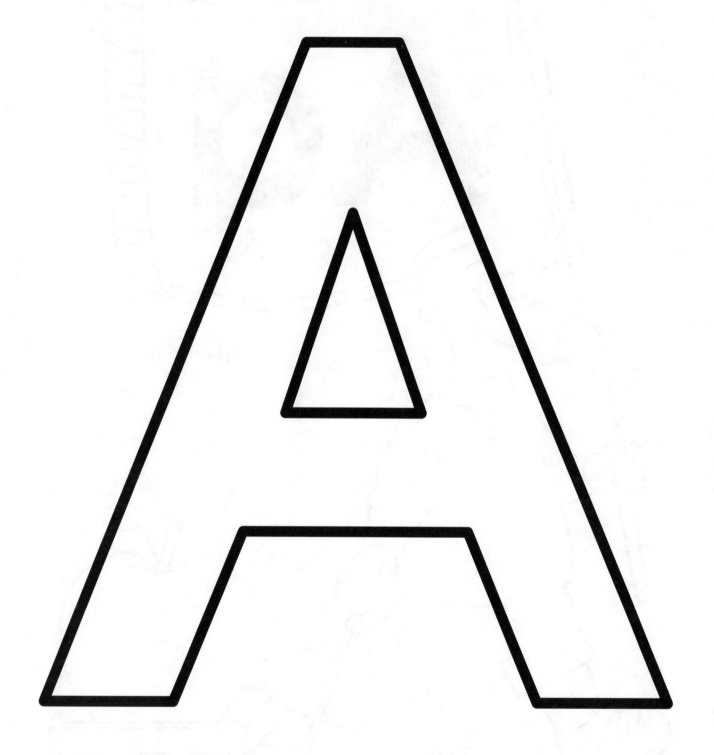

The Letter A

© HighReach Learning® Inc.

Language Activities

Introduce Alvin Alligator and the Letter A

Decorate a copy of the Letter A Display (page 5) as desired. Point to Alvin Alligator on the display. Invite the children to guess what type of animal Alvin is. If necessary explain that he is an alligator. You may wish to share the rhyme below several times and invite the children to join in.

ALVIN ALLIGATOR

Alvin raises apples;
They have lots of juice inside.
But when he sees an ant,
Alvin runs away to hide.

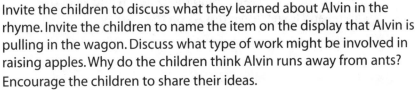

Invite the children to discuss what they learned about Alvin in the rhyme. Invite the children to name the item on the display that Alvin is pulling in the wagon. Discuss what type of work might be involved in raising apples. Why do the children think Alvin runs away from ants? Encourage the children to share their ideas.

Point to both the capital A and the lowercase a on the display. Explain that these are both ways to write the letter. Explain that Alvin likes the letter A best because it is the first letter of his name. Help the children decide if they know anyone whose name begins with A.

Talk About Letter A Words

Invite the children to talk about words they know that begin with the letter A. Write any suggestions down on sentence strips, a large sheet of paper, or chart paper. Attach the words to the wall at the children's eye level. Some familiar word suggestions are:

Short Sounds:
apple
ant
address
astronaut
alphabet

Long Sounds:
ape
apron
acorn

apple   address   astronaut   alphabet   ant

Explain that all of these words begin with the letter A, but the letter A makes more than one sound. In the words *apple* and *ant,* the letter makes the same sound as in Alvin. In the words *acorn* and *apron*, the sound of the letter is the same as its name.

> ☆ *Learning Extension:* Invite the children to clap for the syllables of words that begin with the letter A (ap-ple, ant, a-corn, a-pron, etc.).

Language Activities

Share the Letter A Rebus Rhyme

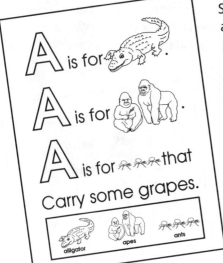

Share the Letter A Rebus Rhyme (page 15) to develop a sense of rhythm and rhyme and to practice naming pictures. Show the display as you recite the rhyme several times. Afterwards, point to each picture on the chart and encourage the children to name it. Discuss each picture and invite the children to share times when they have seen similar items.

☆ **Learning Extension:** Talk about the letter A. Look at all of the words on the display. Help the children locate the letter A. Explain that the letter A can be written more than one way. Point to the capital A on the display and then point to the lowercase a. Help the children find all of the capital and lowercase letter A's on the display.

Create Letter A Rhyme Books

Give each child a copy of the Letter A Rhyme Book (page 16) and crayons or markers. Invite the children to point to the pictures as you read the text. Encourage the children to decorate the pictures as desired. Cut along the dotted lines and stack the pages in order. Staple the pages together. Invite the children to write their names on the rhyme books. Assist the children as needed.

☆ **Learning Extension:** Invite a child to "read" his/her Letter A Rhyme Book to you. Encourage the child to point to the letter A in the book.

Practice Saying Address

Print each child's name and address on an index card. Invite each child to look at the address on the index card. Explain that this is the child's address; you may wish to point out that the word *address* starts with the letter A. Encourage the child to repeat the address after you. Helping the children learn their addresses is an essential safety skill.

The Letter A

8

© HighReach Learning® Inc.

Science Activities

Compare Fresh and Dried Apples

Peel, core, and slice apples. Put the slices in a mixture of equal parts lemon juice and water. Soak for five to ten minutes. Drain well and pat dry. Let the children help you spread the apple slices in a single layer on baking sheets. Invite the children to predict what might happen to the apples if you put them in the oven. Dry the apples in the oven for two to three hours at 150°. Once the apples are dry and have cooled, core and slice some fresh apples. Give each child a slice of fresh apple and a slice of dried apple. Encourage the children to describe how the two types of apples are alike and how they are different, and mention that the word *apple* begins with the letter A. *(Caution: Only an adult should use the knife and put the baking sheets in and out of the oven.)*

Explore Apples on a Balance Scale

Show the children two apples. Encourage the children to look closely at the apples and hold them. Show the children a balance scale. Explain that it is used to find out whether two items weigh the same or not. Ask the children to predict which apple they think is heavier. Invite them to share their ideas. Place an apple on each side of the scale to find out which is heavier. Encourage the children to compare the results to their predictions. Help the children realize that the word *apple* begins with the letter A.

Talk About Air

Learn About Ants

Put a few teaspoons of sugar on a paper plate and a few teaspoons of salt on another paper plate. Label each plate. Take the children outside and show them the paper plates. Explain that one plate has salt on it and the other has sugar on it. Invite the children to predict which paper plate the ants will like best. Leave the paper plates on the ground for several hours or overnight, then take the children back outside to observe the plates. Encourage the children to describe what they see. Most likely, the plate containing the sugar will be covered with ants. Explain that ants like the sweetness of the sugar and that the word *ant* begins with the letter A. *(Caution: Do not let the children try to touch or pick up the plate covered in ants or the ants themselves.)*

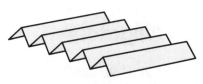

Give each child a sheet of construction paper. If desired, help the child fanfold the paper as shown. Invite the children to wave the fans back and forth in front of their faces. Encourage the children to share what happened. Did they feel the air on their faces when they waved the fans back and forth? During the discussion mention that the word *air* begins with the letter A.

☆ *Learning Extension:* Give the children paper straws and cotton balls. Invite the children to blow the cotton balls with the straws. Help the children notice that the air they are blowing through the straws makes the cotton balls move.

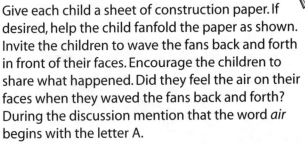

© HighReach Learning® Inc.

The Letter A

Large Muscle Activities

Play Ring Around the Apple

Place a real or plastic apple on the floor and have the children hold hands and form a circle around it. As the children move around the apple, share the song at right and invite them to join in. At the end of the song, invite the children to gently sit down. You may wish to mention that the word *apple* begins with the letter A.

RING AROUND THE APPLE
(tune: "Ring Around the Rosie")

Ring around the apple,
Ring around the apple,
Dipple, dapple,
We all fall down!

Carry Apples on Spoons

Give each child a large spoon. Place an apple on the spoon and invite the child to move across the room without dropping it. Challenge the child to move faster each time he/she moves across the room!

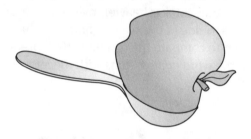

☆ *Learning Extension:* Gather a small group of children to play a game. Divide the children into two teams. Have the teams form lines several feet apart so that the players that are first in line face each other. Give the first player in one line a large spoon and an apple. Ask the child to carry the apple on the spoon across to the first player on the other team. Continue playing the game until each child has had a turn through the line.

Toss Paper Bag Acorns

Create paper bag acorns using small paper lunch bags as shown. Place a laundry basket or small box a few feet away from a child. Invite the child to toss the paper bag acorns into the basket. If the child is having trouble, move the basket closer. If the child needs to be challenged, move the basket farther away. Continue the activity as long as the child shows interest, and mention that the word *acorn* begins with the letter A.

Move Like Alligators

Invite the children to show you how they think an alligator might move. Give suggestions as needed, such as crawling on all fours, pretending to swim, moving fast, etc. As the children move, mention that the word *alligator* begins with the letter A.

The Letter A

© HighReach Learning® Inc.

Art Activities

Create Apples

Give each child a large paper plate and red paint. Provide sponges or paintbrushes for the children to use. Invite the children to decorate the plates to represent apples. The children may also wish to tear or cut pieces of green construction paper to represent leaves. Provide the children with glue or tape to attach the leaves to their apples. Assist the children as needed.

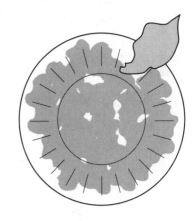

☆ **Learning Extension:** Help a child realize that the word *apple* begins with the letter A. As the child watches, print the word *"Apple"* on an index card. Use a highlighter for the A and crayons for the other letters. Invite the child to trace the letter A. Tape the index card to the back of the child's paper plate apple.

Fingerprint Ants

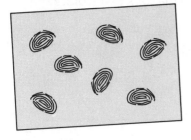

Give the children large sheets of brown construction paper and washable-ink pads. Demonstrate how to press a finger onto the washable-ink pad and make prints on the paper. Invite the children to fingerprint ants on their papers as desired, and mention that the word *ants* begins with the letter A.

Create Tactile Letter A's

Give each child a copy of the capital letter A (page 6), an old paintbrush, and a shallow dish of glue. Invite the children to trace the letter A with their fingers. Encourage the children to spread glue on their letter A's as desired. Provide the children with small bathroom cups filled with sand, salt, or rice. Invite the children to shake the sand, salt, or rice onto the glue. Set aside to dry. After the glue dries, invite the children to trace their tactile letter A's with their fingers. How does the A feel? Use descriptive words such as bumpy, rough, etc. as you interact with the child.

Art Activities

Make Alphabet Soup

Give each child a paper bowl, scissors, and old magazines or newspapers. Explain to the children that they are going to make alphabet soup. You may wish to help the children realize that the word alphabet begins with the letter A. Invite the children to cut or tear letters from the magazine. Give the children old paintbrushes and shallow dishes of glue. Invite the children to spread glue on the inside of the bowl and add the letter cutouts to the glue to create a bowl of alphabet soup.

Trace Arms

Give each child a large sheet of paper. Invite the child to place his/her arm on the paper. Trace around the child's arm with a crayon or marker. After you finish, show the child the tracing. You may wish to help the child realize the word *arm* begins with the letter A. Give the child crayons and markers to decorate the arm as desired.

Make Letter A Collages

Give a child old newspapers or magazines and scissors. Invite the child to search for the letter A in the newspapers or magazines. The child may wish to tear or cut the letters out. Give the child a sheet of paper and a glue stick. Encourage the child to attach the letter A cutouts to the paper as desired. Assist the child as needed.

> ☆ *Learning Extension:* If you are working with a group of children, invite them to work together to make one big letter A collage. If you have bulletin board, butcher, or chart paper, you may even wish to cut the paper in the shape of the letter A. Help the children locate and cut or tear out large examples of the letter from captions and headlines. Have the children glue all the letter cutouts to the paper.

The Letter A

© HighReach Learning® Inc.

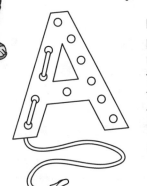

Small Muscle Activities

Explore Letter A Lacing Cards

Draw several block letter A's on posterboard using the pattern on page 6 and cut out. Use a hole punch to make a series of holes around each letter cutout. Vary the number of holes so that some will be easier to lace than others. Tie a length of yarn to one hole and wrap the free end with tape. Be sure the yarn can wrap around the letter twice. Set out the letter A lacing cards. Assist the children as needed as they explore the lacing cards.

Match Felt Apples

Cut simple matching pairs of apple shapes from assorted colors of felt as shown. Provide the children with felt apples and a felt board. Invite the children to place the apples on and off the felt board as desired. Encourage the children to find the matching apples. Assist the children as needed.

☆ *Learning Extension:* Cut enough felt apples to create patterns. Create a simple pattern on the felt board and invite a child to copy the pattern. You may wish to challenge the child to create his/her own pattern.

Create the Letter A With Playdough

Attach several copies of the letter A pattern (page 6) to old file folders or posterboard to create letter A mats. You may wish to laminate the mats or cover them with clear contact paper. Provide the children with playdough and the letter A mats. Invite the children to use the playdough to create letter A's on the mats. Praise the children for their efforts and assist as needed.

Create the Letter A in Damp Sand

Add a small amount of water to a sand table or basin of sand. Invite the children to practice making the letter A in the damp sand. You may need to model how to do this. The children may wish to trace your letter A or attempt to create their own letters in the sand.

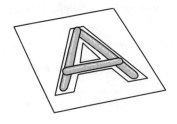

Cooking with Alvin Alligator
Letter A Recipes

ANTS ON A LOG

cream cheese
pretzel rods
raisins

Spread cream cheese on pretzel rods. Provide the children with the pretzel logs and raisins. Encourage the children to arrange the raisins on the pretzel logs to represent ants. You may wish to remind the children that Alvin Alligator does not like ants!

A-PLUS AVOCADO DIP

2 large ripe avocados
8 ounces sour cream
2 medium tomatoes, chopped
1½ Tbsp. lime juice

Show the children an avocado. Invite the children to predict what the avocado looks like inside. Help the children notice that the word *avocado* starts with the letter A. Cut the avocados in half. Show the children the inside of the avocados, remove the pits, and then mash them with a fork. Mix the avocados, sour cream, chopped tomatoes, and lime juice. Cover and chill the dip for several hours. Serve each child avocado dip with crackers, bread, or vegetables for dipping!

AMAZING APPLESAUCE MUFFINS

1 cup flour
1½ tsp. baking powder
¼ cup sugar
¼ tsp. pumpkin pie spice
1 egg
4 Tbsp. butter, melted
1 tsp. vanilla
1 cup applesauce
1 Tbsp. sugar mixed with ½ tsp. cinnamon

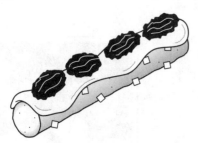

Preheat the oven to 400°. In a small bowl combine flour, baking powder, sugar, and pumpkin pie spice until blended. Add egg, butter, vanilla, and applesauce until well blended. Spoon batter into a muffin tin. Sprinkle with sugar and cinnamon mixture. Bake for about 20 minutes.

Amazing applesauce muffins make a tasty treat!

AWESOME APPLE PIES

1 ready-made pie crust
1 can of apple pie filling
cinnamon sugar

Preheat the oven to 425°. Invite each child to help you with any of the steps that are appropriate as you prepare individual apple pies. Cut two circles of the pie crust using a large round cookie cutter. Put a spoonful of pie filling in the middle of one circle. Place the second dough circle on top and sprinkle with cinnamon sugar. Use a plastic fork to crimp the edges. Use the fork to pierce a few holes in the top of each pie to allow steam to escape. Bake for 10-15 minutes or until brown. Allow the pies to cool. Serve each child an awesome apple pie for a delicious treat!

© HighReach Learning® Inc.

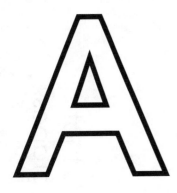 is for  .

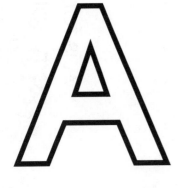 is for  .

 is for that

Carry some grapes.

alligator   apes   ants

A is for alligator.

A is for ants that carry some grapes.

My A Rhyme

Name

A is for apes.

The Letter A

16

© HighReach Learning® Inc.

© HighReach Learning® Inc.

17

The Letter B

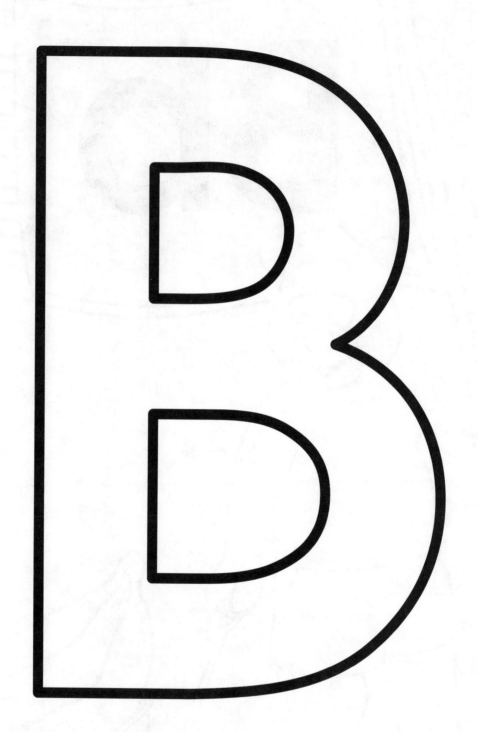

The Letter B

© HighReach Learning® Inc.

Language Activities

Introduce Benny Bear and the Letter B

Decorate a copy of the Letter B Display (page 17) as desired. Point to Benny Bear on the display. Invite the children to guess what type of animal Benny is. If necessary explain that he is a bear. You may wish to share the rhyme below several times and invite the children to join in.

BENNY BEAR

Benny is a bear
Who has a lot of fun.
He pulls around bananas
In the rain or in the sun.

Invite the children to discuss what they learned about Benny in the rhyme. Invite the children to name the item on the display that Benny is pulling in the wagon. Discuss what type of work might be involved in growing bananas. Do the children like to eat bananas? Encourage the children to share their ideas.

Point to both the capital B and the lowercase b on the display. Explain that these are both ways to write the letter. Explain that Benny likes the letter B best because it is the first letter of his name. Help the children decide if they know anyone whose name begins with B.

Talk About Letter B Words

Invite the children to talk about words they know that begin with the letter B. Write any suggestions down on sentence strips, a large sheet of paper, or chart paper. Attach the words to the wall at the children's eye level. Some familiar word suggestions are:

ball	beans	bell	bowling
baker	bear	berry	bubble
banana	bee	bird	butterfly

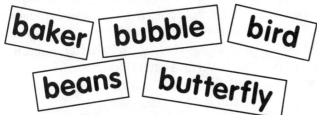

☆ *Learning Extension:* Invite the children to clap for the syllables of words that begin with the letter B (bub-ble, bear, bowl-ing, ba-na-na).

Discuss Foods That Are Baked

Label a sheet of chart paper "Foods We Can Bake." Challenge the children to think of foods that are baked. Write down each child's answer. When the children finish, read their suggestions back to them, and help them realize that the word *bake* begins with B.

Foods We Can Bake

biscuits	cake
bread	meatloaf
brownies	potato
pizza	pie
cookies	

☆ *Learning Extension:* Help the children think of foods that are baked that begin with the letter B. Some examples are biscuits, bagels, brownies, banana bread, and beans.

© HighReach Learning® Inc.

The Letter B

Language Activities

Share the Letter B Rebus Rhyme

Share the Letter B Rebus Rhyme (page 27) to develop a sense of rhythm and rhyme and to practice naming pictures. Show the display as you recite the rhyme several times. Afterwards, point to each picture on the chart and encourage the children to name it. Discuss each picture and invite the children to share times when they have seen similar items.

☆ *Learning Extension:* Talk about the letter B. Look at all of the words on the display. Help the children locate the letter B. Explain that the letter B can be written more than one way. Point to the capital B on the display and then point to the lowercase b. Help the children find all of the capital and lowercase letter B's on the display.

Create Letter B Rhyme Books

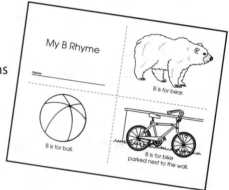

Give each child a copy of the Letter B Rhyme Book (page 28) and crayons or markers. Invite the children to point to the pictures as you read the text. Encourage the children to decorate the pictures as desired. Cut along the dotted lines and stack the pages in order. Staple the pages together. Invite the children to write their names on the rhyme books. Assist the children as needed.

☆ *Learning Extension:* Invite a child to "read" his/her Letter B Rhyme Book to you. Encourage the child to point to the letter B in the book.

Discuss Favorite Books

Invite the children to share their favorite books with the class. Each child can pretend to read the pictures of the book to the class. You may wish to help the children realize that the word *book* begins with the letter B.

☆ *Learning Extension:* Work with a child one-on-one. Invite the child to find the letter B throughout the book. Assist the child as needed.

Imitate Buzzing Patterns

Encourage the children to imitate patterns of buzzing sounds! Invite the children to make buzzing sounds like bees, and mention that the word *buzz* begins with the letter B. Then invite the children to copy your buzzing sounds. Begin with simple patterns and move to more challenging ones as the children are able to imitate you. Some examples are given below. Capital letters indicate loud sounds and lowercase letters indicate soft ones. If possible, record the children making the sounds and then play the recording back to them.

❖ BUZZ buzz
❖ BUZZ BUZZ buzz
❖ buzz buzz BUZZ
❖ BUZZ BUZZ BUZZ <pause> buzz
❖ buzz <pause> BUZZ BUZZ

The Letter B

© HighReach Learning® Inc.

Science Activities

Make Bubble Bottles

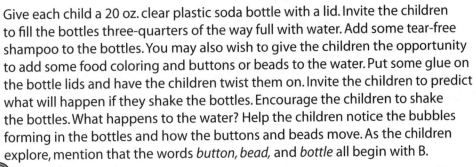

Give each child a 20 oz. clear plastic soda bottle with a lid. Invite the children to fill the bottles three-quarters of the way full with water. Add some tear-free shampoo to the bottles. You may also wish to give the children the opportunity to add some food coloring and buttons or beads to the water. Put some glue on the bottle lids and have the children twist them on. Invite the children to predict what will happen if they shake the bottles. Encourage the children to shake the bottles. What happens to the water? Help the children notice the bubbles forming in the bottles and how the buttons and beads move. As the children explore, mention that the words *button, bead,* and *bottle* all begin with B.

Which Balls Bounce?

Show the children a variety of balls such as basketballs, tennis balls, foam footballs, and soccer balls. Invite the children to explore the balls. Challenge the children to discover which balls bounce and which balls do not bounce. Invite the children to share their ideas about why some of the balls bounce and others do not, and mention that the words *ball* and *bounce* both begin with the letter B.

Listen to Bells

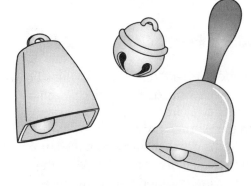

Provide the children with assorted bells such as hand bells, jingle bells, and a cow bell. Invite the children to explore the bells. Encourage the children to talk about how the bells sound. Challenge the children to discuss why they think the bells sound different from one another, and mention that the word *bell* begins with the letter B.

☆ **Learning Extension:** Label a sheet of chart paper "Balls We Like Best." Draw a picture of each ball at the bottom of the paper with a column above the ball. Give each child a coding dot sticker. Encourage the children to put the coding dots above the ball they like best. After the children finish, help them discover which ball people like the best and which ball people like the least.

Balls We Like Best			
		●	
●		●	
●		●	●
●	●	●	●
●	●	●	●
🏀	🏈	🎾	⚽

Large Muscle Activities

Make and Blow Bubbles

Collect or make a variety of bubble makers. To make a bubble wand, twist a loop on one end of a pipe cleaner or chenille stem. To make a giant wand, stretch a coat hanger into a loop. Bend down the hook and wrap well with masking tape. You may also wish to thread string or yarn through two drinking straws as shown. Use the following recipe to make bubble solution: Mix 4 cups water, ½ cup liquid detergent, ¼ cup glycerin, and 2 teaspoons sugar together in a large container with a lid. Take the bubble solution and an assortment of bubble makers outside. Challenge the children to see how many different ways they can make bubbles. Some children can make bubbles while others chase them. You may wish to mention that the word *bubbles* begins with the letter B.

Play Butterfly, Butterfly, Bee

Take the children outside. Have the children sit in a circle. Choose one child to be It. It must walk around the outside of the circle and lightly tap each child on the head while saying "butterfly." At any time, It can say "bee!" When It says "bee," the child that has just been tapped must chase It around the circle. If It reaches the empty spot before the other child, the other child becomes It and the game continues. If It does not reach the space before being tagged by the other child, It continues to be It.

Play a Bowling Game

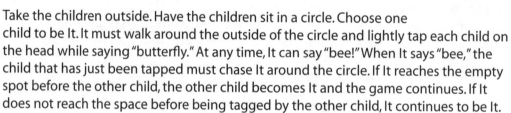
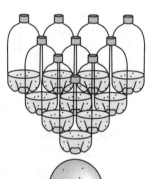

Rinse out ten 2-liter plastic soda bottles and fill them partially with sand. Arrange the bottles like bowling pins. Give the children balls and invite them to practice bowling. Help the children notice how many bottles they knock over as they play. You may also wish to help the children notice that the words *bowling, bottle,* and *ball* all begin with the letter B.

Toss Beanbags on a B

Draw a large bold letter B on a sheet of posterboard. Give the children beanbags. Have the children stand a few feet away from the letter B. Challenge the children to toss their beanbags onto the letter B. Adjust the distance away from the letter B according to the children's abilities. While the children are playing, mention that the word *beanbags* begins with the letter B.

© HighReach Learning® Inc.

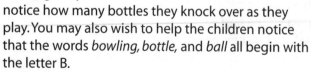

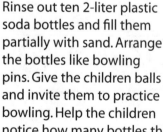

Art Activities

Create Tactile Letter B's

Give each child a copy of the capital letter B (page 18), an old paintbrush, and a shallow dish of glue. Invite the children to trace the letter B with their fingers. Encourage the children to spread glue on their letter B's as desired. Provide the children with small bathroom cups filled with birdseed, sand, or salt. Invite the children to shake the birdseed, sand, or salt onto the glue. Set aside to dry. After the glue dries, invite the children to trace their tactile letter B's with their fingers. How does the B feel? Use descriptive words such as bumpy, rough, and so forth as you interact with the child.

Bubble Wrap Prints

Tape large pieces of bubble wrap to the table. Set out paint, white paper, and paintbrushes near the bubble wrap. Encourage the children to paint on the bubble wrap. They may wish to paint pictures, make designs, or simply spread the paint to coat the bubble wrap. Invite the children to lay the paper on the painted bubble wrap and gently smooth it with their hands. Lift the papers to reveal an interesting design! Encourage the children to describe what they see.

☆ *Learning Extension:* Mention to the children that the word *bubble* begins with the /b/ sound. Challenge the children to think of other words that start with that same sound.

Beautiful Butterflies

Give each child a small zipper-top bag and assorted colors of construction paper scraps. Invite the children to tear the scraps into small pieces and use them to fill their bags. Help the child close the zipper-top bag, pressing out all the air while closing. Next, give each child a spring-type clothespin. Invite the child to use washable markers to decorate the clothespin to represent a butterfly's body. Help the child clip the clothespin to the bag as shown to create a beautiful butterfly, and mention that the words *beautiful* and *butterfly* both begin with the letter B.

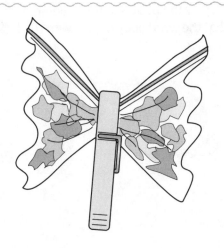

© HighReach Learning® Inc.

The Letter B

Art Activities

Make Letter B Collages

Give a child old newspapers or magazines and scissors. Invite the child to search for the letter B in the newspapers or magazines. The child may wish to tear or cut the letters out. Give the child a sheet of paper and a glue stick. Encourage the child to attach the letter B cutouts to the paper as desired. Assist the child as needed.

☆ *Learning Extension:* If you are working with a group of children, invite them to work together to make one big letter B collage. If you have bulletin board, butcher, or chart paper, you may even wish to cut the paper in the shape of the letter B. Help the children locate and cut or tear out large examples of the letter from captions and headlines. Have the children glue all the letter cutouts to the paper.

Body Tracing

Attach a large sheet of butcher paper to the floor. Invite a child to lie down on the paper. Trace around the child's body. Repeat for all of the children. Give the children crayons and markers and encourage them to decorate their body tracings as desired. Encourage the children to talk about what they are doing as they work. After they finish, cut out each body tracing. Display the bodies at the children's eye level, and mention that the word *body* begins with the letter B.

The Letter B

© HighReach Learning® Inc.

Small Muscle Activities

Explore Letter B Lacing Cards

Draw several block letter B's on posterboard using the pattern on page 18 and cut out. Use a hole punch to make a series of holes around each letter cutout. Vary the number of holes so that some will be easier to lace than others. Tie a length of yarn to one hole and wrap the free end with tape. Be sure the yarn can wrap around the letter twice. Set out the letter B lacing cards. Assist the children as needed as they explore the lacing cards.

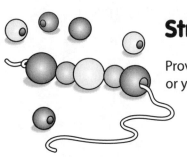

String Beads

Provide assorted sizes of beads and string or yarn. Invite the children to practice stringing the beads as desired. While the children work, mention that the word *bead* begins with the letter B.

> ☆ *Learning Extension:*
> Challenge more advanced children to create patterns with the beads. Start with one characteristic such as size, color, or shape. If the children show readiness, invite them to create more complex patterns with the beads.

Sort Buttons into Bowls

Provide a bag full of buttons and several bowls. Invite the children to sort the buttons as desired into the bowls. They may wish to sort the buttons by size, shape, or color. Assist the children as needed. You may wish to mention that the words *button* and *bowl* both begin with the letter B.

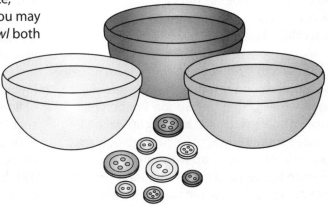

© HighReach Learning® Inc.

The Letter B

Cooking with Benny Bear
Letter B Recipes

FROZEN BUTTERSCOTCH BANANAS

large box of instant butterscotch
    pudding, prepared
bananas

Peel bananas and cut in half. Insert a craft stick into the cut end of each half. Dip each banana in the pudding. Cover a baking sheet with wax paper and arrange the bananas on it. Freeze for two hours or until firm. Serve frozen butterscotch bananas for an un-"B"-table treat!

BODACIOUS BANANA PUDDING

large box of instant vanilla
    pudding, prepared
3-4 bananas
1 box vanilla wafers

Line the bottom of an 8" square pan with vanilla wafers. Top with a layer of sliced bananas. Cover with half the pudding. Repeat layers. Serve each child a bowl of bodacious banana pudding for a delicious treat!

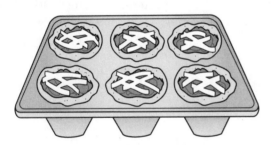

BARBECUE BAKED BEAN BASKETS

1 can refrigerated buttermilk biscuits
1 can barbecue baked beans
½ cup shredded cheese

Preheat the oven to 400°. Put a biscuit into each ungreased muffin cup. Press dough firmly into the bottoms and sides of the cups. Spoon 1 generous tablespoon of beans into each biscuit cup. Bake 11 to 13 minutes or until edges of biscuits are golden brown. Sprinkle each bean cup with shredded cheese. Return to oven and heat 1 minute or until cheese melts. Let cool and serve warm. Serve the children barbecue baked bean baskets for a "B"-licious treat!

BERRY CRISP

⅓ cup sugar
½ cup flour plus 2 Tbsp.
    all-purpose flour, divided
2 cups each sliced strawberries,
    blueberries, and raspberries
¾ cup crushed graham crackers (about 5)
¾ cup quick-cooking oats
½ cup firmly packed light brown sugar
1 tsp. ground cinnamon
1 Tbsp. butter, melted
1 Tbsp. canola oil
1 Tbsp. water
vanilla ice cream or whipped topping

Preheat the oven to 375°. Mix sugar and 2 Tbsp. of flour in a large bowl. Add berries and toss to coat. Place in baking dish. Mix remaining ½ cup flour, crushed graham crackers, oats, brown sugar, cinnamon, butter, canola oil, and water. Sprinkle over berry mixture. Bake for 35 to 40 minutes or until lightly browned. Cool and serve with vanilla ice cream or whipped topping. Serve the children this berry, berry good berry crisp for a tasty snack!

© HighReach Learning® Inc.

B is for .

B is for .

B is for

Parked next to the wall.

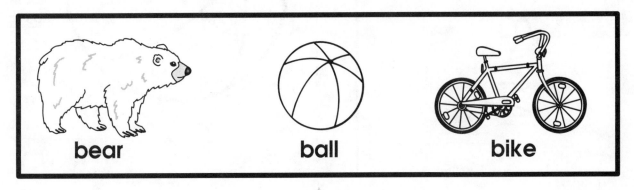

bear   **ball**   **bike**

© HighReach Learning® Inc.

The Letter B

My B Rhyme

Name _____

B is for bear.

B is for bike
parked next to the wall.

B is for ball.

© HighReach Learning® Inc.

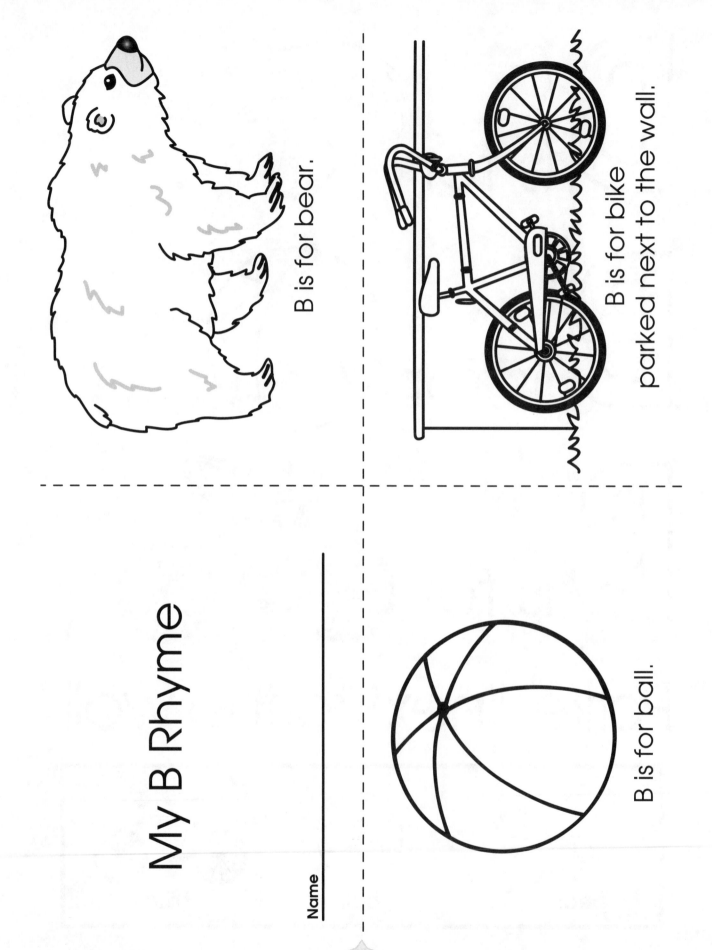

© HighReach Learning® Inc.

29

The Letter C

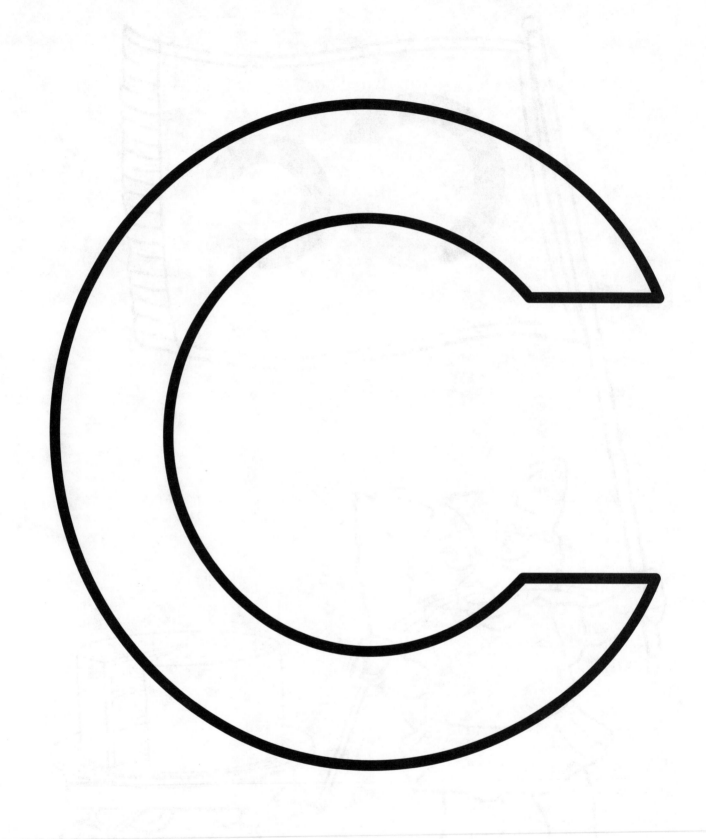

Language Activities

Introduce Callie Cat and the Letter C

Copy and decorate the Letter C Display (page 29) as desired. Point to Callie Cat on the display. Invite the children to guess what type of animal Callie is. If necessary explain that she is a cat. You may wish to share the rhyme below several times and invite the children to join in.

CALLIE CAT

Callie is a cat,
And she can really bake.
She likes to make cookies
And her famous carrot cake.

Invite the children to discuss what they learned about Callie in the rhyme. Invite the children to name the item on the display that Callie is pulling in the wagon. Discuss what type of ingredients might be needed to bake a cake. Encourage the children to share their ideas. You may wish to write the ingredients down. After the children finish, read their ideas back to them.

Point to both the capital C and the lowercase c on the display. Explain that these are both ways to write the letter. Explain that Callie likes the letter C best because it is the first letter of her name. Help the children decide if they know anyone whose name begins with C.

Talk About Letter C Words

Invite the children to talk about words they know that begin with the letter C. Write any suggestions down on sentence strips, a large sheet of paper, or chart paper. Attach the words to the wall at the children's eye level. Some familiar word suggestions are:

cabbage	cent
cake	cereal
carrots	cinnamon
castle	circle
cat	city

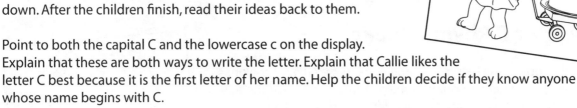

☆ **Learning Extension:** Invite the children to clap for the syllables of words that begin with the letter C (cab-bage, cat, cit-y).

Explain that all of these words begin with the letter C, but the letter C makes more than one sound. In the words *cake* and *carrots* the letter makes the same sound as in Callie. In the words *cereal* and *city,* the sound of the letter is different.

© HighReach Learning® Inc.

The Letter C

Language Activities

Share the Letter C Rebus Rhyme

Share the Letter C Rebus Rhyme (page 39) to develop a sense of rhythm and rhyme and to practice naming pictures. Show the display as you recite the rhyme several times. Afterwards, point to each picture on the chart and encourage the children to name it. Discuss each picture and invite the children to share times when they have seen similar items.

☆ **Learning Extension:** Talk about the letter C. Look at all of the words on the display. Help the children locate the letter C. Explain that the letter C can be written more than one way. Point to the capital C on the display and then point to the lowercase c. Help the children find all of the capital and lowercase letter C's on the display.

Create Letter C Rhyme Books

Give each child a copy of the Letter C Rhyme Book (page 40) and crayons or markers. Invite the children to point to the pictures as you read the text. Encourage the children to decorate the pictures as desired. Cut along the dotted lines and stack the pages in order. Staple the pages together. Invite the children to write their names on the rhyme books. Assist the children as needed.

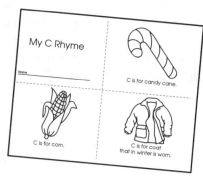

☆ **Learning Extension:** Invite a child to "read" his/her Letter C Rhyme Book to you. Encourage the child to point to the letter C in the book.

Explore Comic Strips and Coupons

Collect several comic strips and coupons. Invite the children to explore the comic strips and coupons as desired, and mention that the words *comic* and *coupons* both begin with the letter C. You may wish to provide scissors and allow the children to cut out the comic strips and coupons.

☆ **Learning Extension:** Invite a child to look for the Letter C in any wording on the comic strips or coupons.

I Spy Colors or Circles

Invite a group of children to play a game with you. To play the game, choose an item that is either a color or circle in the classroom or outdoors. Do not tell the children which item you have chosen. Invite the children to ask yes and no questions about what object you chose until they guess the item. Continue playing the game as the children show interest.

☆ **Learning Extension:** Invite a child to think of words that start with the same sound as the word *colors*. Then invite the child to think of words that begin with the same sound as the word *circles*. Give examples as needed.

© HighReach Learning® Inc.

Science Activities

Mix Colors

Give the children small clear cups of water. Show the children assorted colors of food coloring, and mention that the word *color* begins with the letter C. Drop a few drops of red food coloring in each child's cup. Show the children the blue food coloring. Encourage the children to guess what they think will happen if you add a few drops of blue food coloring to their red water. You may wish to continue this experiment using other colors, such as red and yellow (to make orange) or blue and yellow (to make green).

What Lives in a Cave?

Create a cave for the children. Use a large appliance box or drape a large blanket or sheet over a table. Invite the children to explore the cave. Challenge the children to think of animals that live in caves. Give some examples such as bats, bears, snakes, insects, raccoons, etc. You may want to mention that the word *cave* begins with the letter C.

Clean Copper Coins

Give the children small paper cups. Pour a little vinegar into each child's cup and add a small amount of salt. Have each child place an old penny in the solution and stir with a plastic spoon. The penny should soon become bright and shiny. Have the children rub the clean coins with paper towels to dry. As the children work, explain that pennies are made from a metal called copper. Point out that both the words *coin* and *copper* begin with the letter C. *(Caution: Make sure to closely supervise the children during this activity. Do not let them put the coins in their mouths or drink the mixture.)*

Explore a Coconut

Show the children a fresh coconut. Pass the coconut around the group. You may wish to help the children realize that the word *coconut* begins with the letter C. Invite the children to guess what is inside the coconut. After the children share their ideas, use a hammer and nail to make a hole in each of the three indentations on the end of the coconut. Pour the coconut milk into a pitcher or measuring cup with a handle. Give the children a chance to taste the coconut milk if they are interested. Place the coconut in a shallow dish and bake for 15-30 minutes at 350° to crack the shell. Use the hammer to break apart the coconut. Away from the children, cut the brown skin off using a knife or vegetable peeler. Invite interested children to try a small piece of white coconut meat. *(Caution: Only an adult should use the hammer or knife. Do not allow the children to place the coconut in and out of the oven.)*

© HighReach Learning® Inc.

The Letter C

Large Muscle Activities

Carry Cups of Water

Show the children a plastic bucket and a plastic cup. Challenge the children to predict how many cups of water it will take to fill the bucket. Set the bucket several yards away from the group. Invite one child at a time to carry a cup of water to the bucket and pour it in. If the child spills the water on the way, he/she should go back and refill the cup again. As each cup is added, encourage the children to count aloud with you. After you finish, help the children compare their predictions to the actual number of cups it takes to fill the bucket. Discuss whether the bucket holds more or less than predicted, and mention that the words *carry* and *cup* both begin with the letter C.

Drop Clothespins in a Can

Show the children a coffee can. Give each child a few clothespins. Invite the children to take turns dropping the clothespins in the can. As the children play, help them count the number of clothespins that go into the can and the clothespins that miss. Encourage the children to keep trying as long as they show interest and praise them for their efforts.

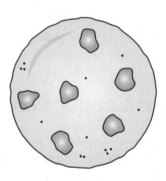

Cookie Hunt

Wrap a cookie in plastic wrap for each child. Hide the cookies in the classroom. Explain to the children that you have hidden a cookie for each one of them somewhere in the classroom, and that the word *cookie* begins with the letter C. As the children look for the cookies, remind each child to find only one cookie. Once everyone has found a cookie, unwrap, eat, and enjoy!

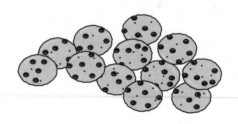

Art Activities

Create Tactile Letter C's

Give each child a copy of the capital letter C (page 30), an old paintbrush, and a shallow dish of glue. Invite the children to trace the letter C with their fingers. Encourage the children to spread glue on their letter C's as desired. Provide the children with small bathroom cups filled with cereal, coconut, or cornmeal. Invite the children to shake the cereal, coconut, or cornmeal onto the glue. Set aside to dry. After the glue dries, invite the children to trace their tactile letter C's with their fingers. How does the C feel? Use descriptive words such as bumpy, rough, and so forth as you interact with the child.

Make Letter C Collages

Give a child old newspapers or magazines and scissors. Invite the child to search for the letter C in the newspapers or magazines. The child may wish to tear or cut the letters out. Give the child a sheet of paper and a glue stick. Encourage the child to attach the letter C cutouts to the paper as desired. Assist the child as needed.

☆ *Learning Extension:* If you are working with a group of children, invite them to work together to make one big letter C collage. If you have bulletin board, butcher, or chart paper, you may even wish to cut the paper in the shape of the letter C. Help the children locate and cut or tear out large examples of the letter from captions and headlines. Have the children glue all the letter cutouts to the paper.

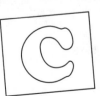

© HighReach Learning® Inc.

The Letter C

Art Activities

Coin Rubbings

Give the children assorted coins, paper, and unwrapped crayons. Invite the children to color over the coins. Help the children notice the designs that appear on the paper. You may also wish to help them notice that the words *crayons* and *coins* both start with the letter C.

☆ *Learning Extension:* Draw a large letter C on the children's papers. The children may wish to trace the letter or try to create their own letters. Assist them as needed.

Colored Cornmeal Creations

Mix assorted colors of powdered tempera paint with cornmeal in separate bowls. Put a small plastic spoon in each bowl of cornmeal. Provide the children with paper, old paintbrushes, and shallow dishes of glue. Invite the children to spread glue on their papers as desired. Show the children the spoons in the cornmeal, and mention that the word *cornmeal* begins with the letter C. Invite the children to sprinkle the cornmeal onto their papers as desired. Shake off the extra cornmeal to reveal the interesting designs the children created.

Create with Cups and Cards

Provide the children with an old deck of playing cards, small paper cups, and tape. Challenge the children to create a structure together using the cups and cards. Assist the children as needed.

☆ *Learning Extension:* Mention that the words *cups* and *cards* begin with the letter C. Challenge the children to think of more words that begin with the same sound.

The Letter C

© HighReach Learning® Inc.

Small Muscle Activities

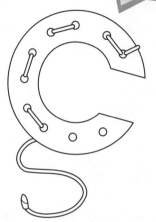

Explore Letter C Lacing Cards

Draw several block letter C's on posterboard using the pattern on page 30 and cut out. Use a hole punch to make a series of holes around each letter cutout. Vary the number of holes so that some will be easier to lace than others. Tie a length of yarn to one hole and wrap the free end with tape. Be sure the yarn can wrap around the letter twice. Set out the letter C lacing cards. Assist the children as needed as they explore the lacing cards.

Practice Cutting the Letter C

Give each child a copy of the letter C pattern (page 30). Provide crayons or markers and invite the children to decorate the letter C's as desired. Provide scissors and invite the children to practice cutting the letter C.

Create with Cereal

Provide the children with several lengths of string or yarn and a bowl of fruit-flavored round cereal. Encourage the children to practice stringing the cereal onto the string or yarn. They may wish to create bracelets or necklaces. Prior to stringing the pieces, you may wish to tie a piece of cereal to the end of each child's string or yarn as shown to keep the rings from slipping off. You may also wish to help the children realize that the words *circle* and *cereal* both start with the same sound.

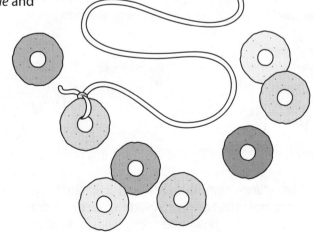

☆ *Learning Extension:* Provide assorted colors of round cereal. Invite the children who show readiness to create patterns with the cereal on the string. You may wish to start with a simple pattern that the children can copy. Increase the difficulty of the pattern according to each child's abilities.

Cooking with Callie Cat
Letter C Recipes

CARROT AND CUCUMBER CATERPILLARS

cucumber slices
matchstick carrot strips
raisins

Give the children cucumber slices, carrot strips, and raisins. Invite the children to create caterpillars with the materials. Assist the children as needed in making this healthy and delicious treat!

COCOA CAKE

Cake:

2 sticks butter or margarine	1¾ cups sugar
1 cup water	1 tsp. baking soda
¼ cup cocoa	½ tsp. salt
2 cups all-purpose flour	2 eggs
	½ cup sour cream

Preheat the oven to 350°. Grease and flour a 13" x 9" x 2" baking pan. Combine butter, water, and cocoa in a small saucepan. Cook over medium heat, stirring constantly, until mixture boils; remove from heat. Stir together flour, sugar, baking soda, and salt in a large bowl. Stir in hot cocoa mixture. Add eggs and sour cream; beat on medium speed until well blended. Pour batter into prepared pan. Bake 30 or 35 minutes. Leave cake in pan and frost while hot. Cool completely in pan on wire rack before serving.

Frosting:

½ stick butter or margarine	dash of salt
¼ cup milk	½ tsp. vanilla extract
2 Tbsp. cocoa	2 cups powdered sugar

Combine butter, milk, cocoa, and salt in a small saucepan. Cook over medium heat, stirring constantly, until mixture is smooth and slightly thickened. Remove from heat and stir in vanilla. Place powdered sugar in medium bowl; add cocoa mixture. Beat until smooth and pour over hot cake in pan.

CARROT CAKE COOKIES

1 cup packed light brown sugar
2 sticks unsalted butter, room temperature
2 large eggs, room temperature
1 tsp. vanilla extract
1½ cups all-purpose flour
1 tsp. baking soda
1 tsp. baking powder
¼ tsp. salt
1 tsp. ground cinnamon
½ tsp. ground nutmeg
½ tsp. ground ginger
2 cups old-fashioned rolled oats
1½ cups finely grated carrots (about 3 large carrots)
1 cup raisins
1 can cream cheese frosting

Preheat the oven to 350°. Combine brown sugar, butter, eggs, and vanilla in a large bowl. Beat until well combined. Add flour, baking soda, baking powder, salt, cinnamon, nutmeg, and ginger. Mix on low speed until blended. Then add oats, carrots, and raisins. Chill dough in refrigerator for 30 minutes. Scoop several spoonfuls of dough onto a greased cookie sheet. Leave 2 inches between each scoop. Cook for 10-12 minutes until browned and crisp. When baked, transfer to a wire baking rack. Once cooled, use a spatula to frost with cream cheese frosting.

CORN CASSEROLE

1 can whole kernel corn
1 can cream style corn
1 stick butter
1 package (8 oz.) cream cheese, room temperature
4 eggs
1 package corn bread mix
shredded cheddar cheese

Preheat the oven to 350°. Mix all ingredients (except cheddar cheese) and pour into greased casserole dish. Sprinkle with shredded cheese and bake for 1 hour. Cool and serve.

© HighReach Learning® Inc.

C is for .

C is for .

C is for

That in winter is worn.

candy cane   corn   coat

My C Rhyme

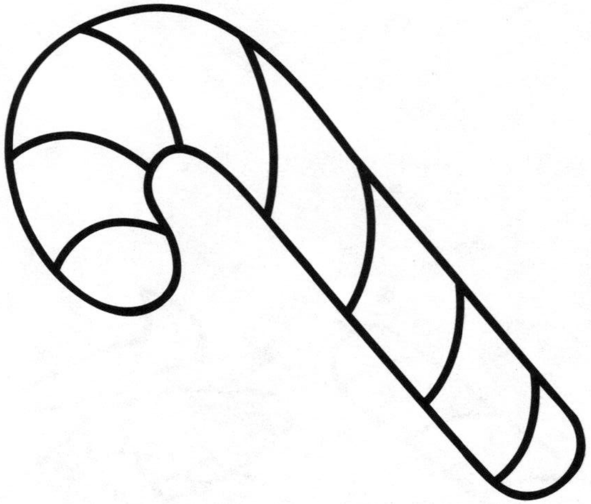

C is for candy cane.

C is for coat
that in winter is worn.

C is for corn.

Name

The Letter C

40

© HighReach Learning® Inc.

© HighReach Learning® Inc.

The Letter D

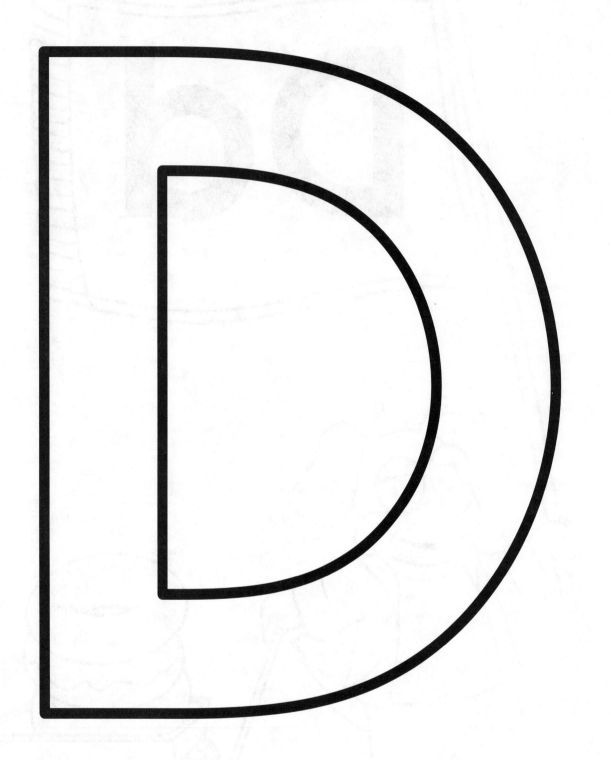

Language Activities

Introduce Devon Dog and the Letter D

Copy and decorate the Letter D Display (page 41) as desired. Point to Devon Dog on the display. Invite the children to guess what type of animal Devon is. If necessary explain that he is a dog. You may wish to share the rhyme below several times and invite the children to join in.

DEVON DOG

Devon is a dog
Who really likes to eat.
He thinks delicious doughnuts
Are a most delightful treat.

Invite the children to discuss what they learned about Devon in the rhyme. Invite the children to name the items on the display that Devon is pulling in the wagon. Invite the children to discuss if they have ever eaten doughnuts. What are their favorite kinds of doughnuts? Encourage the children to share their ideas.

Point to both the capital D and the lowercase d on the display. Explain that these are both ways to write the letter. Explain that Devon likes the letter D best because it is the first letter of his name. Help the children decide if they know anyone whose name begins with D.

Talk About Letter D Words

Invite the children to talk about words they know that begin with the letter D. Write any suggestions down on sentence strips, a large sheet of paper, or chart paper. Attach the words to the wall at the children's eye level. Some familiar word suggestions are:

dancer   dentist   dish
day   dinosaur   doctor
deer   dirt

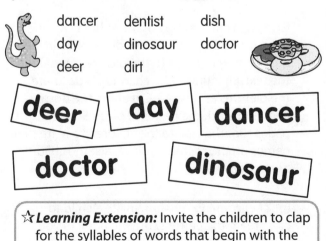

☆ **Learning Extension:** Invite the children to clap for the syllables of words that begin with the letter D (den-tist, day, di-no-saur, doc-tor).

Discuss Visiting the Doctor

Discuss going to the doctor with the children, and mention that the word *doctor* begins with the letter D. Invite the children to share times when they have been to the doctor when they may have been sick or for well checkups. Show the children a toy medical kit. Discuss the name of each item and invite the children to talk about how they think a doctor may use the item. Write down what the children say on a sheet of chart paper. You may also want to discuss that doctors give medication and help us when we are sick. Invite the children to share times when they may have been sick and gone to the doctor's office or hospital.

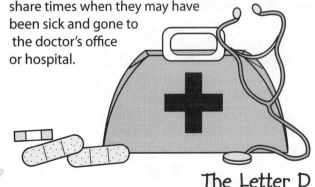

© HighReach Learning® Inc.

The Letter D

Language Activities

Share the Letter D Rebus Rhyme

Share the Letter D Rebus Rhyme (page 51) to develop a sense of rhythm and rhyme and to practice naming pictures. Show the display as you recite the rhyme several times. Afterwards, point to each picture on the chart and encourage the children to name it. Discuss each picture and invite the children to share times when they have seen similar items.

> ☆ *Learning Extension:* Talk about the letter D. Look at all of the words on the display. Help the children locate the letter D. Explain that the letter D can be written more than one way. Point to the capital D on the display and then point to the lowercase d. Help the children find all of the capital and lowercase letter D's on the display.

Talk About Delivering Packages

Put a sheet of reward stickers in a shoe box or medium-sized box with a lid. Write the children's names on index cards and place them in a small paper lunch bag. Have the children sit in a circle. Show the children the box. Invite the children to discuss things that they think might be delivered in a box, and mention that the word *deliver* begins with the letter D. Encourage the children to talk about delivery people. You may wish to give examples such as packages, flowers, pizza, etc. Invite the children to play a delivery game. Choose a child to come up and pull a name from the paper lunch bag. Show the card to all of the children and help them determine whose name it is. Have the child who pulled the name from the bag deliver the box to the child whose name is on the card. Invite the child who received the package to step away from the group, open the box, look inside, but not tell anyone what is in the box. Continue to play the game in this manner until everyone has seen what is in the box. After the last child is finished, reward all of the children with a sticker.

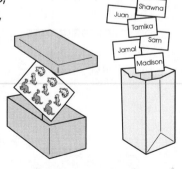

Create Letter D Rhyme Books

Give each child a copy of the Letter D Rhyme Book (page 51) and crayons or markers. Invite the children to point to the pictures as you read the text. Encourage the children to decorate the pictures as desired. Cut along the dotted lines and stack the pages in order. Staple the pages together. Invite the children to write their names on the rhyme books. Assist the children as needed.

> ☆ *Learning Extension:* Invite a child to "read" the Letter D Rhyme Book to you. Encourage the child to point to the letter D in the book.

The Letter D

44

© HighReach Learning® Inc.

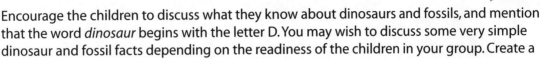

Science Activities

Discuss Dinosaurs and Fossils

Encourage the children to discuss what they know about dinosaurs and fossils, and mention that the word *dinosaur* begins with the letter D. You may wish to discuss some very simple dinosaur and fossil facts depending on the readiness of the children in your group. Create a coffee dough fossil. Encourage the children to help you mix the following ingredients using their hands.

1½ cups flour
1 cup dried coffee grounds
½ cup salt
1½ cups water
¼ cup sand

As the children mix the ingredients, encourage them to talk about the way the dough feels, looks, and smells. After each child has had a chance to touch the mixture, form it into a ball and place it on a piece of wax paper. Encourage the children to tell you what they think will happen to the dough. When the children are not looking, place your thumb in the center of the ball to make a hole. Place a small plastic dinosaur inside the hole. Cover the hole with dough. Place the dough out of the children's reach and allow to completely dry. After the dough dries, pass it around the group and encourage the children to make observations about the way the dough looks and feels. After all of the children have had a chance to explore the dough, remind them that fossils found in mud, rocks, and other places help us learn about animals and plants that lived long ago. Encourage the children to tell how they think dinosaur fossils end up in rocks, mud, and other places. Then break the dough apart to reveal the dinosaur inside. Encourage the children to tell you how they think the dinosaur got inside the ball of dough.

Discuss Different Types of Dogs

Show the children assorted nonfiction books about dogs, and mention that the word *dog* begins with the letter D. Invite the children to talk about the pictures in the books. Challenge the children to tell you how the dogs are alike and how they are different.

☆ *Learning Extension:* Create a chart featuring characteristics of dogs such as color, size, long-hair, short-hair, etc. Encourage the children to discuss the characteristics of several types of dogs.

Explore Dirt

Give each child a cup of untreated dirt (organic, non-chemically treated potting soil), and mention that the word *dirt* begins with the letter D. Invite the children to discuss what they think the dirt could be used for. Invite the children to make small holes in their dirt. Help the children pour grass seed into the holes and cover with the dirt. Challenge the children to predict what will happen if they water the seeds. Encourage the children to monitor the cups over the next several days. Help them notice what happens to the seeds.

© HighReach Learning® Inc.

The Letter D

Large Muscle Activities

Dance to Disco Music

Play some disco music and invite the children to dance. An example of this type of music is "Disco Duck" from *A Child's Celebration of Disco* by Rhino Music (2002). You may wish to help the children notice the words *disco* and *dance* both start with the same sound.

Dodge Ball

Explan to the children that you are going to play a game called dodge ball add that the word *dodge* begins with the letter D. Divide the children into two groups. Have one group form a circle around the children in the other group. Have the children in the outer circle roll a soft playground ball back and forth across the circle. Any child the ball touches should move to the outer circle. Continue in this fashion until all the children are in the outer circle. Then have the children who began the game in the outer circle move inside the circle and play again.

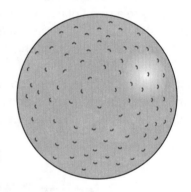

Doggie, Doggie, Where Is Your Dish?

Have the children sit in a semicircle. Choose one child to be Doggie and sit in a chair facing away from the others, covering his/her eyes. Place a plastic bowl under Doggie's chair. Tap a child from the group to quietly come forward, pick up the dish, and return to his/her place, hiding the dish behind his/her back. Have all of the children put their hands behind their backs as well. Once the child has hidden the dish, the group chants, "Doggie, Doggie, don't you wish, that you knew who took your dish?" Doggie turns around to the group and has three guesses to find out who has the dish. If Doggie guesses correctly, the child with the dish becomes Doggie. If Doggie does not guess correctly after three guesses, another child is chosen to be Doggie and play continues. As the children play the game, mention that the words *doggie* and *dish* both begin with the letter D.

The Letter D

46

© HighReach Learning® Inc.

Art Activities

Create Tactile Letter D's

Give each child a copy of the capital letter D (page 42), an old paintbrush, and a shallow dish of glue. Invite the children to trace the letter D with their fingers. Encourage the children to spread glue on their letter D's as desired. Provide the children with small bathroom cups filled with rice, sand, or salt. Invite the children to shake the rice, sand, or salt onto the glue. Set aside to dry. After the glue dries, invite the children to trace their tactile letter D's with their fingers. How does the D feel? Use descriptive words such as bumpy, rough, and so forth as you interact with the child.

Dinosaur Bones

Create self-hardening dough using the following ingredients:

1½ cups salt
4 cups flour
1 tsp. alum (found in the baking section of stores)
1½ cups water

Mix salt, flour, and alum in a bowl. Gradually add water. Knead the dough and add water until the dough forms a ball and no longer crumbles. Store in a sealed plastic bag in the refrigerator. Allow the dough to come to room temperature before using. Give each child some dough. Invite the children to make dinosaur bones with the dough. You may wish to help the children realize that the word *dinosaur* begins with the letter D. After the children finish, place their creations on wax paper and allow to dry for a few days.

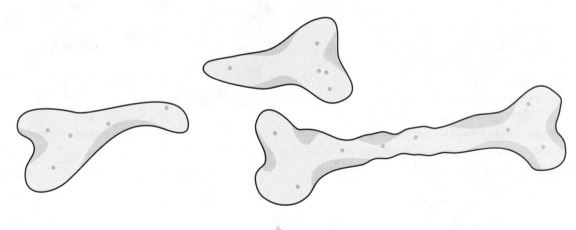

© HighReach Learning® Inc.

The Letter D

Art Activities

Make Letter D Collages

Give a child old newspapers or magazines and scissors. Invite the child to search for the letter D in the newspapers or magazines. The child may wish to tear or cut the letters out. Give the child a sheet of paper and a glue stick. Encourage the child to attach the letter D cutouts to the paper as desired. Assist the child as needed.

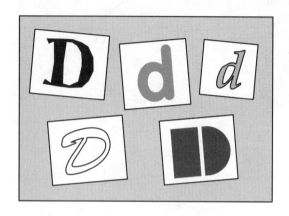

☆ **Learning Extension:** If you are working with a group of children, invite them to work together to make one big letter D collage. If you have bulletin board, butcher, or chart paper, you may even wish to cut the paper in the shape of the letter D. Help the children locate and cut or tear out large examples of the letter from captions and headlines. Have the children glue all the letter cutouts to the paper.

Dot Art

Provide the children with paper, coding dot stickers, and assorted dot art markers. Invite the children to design pictures with dots. You may wish to mention that the word *dot* begins with the letter D.

☆ **Learning Extension:** Help a child realize that the word *dot* begins with the letter D. As the child watches, print the word *dot* on an index card. Use a highlighter for the D and crayons for the other letters. Invite the child to trace the letter D. Tape the index card to the back of the child's paper.

© HighReach Learning® Inc.

Small Muscle Activities

Explore Letter D Lacing Cards

Draw several block letter D's on posterboard using the pattern on page 42 and cut out. Use a hole punch to make a series of holes around each letter cutout. Vary the number of holes so that some will be easier to lace than others. Tie a length of yarn to one hole and wrap the free end with tape. Be sure the yarn can wrap around the letter twice. Set out the letter D lacing cards. Assist the children as needed as they explore the lacing cards.

Match Dots on Dominos

Provide the children with a set of dominoes. Encourage the children to line up the dominoes by matching the sets of dots. As the children explore the dominoes, you may wish to mention that the words *dominoes* and *dots* both begin with the letter D.

Diamond Stencils

Draw several diamond shapes onto posterboard or old file folders. With a utility knife or sharp scissors, carefully cut out the diamond shapes to create diamond stencils. Provide the children with paper and colored pencils or markers. Invite the children to create diamonds with the stencils as desired, and mention that the word *diamond* begins with the letter D.

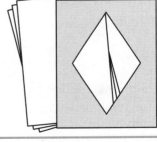

Explore Dice

Create a pair of large dice by covering two facial tissue boxes with paper as shown. Add large bold dots to the tissue boxes with a nontoxic permanent marker. Invite the children to take turns rolling the dice. After the dice stop rolling, help the children count the number of dots on the dice. Continue playing as long as the children show interest, and mention that the word *dice* begins with the letter D.

☆ *Learning Extension:* Write the word *diamond* next to the each diamond stencil. Invite the children to point to the letter D's in the word. The children may also wish to practice making the letter D on their papers.

© HighReach Learning® Inc.

The Letter D

Cooking with Devon Dog
Letter D Recipes

DELIGHTFUL DIP

1 package (8 oz.) cream cheese, room temperature
¾ cup brown sugar
¼ cup sugar
1 tsp. vanilla

Blend all ingredients together well. Serve with fresh fruit or vegetables for dipping such as baby carrots, strawberries, or apple slices.

DOUGHNUT DOTS

⅓ cup butter
½ cup sugar
1 egg, beaten
1½ cups flour
2¼ tsp. baking powder
¼ tsp. salt
¼ tsp. nutmeg
½ cup milk

Doughnut Topping:
½ cup melted butter
1 cup sugar mixed with 2 tsp. cinnamon

Preheat oven to 350°. Cream butter and sugar together. Add in beaten egg and mix well. Mix in dry ingredients and milk. Fill greased muffin tins half full. Bake for 20-30 minutes until golden brown. Dip the doughnuts in the melted butter, then roll in cinnamon sugar mixture.

DELICIOUS DIRT

1 package black and white sandwich cookies
  (grind in blender or food processor)
1 package (8 oz.) cream cheese,
  room temperature
½ stick butter
1 cup powdered sugar
3½ cups milk
2 packages instant vanilla pudding
1 container (12 oz.) whipped topping
OPTIONAL: gummy worms

Mix cream cheese, butter, and powdered sugar until blended. Add pudding mix and milk into the cream cheese mixture and beat on low until thick. Gently stir in whipped topping into cream cheese/pudding mixture. Alternate layers of cookie crumbs and cream cheese/pudding mixture in a clean flowerpot or baking pan. Top with gummy worms if desired.

© HighReach Learning® Inc.

D is for .

D is for .

D is for that

Lies on the floor.

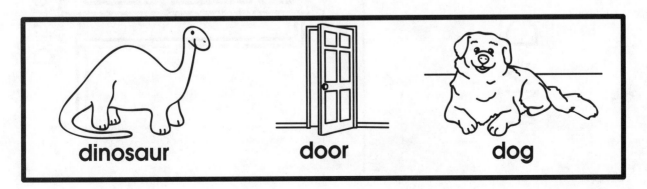

dinosaur   door   dog

© HighReach Learning® Inc.   The Letter D

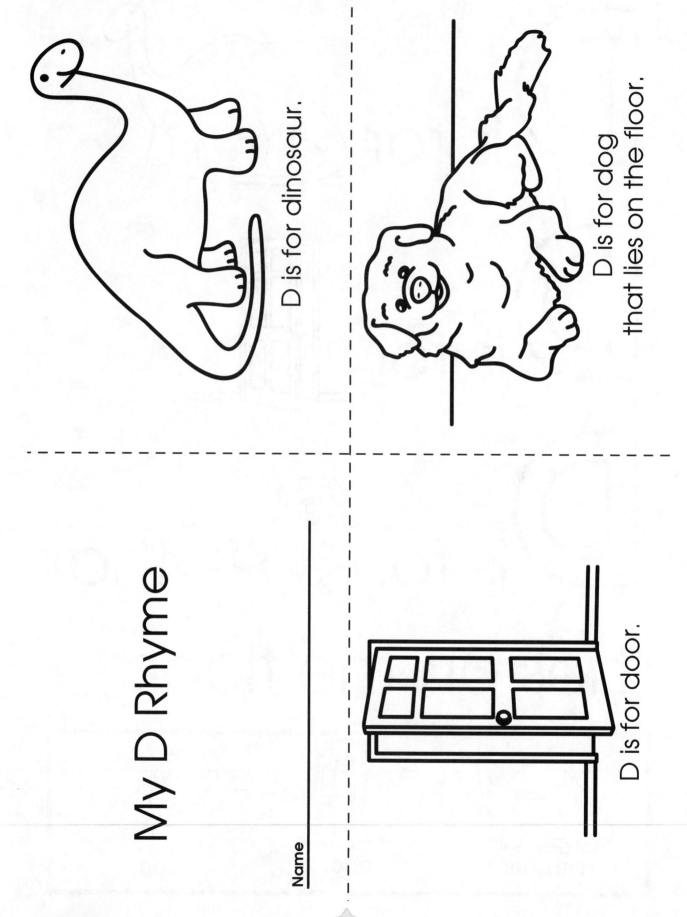

D is for dinosaur.

D is for dog
that lies on the floor.

My D Rhyme

Name

D is for door.

52

© HighReach Learning® Inc.

© HighReach Learning® Inc.

53

The Letter E

The Letter E

© HighReach Learning® Inc.

Language Activities

Introduce Evelyn Elephant and the Letter E

Decorate a copy of the Letter E Display (page 53) as desired. Point to Evelyn Elephant on the display. Invite the children to guess what type of animal Evelyn is. If necessary explain that she is an elephant. You may wish to share the rhyme below several times and invite the children to join in.

EVELYN ELEPHANT

Evelyn gathers eggs
Every single day.
She sells the eggs to everyone
Who has the cash to pay.

Invite the children to discuss what they learned about Evelyn in the rhyme. Invite the children to name the items on the display that Evelyn is pulling in the wagon. Discuss where eggs come from. How much do the children think eggs cost? Encourage the children to share their ideas.

Point to both the capital E and the lowercase e on the display. Explain that these are both ways to write the letter. Explain that Evelyn likes the letter E best because it is the first letter of her name. Help the children decide if they know anyone whose name begins with E.

Talk About Letter E Words

Invite the children to talk about words they know that begin with the letter E. Write any suggestions down on sentence strips, a large sheet of paper, or chart paper. Attach the words to the wall at the children's eye level. Some familiar word suggestions are:

Short Sounds: Long Sounds:

  egg   eel

  echo   enormous

  eggplant   erase

egg

echo

eggplant

Explain that all of these words begin with the letter E, but the letter E makes more than one sound. In the words *echo* and *egg,* the letter makes the same sound as in Evelyn. In the words *enormous* and *erase,* the sound of the letter is the same as its name.

> ☆ *Learning Extension:* Invite the children to clap for the syllables of words that begin with the letter E (e-cho, east, ea-sy, e-vap-o-rate).

Play Guess What's in the Egg?

Invite the children to sit in a circle. Place an item inside a large plastic egg and seal with tape. Toss the egg around the group. Help the children realize that the word *egg* begins with the letter E. Invite the children to guess what item is hidden inside the egg. You may wish to give the children clues about what is inside the egg. After they guess correctly, remove the tape and open the egg. Continue playing using different items as long as the children show interest.

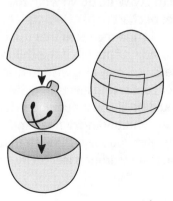

© HighReach Learning® Inc.

The Letter E

Language Activities
Share the Letter E Rebus Rhyme

Share the Letter E Rebus Rhyme (page 63) to develop a sense of rhythm and rhyme and to practice naming pictures. Show the display as you recite the rhyme several times. Afterwards, point to each picture on the chart and encourage the children to name it. Discuss each picture and invite the children to share times when they have seen similar items.

> ☆ *Learning Extension:* Talk about the letter E. Look at all of the words on the display. Help the children locate the letter E. Explain that the letter E can be written more than one way. Point to the capital E on the display and then point to the lowercase e. Help the children find all of the capital and lowercase letter E's on the display.

Create Letter E Rhyme Books

Give each child a copy of the Letter E Rhyme Book (page 64) and crayons or markers. Invite the children to point to the pictures as you read the text. Encourage the children to decorate the pictures as desired. Cut along the dotted lines and stack the pages in order. Staple the pages together. Invite the children to write their names on the rhyme books. Assist the children as needed.

> ☆ *Learning Extension:* Invite a child to "read" his/her Letter E Rhyme Book to you. Encourage the child to point to the letter E in the book.

Talk About Electricity

Discuss electricity with the children. Help the children realize that the word *electricity* begins with the letter E. Invite the children to share their ideas about what electricity is and things that run by using electricity. Write down what the children say on a sheet of chart paper. Help the children think of items around the room that use electricity, such as lights, radios, fans, etc. If the children show readiness, you may also wish to discuss the importance of conserving electricity. Give examples of what it would be like without electricity, such as no lights, air conditioning or heat, and in some cases no hot water. You may also wish to talk to the children about safety around electricity, using some of the suggestions listed.

❖ Never touch wires you see lying on the ground.

❖ Never put your fingers or any other object into electrical outlets.

❖ Always let adults plug things in and unplug things.

❖ When you are wet, do not touch anything that is electrical.

> ☆ *Learning Extension:* Choose a child to be the electric patrol each week. The child will help the other children remember to turn off lights and other things, such as fans, radios, etc., during recess or when away from the room.

Science Activities

Talk About Evaporation

Give each child a paper towel. Invite the children to wet the paper towels at the sink. Choose a place in the classroom for the children to put their paper towels. Invite the children to crumple up the paper towels in a ball or lay them flat. Invite the children to predict how long it will take for the paper towels to dry and which paper towels they think will dry faster. Discuss evaporation. Explain to the children that when the paper towels dry, the water evaporates into the air. Help the children realize that the word *evaporation* begins with the letter E. After a few hours, invite the children to check the paper towels. Are all of them dry? Discuss with the children which paper towels dried first and suggest reasons why. Some factors may include whether the paper towels were near a source of light, whether they got air circulation, etc.

☆ *Learning Extension:* Give each child a clear plastic cup. Have the child fill the cup with water. Mark the level of the water with a nontoxic permanent marker. Each day, invite the child to check the water level and mark it again. Help the child discover that the water is evaporating into the air a little bit each day.

Talk About Echoes

Show the children a large metal bucket. Say a word into the bucket and invite the children to discuss what happens. Did they hear the word twice? Explain that this is called an echo. Help the children realize that the word *echo* begins with the letter E. Give each child a chance to practice making echoes in the metal bucket.

© HighReach Learning® Inc.

The Letter E

Large Muscle Activities

Perform an Egg Experiment

Show the children a clear plastic jar or container filled with water. Gently drop a hard-boiled egg into the water. Encourage the children to think of ways to make the egg come to the top of the jar. Next, show the children some salt. Ask the children to predict what they think might happen when salt is added to the water. Use a spoon to add salt to the water. Invite the children to help you count the spoonfuls of salt and observe what happens to the egg. It will eventually float to the top of the container. After you finish, invite the children to discuss why they think the salt made the egg float to the top of the water. You may wish to mention that the word *egg* begins with the letter E.

salt

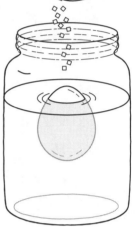

Explore an Eggplant

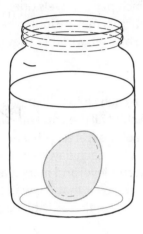

Show the children an eggplant, and mention that the word *eggplant* begins with the letter E. Pass the eggplant around the group and encourage the children to look at it closely. Encourage them to notice its color, its smooth texture, and its shiny surface. Invite the children to guess how they think the eggplant will look on the inside. Discuss what color may be on the inside, whether or not there may be seeds, whether it will be dry or juicy, and so forth. Cut open the eggplant and encourage the children to touch the surface and look closely. Talk about how it looks and feels. Invite the children to use unbreakable magnifying glasses for a closer look at the seeds. The children may notice that the flesh of the eggplant is beginning to turn darker as it is exposed to the air.

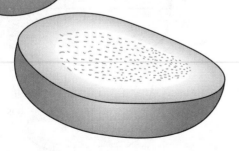

☆ *Learning Extension:* As the children explore the eggplant, mention that the words *eggplant* and *explore* begin with the same sound as Evelyn Elephant's name. Challenge the children to think of other words that begin with the sound of *Evelyn* and *eggplant*.

The Letter E

58

© HighReach Learning® Inc.

Art Activities

Move Like Elephants

Encourage the children to share what they know about elephants, and mention that the word *elephant* begins with the letter E. Have they ever seen elephants in the circus or in a parade? Suggest that the children have their own elephant parade. Invite them to line up. Have each child reach a hand back through his/her legs and grasp a hand of the child behind as if walking "trunk to tail." Challenge the children to try to walk around the classroom or outside without breaking the line.

Roll Eggs

Mark a start and finish line in the classroom with masking tape or outside with sidewalk chalk. Give each child a long-handled spoon and a plastic egg. Invite the children to put their plastic eggs on the start line. Explain to the children that when you say "Go," they should push the egg with the spoon to roll it to the finish line.

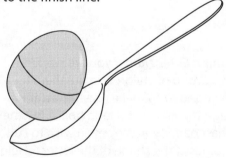

☆ *Learning Extension:* Use a timer to time an individual child rolling the egg from start to finish. Challenge the child to try to beat his/her own time. Give as many tries as needed.

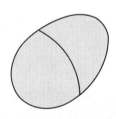

Egg Toss

Invite the children to choose partners. Give one child in each pair a plastic egg. Have the pair stand a few feet apart from each other. Encourage the children to toss their plastic eggs to their partners. Each time the children catch the egg, invite them to take one step back. Continue playing until the children cannot catch the eggs anymore!

☆ *Learning Extension:* Invite the children to count as high as they can as they toss the plastic eggs back and forth.

Art Activities

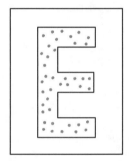

Eggshell Art

Give each child a large sheet of construction paper and crayons or markers. Set out several dishes of crumbled eggshells from hard-boiled eggs and bottles of glue. Invite the children to create pictures as desired with the crayons or markers. Encourage the children to use the eggshells and glue to decorate the designs on their papers. You may need to demonstrate how to do this for the children, and assist them as needed. Talk with the children as they create. Encourage them to describe how the eggshells look and feel. As the children work, you many wish to point out that the words *egg* and *eggshell* begin with the letter E.

Create Tactile Letter E's

Give each child a copy of the capital letter E (page 54), an old paintbrush, and a shallow dish of glue. Invite the children to trace the letter E with their fingers. Encourage the children to spread glue on their letter E's as desired. Provide the children with small bathroom cups filled with sand, salt, or rice. Invite the children to shake the sand, salt, or rice onto the glue. Set aside to dry. After the glue dries, invite the children to trace their tactile letter E's with their fingers. How does the E feel? Use descriptive words such as bumpy, rough, etc. as you interact with the child.

Make Letter E Collages

Give a child old newspapers or magazines and scissors. Invite the child to search for the letter E in the newspapers or magazines. The child may wish to tear or cut the letters out. Give the child a sheet of paper and a glue stick. Encourage the child to attach the letter E cutouts to the paper as desired. Assist the child as needed.

> ☆ *Learning Extension:* If you are working with a group of children, invite them to work together to make one big letter E collage. If you have bulletin board, butcher, or chart paper, you may even wish to cut the paper in the shape of the letter E. Help the children locate and cut or tear out large examples of the letter from captions and headlines. Have the children glue all the letter cutouts to the paper.

© HighReach Learning® Inc.

Small Muscle Activities

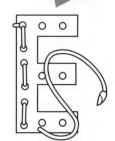

Explore Letter E Lacing Cards

Draw several block letter E's on posterboard using the pattern on page 54 and cut out. Use a hole punch to make a series of holes around each letter cutout. Vary the number of holes so that some will be easier to lace than others. Tie a length of yarn to one hole and wrap the free end with tape. Be sure the yarn can wrap around the letter twice. Set out the letter E lacing cards. Assist the children as needed as they explore the lacing cards.

Make Bubbles with an Eggbeater

Fill the sand/water table or a basin with water. Show a child a hand-operated eggbeater, and mention that the word *eggbeater* begins with the letter E. Put some tear-free shampoo in the water. Invite the child to crank the eggbeater in the water. Encourage the child to describe what happens while using the eggbeater. **Note: Supervise this activity closely to avoid pinched fingers.**

Craft Stick Letter E's

Draw several large capital letter E's on old file folders or cardboard. Give the children several craft sticks. Invite them to use the craft sticks to make capital letter E's. Assist the children as needed.

> ☆ **Learning Extension:** Invite children that show readiness to make the letter E with craft sticks on their own.

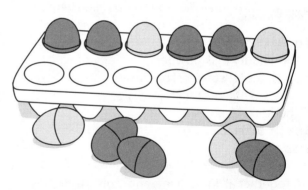

Pattern Plastic Eggs

Set out several sanitized egg cartons and assorted colors of plastic eggs. If they show readiness, invite the children to create patterns with the eggs in the egg cartons. You may wish to model a simple pattern for the children and invite them to copy the pattern. The children may also wish to sort the eggs by color into the egg carton sections.

> ☆ **Learning Extension:** Invite a child to count the number of eggs in the egg carton sections. Assist the child as needed.

© HighReach Learning® Inc.

The Letter E

Cooking with Evelyn Elephant
Letter E Recipes

EGGPLANT SNACKS

1 large eggplant (1 pound) or
    2 small Japanese eggplants
vegetable oil
mayonnaise
garlic salt
1 tsp. oregano
grated Parmesan cheese
OPTIONAL: crackers

Preheat the oven to 425°. Show the children the eggplant(s). Invite the children to guess what the eggplant looks like inside. Help the children notice that the word *eggplant* starts with the letter E. Remove and discard the ends of the eggplant. Cut into ⅛″ slices. Place on an oiled baking sheet and brush with oil. Top each slice with a small amount of mayonnaise. Sprinkle with garlic salt, oregano, and cheese. Put in oven and bake until lightly browned, or about 10 minutes. Cool until slices can be safely handled. Serve plain or on crackers.

EASY EGGNOG

3 quart package instant
    nonfat dry milk powder
2 packages (4½ ounces) no-bake
    custard mix or French vanilla
    pudding mix
6 oz. jar coffee creamer
2 tsp. nutmeg

Stir together all ingredients and store in a tightly covered container. To serve warm, stir ½ cup mix into a cup of warm water for each serving. To serve cold, blend equal parts mix, water, and ice cubes at high speed in a blender until slushy.

EGG SALAD

eggs
mustard
mayonnaise
salt
pepper
crackers or pita bread

Hard-boil enough eggs to allow two for each child in your group. After they cool a bit, invite the children to crack the shells and peel the eggs. Assist the children as necessary. Set aside the discarded eggshells, as you may wish to use them for another activity. Rinse eggs and refrigerate overnight before use. Give each child a bowl, a plastic spoon, and two hard-boiled eggs. Encourage the children to talk about how the eggs feel in their hands. Then invite the children to use their plastic spoons to chop up the eggs in their bowls. Ask the children if they would like you to add any mustard or mayonnaise to the chopped egg. Have the children mix in the mustard or mayonnaise or both. Add a small amount of salt and pepper to each child's mixture if desired. Invite the children to spread their egg salad on crackers or pita bread. Enjoy!

© HighReach Learning® Inc.

E is for 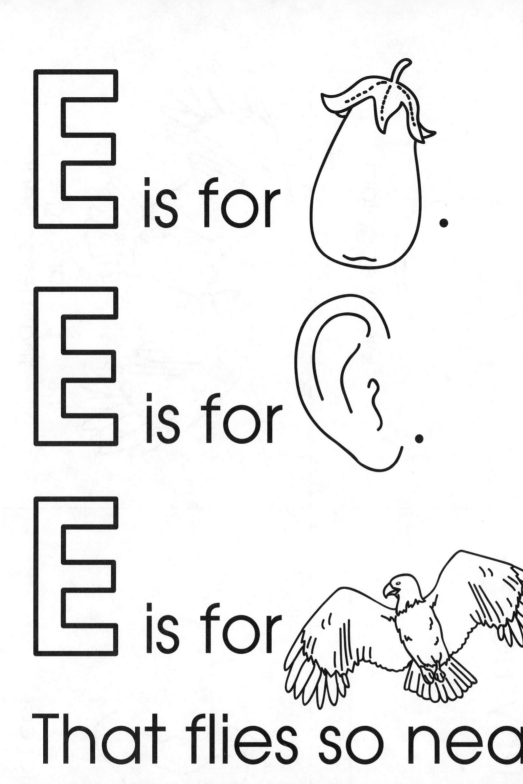.

E is for .

E is for .

That flies so near.

eggplant   ear   eagle

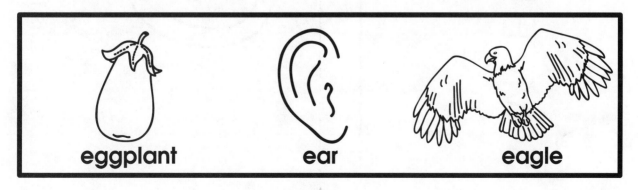

© HighReach Learning® Inc.

63

The Letter E

E is for eggplant.

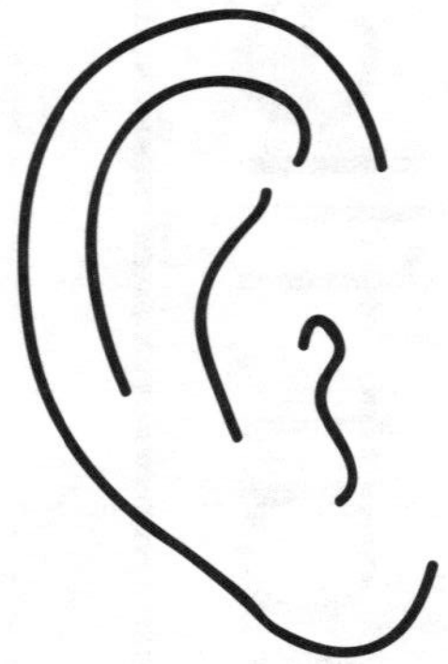

E is for eagle
that flies so near.

My E Rhyme

Name

E is for ear.

The Letter E

© HighReach Learning® Inc.

© HighReach Learning® Inc.

The Letter F

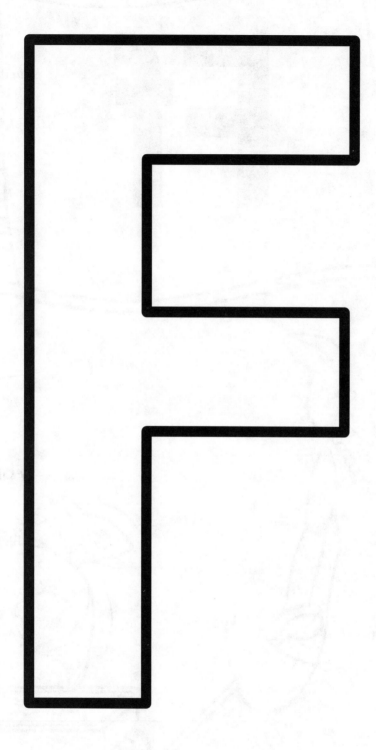

The Letter F

© HighReach Learning® Inc.

Language Activities

Introduce Farrah Fox and the Letter F

Decorate a copy of the Letter F Display (page 65) as desired. Point to Farrah Fox on the display. Invite the children to guess what type of animal Farrah is. If necessary explain that Farrah is a fox. You may wish to share the rhyme below several times and invite the children to join in.

FARRAH FOX

Farrah Fox carries fish
In a wagon that she found.
She feels her fish are fabulous
And fun to have around.

Invite the children to discuss what they learned about Farrah in the rhyme. Invite the children to name what Farrah is pulling in the wagon. Invite the children to talk about fish. Have they ever seen fish in the water? Have they ever been fishing? Encourage the children to share their ideas.

Point to both the capital F and the lowercase f on the display. Explain that these are both ways to write the letter. Explain that Farrah likes the letter F best because it is the first letter of her name. Help the children decide if they know anyone whose name begins with F.

Talk About Letter F Words

Invite the children to talk about words they know that begin with the letter F. Write any suggestions down on sentence strips, a large sheet of paper, or chart paper. Attach the words to the wall at the children's eye level. Some familiar word suggestions are:

fabric	feather	football
fade	fish	fox
family	five	funny

fabric fox five

football feather

☆*Learning Extension:* Invite the children to clap for the syllables of words that begin with the letter F (foot-ball, fab-ric, fade).

Talk About Families

Invite the children to talk about their families. Help the children realize that the word *family* begins with the letter F. The children may talk about who is in their families, what types of things they like to do, and where they live.

☆*Learning Extension:*
Invite a child to name the people in his/her family. Give the child a sheet of construction paper and coding dots or stickers. As the child names family members, invite him/her to add a coding dot or sticker for each. When finished, help the child count all of the coding dots or stickers that represent the members of his/her family. The child may wish to use a fine-tip marker to draw faces on the dots or even add bodies to them.

Language Activities
Share the Letter F Rebus Rhyme

Share the Letter F Rebus Rhyme (page 75) to develop a sense of rhythm and rhyme and to practice naming pictures. Show the display as you recite the rhyme several times. Afterwards, point to each picture on the chart and encourage the children to name it. Discuss each picture and invite the children to share times when they have seen similar items.

> ☆ *Learning Extension:* Talk about the letter F. Look at all of the words on the display. Help the children locate the letter F. Explain that the letter F can be written more than one way. Point to the capital F on the display and then point to the lowercase f. Help the children find all of the capital and lowercase letter F's on the display.

Create Letter F Rhyme Books

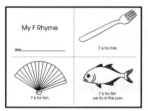

Give each child a copy of the Letter F Rhyme Book (page 76) and crayons or markers. Invite the children to point to the pictures as you read the text. Encourage the children to decorate the pictures as desired. Cut along the dotted lines and stack the pages in order. Staple the pages together. Invite the children to write their names on the rhyme books. Assist the children as needed.

> ☆ *Learning Extension:* Invite a child to "read" his/ her Letter F Rhyme Book to you. Encourage the child to point to the letter F in the book.

Discuss Firefighters and Fire Safety

Invite the children to tell you what they know about firefighters, and mention that the word *firefighter* begins with the letter F. You may wish to explain that firefighters help keep people safe from fire. Listen closely to what the children say and try to answer any questions that they may have about firefighters. Some suggestions you may wish to add to the discussion about firefighters are listed below.

FIREFIGHTERS:
❖ Teach people ways to be safe
❖ Drive trucks to places where there are fires
❖ Work very hard to put out fires
❖ Rescue people from fires
❖ Wear special clothing when they fight fires

Encourage the children to share what they know about preventing fires. As you talk together, you may want to share some of the tips listed below.

❖ If you see matches lying around, don't touch them. Tell a grown-up.
❖ Never play with electrical cords
❖ Do not put anything on the top of a lamp
❖ Do not play or get close to things that are hot, such as fireplaces, campfires, stoves, or grills

The Letter F

68

© HighReach Learning® Inc.

Science Activities

Find Out About Fading

Give the children sheets of assorted colors of construction paper and crayons or markers. Invite the children to write their names on their papers. Explain to the children that they are going to try an experiment. Encourage half of the children to put their papers near a window and have the other half of the group put their papers in their cubbies. Be sure to have some of the same color sheets in both places. Invite the children to predict what they think will happen to the papers in the direct light and what will happen to the papers not in the lighted areas. After a few days, invite the children to collect their papers. Put all of the papers on the table and talk about what happened to the papers that were in the lighted areas. Did the papers fade? Invite the children to discuss why they think this happened. Help the children realize that the word *fade* begins with the letter F.

Washable Ink

Examine Fingerprints

Set out washable-ink pads and white paper. Encourage the children to press their fingers onto the ink pads and then onto the white paper to make fingerprints. After the children wash their hands, provide unbreakable magnifying glasses that they can use to examine the fingerprints. You may wish to explain that everyone's fingerprints are different. You may also wish to mention that the word *fingerprint* begins with the letter F.

Which Animals Have Fur?

Challenge the children to brainstorm a list of animals that have fur, and mention that the word *fur* begins with the letter F. Write the children's responses on a sheet of chart paper. You may wish to help the children get started by giving suggestions. If you have access to the Internet, you may wish to extend the activity and look for pictures of the animals the children named. Invite the children to talk about the characteristics of the animals.

☆ *Learning Extension:* Invite the children to think of animals that have fur that begin with the letter F. Some examples are foxes and ferrets.

© HighReach Learning® Inc.

The Letter F

Large Muscle Activities

Follow Footprints

Cut several footprint shapes from construction paper. You may want to use the bottom of a shoe as a pattern. Attach the footprints to the floor or sidewalk to create a trail. You can add variety to the trail by putting some of the footprints close together and some far apart as shown. Invite the children to follow the footprints by placing a foot on each one. As they do so, you may wish to mention that the words *follow* and *footprint* both begin with the letter F.

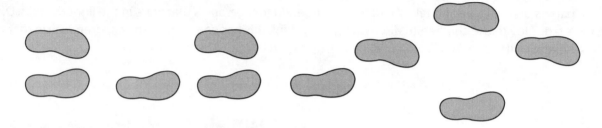

Play a Fishing Game

Cut several fish shapes from plastic-foam paper plates. Use a nontoxic permanent marker to draw capital letter F's on some of the fish and lowercase letter f's on others. Put the fish in a water table or basin of water. Invite the children to go fishing for the letter F. When a child catches a fish, invite the child to tell you if it is a lowercase or capital letter F. Continue playing until all of the children have had a chance to go fishing.

☆**Learning Extension:** Create more fish shapes labeled with assorted letters. Invite the children to identify the letters as they go fishing.

Play Follow the Fox

Create a fox mask by cutting a paper plate as shown. Decorate the mask with orange markers or paint. Add two orange construction paper triangles to the mask for ears. Add a black construction paper circle or pom-pom to create a nose. Finish the mask by taping a piece of elastic string to the back of the mask. Invite the children to play a game. Remind the children that Farrah is a fox and the word *fox* begins with the letter F. Choose one child to wear the fox mask. Invite the fox to move around the classroom or on the playground in different ways, such as crawling, hopping, skipping, etc., and have the other children imitate the movements. Continue playing, giving the children turns being the fox.

© HighReach Learning® Inc.

Art Activities

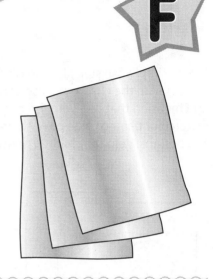

Foil Sculptures

Show the children some foil. Help the children notice that the word *foil* begins with the letter F. Give the children several sheets of foil and invite them to crumple, twist, and shape the foil to make sculptures as desired.

Make Letter F Collages

Give a child old newspapers or magazines and scissors. Invite the child to search for the letter F in the newspapers or magazines. The child may wish to tear or cut the letters out. Give the child a sheet of paper and a glue stick. Encourage the child to attach the letter F cutouts to the paper as desired. Assist the child as needed.

☆ *Learning Extension:* If you are working with a group of children, invite them to work together to make one big letter F collage. If you have bulletin board, butcher, or chart paper, you may even wish to cut the paper in the shape of the letter F. Help the children locate and cut or tear out large examples of the letter from captions and headlines. Have the children glue all the letter cutouts to the paper.

Feather Art

Set out a large container of craft feathers, shallow dishes of glue, old paintbrushes, and construction paper. Invite the children to explore the feathers and discuss how they feel in their hands. Encourage the children to spread glue onto their papers and then make designs by placing the feathers in the glue. As the children work, you may wish to help them notice that the word *feather* begins with the letter F.

Art Activities

Fabulous Fish!

Create simple fish stencils from old file folders as shown. Give the children white construction paper. Invite the children to use crayons to create fish using the stencils on top of the paper, and mention that the word *fish* begins with the letter F. After the children finish, provide blue watercolor paint or blue paint thinned with water in a shallow dish. Encourage the children to paint over their fish designs. Help the children notice what happens to the crayon marks when they paint over the fish.

☆ *Learning Extension:* Invite the children that show readiness to create their own fish without using the stencils.

Make F's in Finger Paint

Give each child a sheet of finger-paint paper. Help the child rub over the paper with a damp sponge to moisten it. Offer several colors of finger paint to the children. Spoon the color each child chooses onto the finger paint paper. Encourage the children to use their fingers to spread the paint across the paper. Invite the children to practice making the letter F in the wet finger paint. Keep in mind that the children may wish to use the paint in other ways, and that is okay too! As the children work, you may wish to mention that the word *finger* begins with the letter F.

    © HighReach Learning® Inc.

Small Muscle Activities

Practice Folding Paper

Give the children several sheets of scrap paper. Invite the children to practice folding the paper. Invite the children to fold the paper into four sections or fanfold them. You may need to demonstrate how to do this for the children. As the children practice folding their papers, you may wish to share that the words *fold, four,* and *fan* all begin with the letter F.

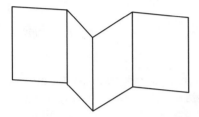
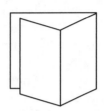
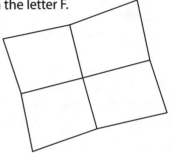

Explore Letter F Lacing Cards

Draw several block letter F's on posterboard using the pattern on page 66 and cut out. Use a hole punch to make a series of holes around each letter cutout. Vary the number of holes so that some will be easier to lace than others. Tie a length of yarn to one hole and wrap the free end with tape. Be sure the yarn can wrap around the letter twice. Set out the letter F lacing cards. Assist the children as needed as they explore the lacing cards.

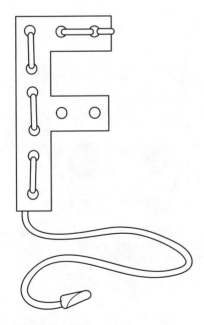

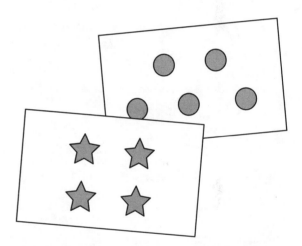

Find Sets of Four and Five

Attach four and five matching stickers to several index cards. Mix the cards together. Explain to the children that there are four and five matching stickers on the cards. Hold up a card with four stickers on it and count the stickers with the children. Then hold up a card with five stickers on it and count the stickers again. Mix up the cards and invite the children to choose one card each. Encourage the children to show the group their cards one at a time. Decide together if the card has four or five stickers on it. You may wish to help the children notice that the words *four* and *five* begin with the letter F.

© HighReach Learning® Inc.

The Letter F

Cooking with Farrah Fox
Letter F Recipes

Ff

FUNNY FACES

rice cakes
cream cheese
raisins or chocolate chips

Spread cream cheese on a rice cake for each child. Give the child several raisins or chocolate chips. Invite the child to make a funny face on the rice cake using the raisins or chocolate chips.

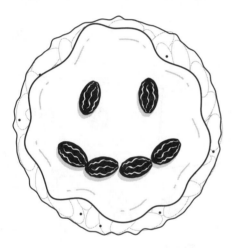

FABULOUS FAST FUDGE

3⅔ cups confectioners' sugar
½ cup cocoa
¼ cup milk
½ cup butter
1 Tbsp. vanilla

Combine confectioners' sugar, cocoa, milk, and butter in a microwave-safe bowl. Microwave on high power about 2 to 3 minutes, or until melted. Blend in vanilla. Spread into a buttered 8-inch square pan. Refrigerate for several hours. Cut into small squares and serve.

FOX FACES

pear halves
cheese triangles
chocolate chips

Cut cheese slices into small triangles. Place a pear half cut side down on a small paper plate. Arrange chocolate chips on the pear half to make eyes and a nose as shown. Place the cheese triangles at the top for ears.

The Letter F

© HighReach Learning® Inc.

F is for .

F is for .

F is for

We fry in the pan.

fork   fan   fish

F is for fork.

F is for fish
we fry in the pan.

My F Rhyme

Name

F is for fan.

© HighReach Learning® Inc.

© HighReach Learning® Inc.

The Letter G

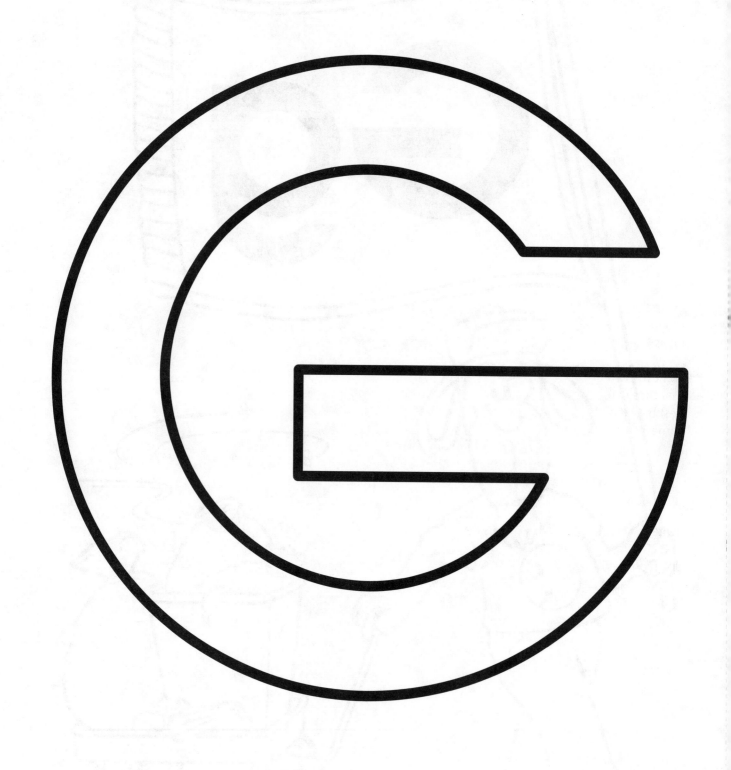

The Letter G

© HighReach Learning® Inc.

Language Activities

Introduce Gilbert Goat and the Letter G

Decorate a copy of the Letter G Display (page 77) as desired. Point to Gilbert Goat on the display. Invite the children to guess what type of animal Gilbert is. If necessary explain that Gilbert is a goat. You may wish to share the rhyme below several times and invite the children to join in.

GILBERT GOAT

Gilbert is a goat,
Who goes all over town.
He gathers all the garbage,
When he sees it on the ground.

Invite the children to discuss what they learned about Gilbert in the rhyme. Invite the children to name what Gilbert is pulling in the wagon. Invite the children to discuss who gathers the garbage where they live. Where does their garbage go? Encourage the children to share their ideas.

Point to both the capital G and the lowercase g on the display. Explain that these are both ways to write the letter. Explain that Gilbert likes the letter G best because it is the first letter of his name. Help the children decide if they know anyone whose name begins with G.

Talk About Letter G Words

Invite the children to talk about words they know that begin with the letter G. Write any suggestions down on sentence strips, a large sheet of paper, or chart paper. Attach the words to the wall at the children's eye level. Some familiar word suggestions are:

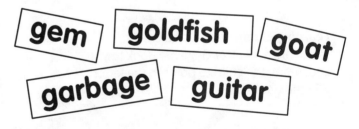

goat   gem
garbage   giraffe
goldfish   gingerbread
guitar
gallop

Explain that all of these words begin with the letter G, but the letter G makes more than one sound. In the words *goat* and *guitar*, the letter makes the same sound as in Gilbert. In the words *gem* and *giraffe*, the sound of the letter is different.

> ☆**Learning Extension:** Invite the children to clap for the syllables of words that begin with the letter G (gin-ger-bread, gem, gui-tar).

© HighReach Learning® Inc.

The Letter G

Language Activities

Share the Letter G Rebus Rhyme

Share the Letter G Rebus Rhyme (page 87) to develop a sense of rhythm and rhyme and to practice naming pictures. Show the display as you recite the rhyme several times. Afterwards, point to each picture on the chart and encourage the children to name it. Discuss each picture and invite the children to share times when they have seen similar items.

☆ *Learning Extension:* Talk about the letter G. Look at all of the words on the display. Help the children locate the letter G. Explain that the letter G can be written more than one way. Point to the capital G on the display and then point to the lowercase g. Help the children find all of the capital and lowercase letter G's on the display.

Create Letter G Rhyme Books

Give each child a copy of the Letter G Rhyme Book (page 88) and crayons or markers. Invite the children to point to the pictures as you read the text. Encourage the children to decorate the pictures as desired. Cut along the dotted lines and stack the pages in order. Staple the pages together. Invite the children to write their names on the rhyme books. Assist the children as needed.

☆ *Learning Extension:* Invite a child to "read" his/her Letter G Rhyme Book to you. Encourage the child to point to the letter G in the book.

Play the Game Don't Giggle!

Invite the children to play a game. Explain that the word *giggle* begins with the letter G, and that giggle is another word for laugh. Invite one of the children to be It. Everyone else should try to make It laugh. You may want to suggest that the children make faces or tell jokes to It, but they cannot touch or tickle It. Once It giggles, choose a new child to be It and play again.

Talk About Favorite Games

Invite the children to discuss their favorite games. Encourage the children to give you details about the game, such as how many players are needed, or if the game is played inside or outside. Write what the children say on a sheet of chart paper. Help the children realize that the word *game* begins with the letter G. After they finish, read the children's responses back to them. Make it a point to incorporate some of the children's favorite games into your lesson plans.

The Letter G

80

© HighReach Learning® Inc.

Science Activities

How Many Cups of Water Are in a Gallon?

Show the children a full gallon container of water and an empty gallon container. Place a funnel in the empty container. Show the children a measuring cup and invite them to guess how many cups of water will fill the gallon container. Invite one child at a time to pour a measuring cup full of water into the funnel. Count with the children as you fill the container. As the children pour the water, you may wish to mention that the word *gallon* begins with the letter G. How many cups did it take to fill the gallon? The actual measurement should be close to 16 cups of water. Were the children's guesses accurate?

Observe a Goldfish

Show the children a goldfish. Help the children realize the word *goldfish* begins with the letter G. Invite the children to share their observations about the goldfish. Does the goldfish swim in the water? How does the goldfish move? Does the goldfish breathe under the water? Do the best you can to answer any questions that the children have as they make their observations.

☆ *Learning Extension:* Invite the children that show readiness to talk about the goldfish's characteristics, such as color, body parts, etc.

Explore Gems

Show the children assorted craft gems and magnifying glasses. As the children explore, help them realize that the word *gem* begins with the letter G. What color are the gems? What happens when the children hold the gems in the sunlight? Why do the gems sparkle? Try to answer any questions that the children may have as they explore.

☆ *Learning Extension:* Set up a gem panning area near the water table. Bury the toy gems in several buckets of sand. Provide the children with sand sifters. Pour some of the sand into each sand sifter over the water table. Help the children pan or sift the sand in the water to look for the gems. You may wish to mention that when people look for real gems, they usually look for them by panning or washing away the sand with water.

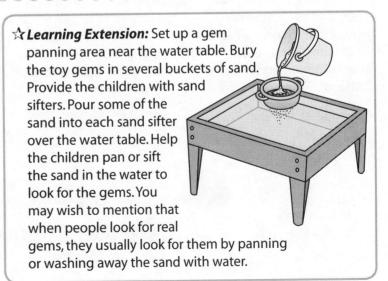

© HighReach Learning® Inc.

81

The Letter G

Large Muscle Activities

Dance to Guitar Music

Show the children a toy or real guitar. Help the children notice the sounds the guitar makes when it is played. Invite the children to gently strum the guitar strings. You may wish to mention that the word *guitar* begins with the letter G. Play some music featuring guitars. As the music plays, invite the children to dance or move to the music. They may even wish to pretend to play guitars.

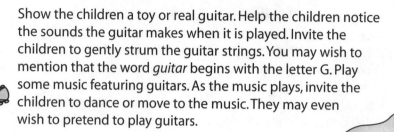

Gallop Outside

Show the children how to gallop by leading with one foot. Help the children realize the word *gallop* begins with the letter G. Encourage the children to gallop as they move around the area where they are playing.

Play a Golf Game

Create a golf set. For each golf club, stack several sheets of newspaper, roll tightly, and secure with tape to form a shaft. Cut a rectangle from heavy cardboard and tape it to the end of the shaft. Use small plastic balls for golf balls. Cut a hole in the center of a large sturdy paper plate. Attach the plate upside down to a sheet of green posterboard. Show the children the golf set. Invite the children to share what they know about playing golf. After the children share, help them realize that *golf* begins with the letter G. Demonstrate how to hit the ball in the hole. Give each child a chance to try to hit the ball into the hole.

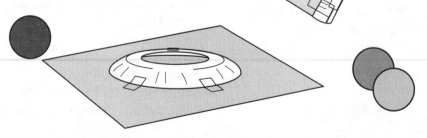

The Letter G

© HighReach Learning® Inc.

Art Activities

Create Tactile Letter G's

Give each child a copy of the capital letter G (page 78), an old paintbrush, and a shallow dish of glue. Invite the children to trace the letter G with their fingers. Encourage the children to spread glue on their letter G's as desired. Provide the children with small bathroom cups filled with nonmetallic gold glitter, salt, or rice. Invite the children to shake the gold glitter, salt, or rice onto the glue. Set aside to dry. After the glue dries, invite the children to trace their tactile letter G's with their fingers. How does the G feel? Use descriptive words such as bumpy, rough, etc. as you interact with the child.

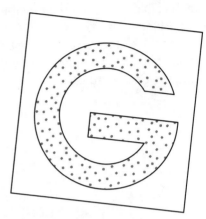

Make Gift Bags

Give each child a paper bag, glue, crayons or markers, and assorted collage materials. Invite the children to create gift bags with the materials. The children may wish to discuss items they like to give or receive as gifts. As the children, work you may wish to mention that the word *gift* begins with the letter G.

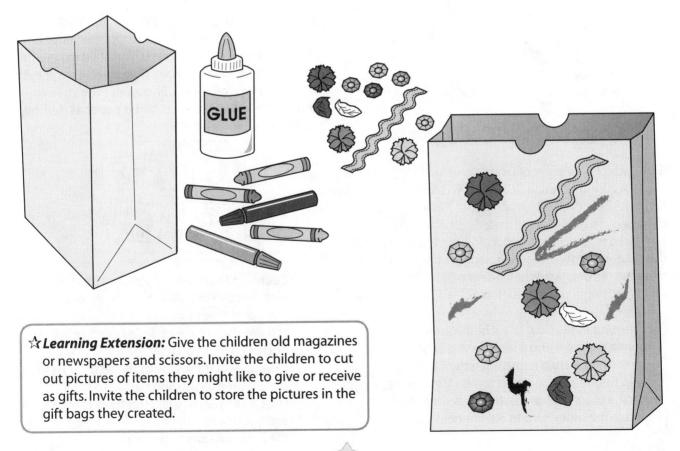

☆ *Learning Extension:* Give the children old magazines or newspapers and scissors. Invite the children to cut out pictures of items they might like to give or receive as gifts. Invite the children to store the pictures in the gift bags they created.

© HighReach Learning® Inc.

The Letter G

Art Activities

Make Garbage Structures

Give the children assorted recyclable items such as scrap paper, old newspapers, old boxes, etc., and masking tape. Invite the children to work together to create a garbage structure using the items. As the children work, you may wish to remind the children that Gilbert Goat likes to gather garbage because the word *garbage* begins with the letter G. When they finish, invite the children to describe their garbage structures.

Create Gold Collages

Give each child a sheet of white construction paper. As the children watch, print "G is for gold" on each sheet of construction paper. Provide the children with gold collage materials, such as sticky stars, art tissue, rickrack, ribbon, foil, etc. Encourage the children to decorate their papers with the gold materials. As they work, help them realize that the word *gold* begins with the letter G.

☆ *Learning Extension:* Use a highlighter and print a capital G and a lowercase g on index cards. Have a child name the letters, and help the child trace the letters on the card as he/she shows readiness. Then have the child attach the index card to his/her gold collage.

Make Letter G Collages

Give a child old newspapers or magazines and scissors. Invite the child to search for the letter G in the newspapers or magazines. The child may wish to tear or cut the letters out. Give the child a sheet of paper and a glue stick. Encourage the child to attach the letter G cutouts to the paper as desired. Assist the child as needed.

☆ *Learning Extension:* If you are working with a group of children, invite them to work together to make one big letter G collage. If you have bulletin board, butcher, or chart paper, you may even wish to cut the paper in the shape of the letter G. Help the children locate and cut or tear out large examples of the letter from captions and headlines. Have the children glue all the letter cutouts to the paper.

The Letter G

© HighReach Learning® Inc.

Small Muscle Activities

Explore Letter G Lacing Cards

Draw several block letter G's on posterboard using the pattern on page 78 and cut out. Use a hole punch to make a series of holes around each letter cutout. Vary the number of holes so that some will be easier to lace than others. Tie a length of yarn to one hole and wrap the free end with tape. Be sure the yarn can wrap around the letter twice. Set out the letter G lacing cards. Assist the children as needed as they explore the lacing cards.

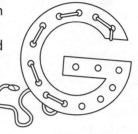

Drive Cars to Garages

Create garages using three shoe boxes as shown. Label the boxes with the numerals 1–3 using a nontoxic permanent marker. Use coding dot stickers to label three cars with the numerals 1–3 to match the garages. Show the children the cars and the garages. Invite the children to drive each car to its matching number on the box garage. Assist the children as needed. As the children play, you may wish to mention that the word *garage* begins with the letter G.

☆ *Learning Extension:* You may wish to create more garages and cars for higher numerals depending on the abilities of the children in your class.

Explore Gift Boxes

Provide the children with assorted sizes of gift boxes with lids. The children may wish to stack the gift boxes, sort them by size, or use them in another way. As the children explore the boxes, you may wish to help them realize that the word *gift* begins with the letter G.

☆ *Learning Extension:* Show the children the gift boxes without the lids. Challenge the children to match the lids to the gift boxes.

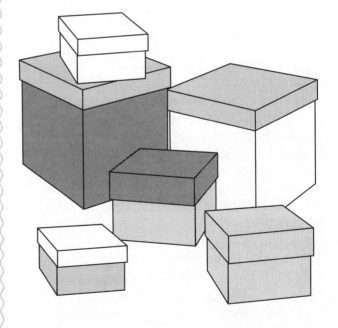

© HighReach Learning® Inc.

The Letter G

Cooking with Gilbert Goat
Letter G Recipes

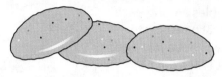

Gingerbread Cookies

1 (6 oz.) package of butterscotch pudding mix
¾ cup butter
¾ cup firmly packed brown sugar
1 egg
2¼ cups all-purpose flour
1 tsp. baking soda
1 Tbsp. ground ginger
1½ tsp. ground cinnamon

Cream pudding mix with butter and sugar; add egg and blend well. Combine flour, baking soda, ginger, and cinnamon; blend into pudding mixture. Chill dough for 1 hour. Roll dough on floured board to quarter inch thickness and cut with cookie cutter. Place on greased baking sheet and bake at 350° for 10–12 minutes.

Garlic Cheese Bread

1 (8 oz.) package shredded
   mozzarella cheese
1 stick softened butter or margarine
2 cloves of minced garlic
1 Tbsp. chopped fresh parsley
¼ tsp. black pepper
1 (16 oz.) loaf of Italian bread

Preheat oven to 425°. Invite the children to help you mix all ingredients, excluding the bread, into a large mixing bowl. Slice bread at ¾-inch intervals almost all the way through, but stopping just before the bottom. Invite the children to help you spread one side of each slice with the cheese mixture using spatulas or spoons. Wrap in foil and bake for 25 minutes. Serve warm.

Giggling Gelatin

2½ cups boiling water
2 (8 oz.) packages of your
   favorite flavored gelatin mix
1 cup cold milk
1 (4 oz) package of vanilla instant pudding mix

Stir gelatin mix in boiling water for 3 minutes, or until dissolved. Away from the stove, invite the children to help you mix together the cold milk and instant pudding mix in another bowl. Then pour the pudding into the cooled gelatin mixture. Beat with a whisk for one minute. Pour the mix into a lightly greased 9" x 13" pan. Use a smaller pan for thicker servings. Refrigerate at least 3 hours or until firm. You may wish to invite the children to use cookie cutters to make gigglers or simply cut into squares. Lift from pan and put on plate.

Gourmet Gumbo

4 Tbsp. butter
4 Tbsp. flour
2 tsp. minced garlic
1½ cups sliced okra
¼ cup diced celery
¼ cup peeled and diced carrots
3 cups vegetable broth
3 cups water
2 cups cooked rice

Melt butter in pot. Add flour and stir frequently over low heat until brown. Away from the stove, invite the children to help measure out the vegetables for the gumbo. When finished, add the garlic and the vegetables and stir. Cook for 2 minutes, then add broth and water. Bring to a boil, reduce the heat and simmer for 1½ hours. Serve over rice.

© HighReach Learning® Inc.

G is for .

G is for .

G is for who

Wears a new coat.

| goose | goat | girl |

© HighReach Learning® Inc.

The Letter G

My G Rhyme

G is for goose.

G is for girl who wears a new coat.

G is for goat.

Name _____

© HighReach Learning® Inc.

Language Activities

Introduce Holly Hippo and the Letter H

Decorate a copy of the Letter H Display (page 89) as desired. Point to Holly Hippo on the display. Invite the children to guess what type of animal Holly is. If necessary explain that Holly is a hippo. You may wish to share the rhyme below several times and invite the children to join in.

HOLLY HIPPO

Holly is a hippo,
Who has a lot to say.
She hauls around her doll's house,
As she hurries down the way!

Invite the children to discuss what they learned about Holly in the rhyme. Invite the children to name what Holly is pulling in the wagon. Invite the children to talk about their homes. What type of home do they think a hippo needs?

Point to both the capital H and the lowercase h on the display. Explain that these are both ways to write the letter. Explain that Holly likes the letter H best because it is the first letter of her name. Help the children decide if they know anyone whose name begins with H.

Talk About Letter H Words

Invite the children to talk about words they know that begin with the letter H. Write any suggestions down on sentence strips, a large sheet of paper, or chart paper. Attach the words to the wall at the children's eye level. Some familiar word suggestions are:

hamburger	heartbeat	hot dog
hand	hippo	hula hoop
happy	hole	
hat	home	

☆**Learning Extension:** Invite the children to clap for the syllables of words that begin with the letter H (hat, ham-burg-er, heart-beat).

Talk About Homes

Invite the children to talk about their homes. They may live in apartments, townhomes, houses, trailers, or other types of homes. As the children discuss their homes, help them realize that the word *home* begins with the letter H.

☆**Learning Extension:** Provide assorted blocks and invite the children to build homes. As the children work, encourage them to talk about their creations.

© HighReach Learning® Inc.

The Letter H

Language Activities

Share The Letter H Rebus Rhyme

H is for [hand] .

H is for [hay] .

H is for [horse] that Likes to run and play.

hand   hay   horse

Share the Letter H Rebus Rhyme (page 99) to develop a sense of rhythm and rhyme and to practice naming pictures. Show the display as you recite the rhyme several times. Afterwards, point to each picture on the chart and encourage the children to name it. Discuss each picture and invite the children to share times when they have seen similar items.

☆ *Learning Extension:* Talk about the letter H. Look at all of the words on the display. Help the children locate the letter H. Explain that the letter H can be written more than one way. Point to the capital H on the display and then point to the lowercase h. Help the children find all of the capital and lowercase letter H's on the display.

What Makes You Happy?

Invite the children to talk about things that make them feel happy. As the children share ideas, write what they say on a sheet of chart paper. After they finish, read the chart back to the children. Help the children notice that the word *happy* begins with the letter H.

What Makes You Happy

friends
holidays
puppies
hot dogs
zoo
presents

☆ *Learning Extension:* Invite the children that show readiness to find and point to the letter H where it is written on the chart.

My H Rhyme

Name _____

H is for hand.

H is for hay.

H is for horse that likes to run and play.

Create Letter H Rhyme Book

Give each child a copy of the Letter H Rhyme Book (page 100) and crayons or markers. Invite the children to point to the pictures as you read the text. Encourage the children to decorate the pictures as desired. Cut along the dotted lines and stack the pages in order. Staple the pages together. Invite the children to write their names on the rhyme books. Assist the children as needed.

☆ *Learning Extension:* Invite a child to "read" his/her Letter H Rhyme Book to you. Encourage the child to point to the letter H in the book.

The Letter H

© HighReach Learning® Inc.

Science Activities

Graph Hair Color

Add four columns to a sheet of chart paper. Use brown, yellow, red, and black markers to label the columns *brown, blond, red,* and *black.* Invite one child at a time to look at his/her hair color in an unbreakable mirror. Ask the child to describe the colors he/she sees. Help the child determine his/her hair color. Use the corresponding colored marker and print the child's name in the appropriate column. For example, if the child has brown hair, use the brown marker to print that child's name in the column labeled brown. You may wish to mention that the word *hair* begins with the letter H. Afterwards, look at the chart as a group. Help the children determine which column has the most names in it.

Lane			
Dave	Kerry	Lance	Jamal
Amy	Alex	Holly	Kim
brown	blond	red	black

> ☆ *Learning Extension:* Invite a child to help you count the number of names in each column. Which column has the most names? The fewest?

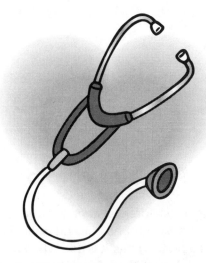

Listen to Heartbeats

Show the children a real or toy stethoscope. Explain to the children that the stethoscope is used to listen to your heartbeat. Invite one child at a time to listen to his/her heartbeat. What does a heartbeat sound like? You may also wish to mention that the word *heartbeat* starts with the letter H.

Measure Height

Tape a long strip of adding machine tape to the wall or back of a door. Have each child stand in front of the adding machine tape. Mark the child's height. Write the child's name beside the mark. Explain to the children that you are marking their height, or how tall they are. Use a measuring tape to determine how tall each child is. Be sure to tell the children how tall they are. You may wish to mention that the word *height* begins with the letter H.

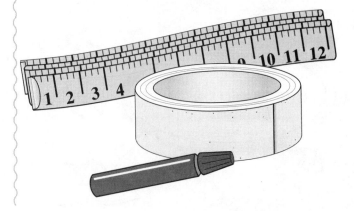

© HighReach Learning® Inc.

The Letter H

Large Muscle Activities

Hop Along a Letter H

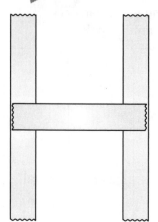

Use masking tape or chalk to create a large letter H on the sidewalk or other outdoor surface. Show the children the large letter H. Encourage the children to take turns hopping along the lines of the letter. As they play, help the children realize the word *hop* begins with the letter H.

☆ **Learning Extension:** If the children show readiness, invite them to hop on one foot along the lines of the letter H.

Toss Beanbags in a Hula Hoop

Show the children a hula hoop. Encourage the children to stand a few feet away from the hula hoop. Give each child a beanbag. Invite the children to toss the beanbags into the hula hoop. How many beanbags went into the hula hoop? How many landed outside the hula hoop? Invite the children to help you count. Challenge the children to step a little farther away from the hula hoop each time their beanbags land inside. As the children play, you may wish to mention that the term *hula hoop* starts with the letter H.

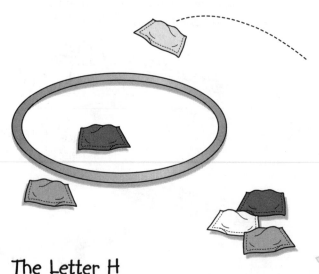

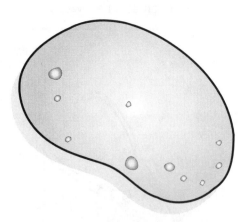

Play Hot Potato

Encourage the children to stand in a circle. Show the children a playground ball and explain that they should pretend that it is hot! When the children get the ball they should toss it quickly to the person beside them. Help the children realize that the word *hot* begins with the letter H. Continue playing the game as long as the children show interest.

The Letter H

94

© HighReach Learning® Inc.

Art Activities

Create Tactile Letter H's

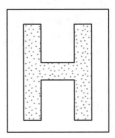

Give each child a copy of the capital letter H (page 90), an old paintbrush, and a shallow dish of glue. Invite the children to trace the letter H with their fingers. Encourage the children to spread glue on their letter H's as desired. Provide the children with small bathroom cups filled with sand, salt, or rice. Invite the children to shake the sand, salt, or rice onto the glue. Set aside to dry. After the glue dries, invite the children to trace their tactile letter H's with their fingers. How does the H feel? Use descriptive words such as bumpy, rough, etc. as you interact with the child.

Make Hats

Provide various materials such as whipped topping bowls, large sheets of construction paper, old newspapers, stickers, and crayons or markers. Encourage the children to use the materials to make hats. As the children work, help them realize that the word *hat* begins with the letter H.

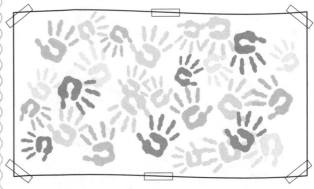

Make a Handprint Mural

Attach a long sheet of butcher paper to a table or to the classroom floor. Place sponges in shallow dishes and soak each with a different color of paint. Invite the children to press their hands onto the paint-soaked sponges and then onto the butcher paper to make a handprint mural. As the children work, be sure to point out that *handprint* is another word that begins with the letter H. When they are finished, display the mural in the classroom or hallway.

☆ *Learning Extension:* Invite a child to trace his/her own hands. Assist the child as needed. Provide crayons or markers and scissors. Invite the child to decorate the hands and then cut them out. Attach the hand cutouts to the butcher paper to create a mural.

Art Activities

Create Hole Punch Art

Provide assorted colors of construction paper and several hole punches for the children to use. *Caution: Be sure to provide close supervision while the children use the hole punches, as they can be a pinching hazard.* Encourage the children to punch holes in the construction paper and collect the circle punch-outs. Encourage the children to spread a thin layer of glue on a sheet of construction paper with an old paintbrush. Then invite the children to use the cutouts to create designs in the glue. As the children work, you may wish to mention that the word *hole* begins with the letter H.

Make Letter H Collages

Give a child old newspapers or magazines and scissors. Invite the child to search for the letter H in the newspapers or magazines. The child may wish to tear or cut the letters out. Give the child a sheet of paper and a glue stick. Encourage the child to attach the letter H cutouts to the paper as desired. Assist the child as needed.

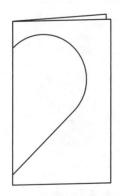

Make Blob Art Hearts

Fold sheets of construction paper in half. Use a nontoxic permanent marker to draw half of a heart pattern along the fold line as shown. Provide scissors and the folded paper and encourage the children to cut along the bold line. Assist children as needed. When they finish, open up the papers to reveal the hearts. You may wish to mention that the word *heart* begins with the letter H. Put assorted colors of paint in cups with plastic spoons. Invite each child to choose a few colors of paint. Encourage the children to put a few spoonfuls of the paint onto their hearts. Help the children fold their heart shapes in half and rub their hands over the outside. Then open up the hearts to reveal the interesting paint designs.

☆ *Learning Extension:* If you are working with a group of children, invite them to work together to make one big letter H collage. If you have bulletin board, butcher, or chart paper, you may even wish to cut the paper in the shape of the letter H. Help the children locate and cut or tear out large examples of the letter from captions and headlines. Have the children glue all the letter cutouts to the paper.

The Letter H

96

© HighReach Learning® Inc.

Small Muscle Activities

Make Playdough Hot Dogs and Hamburgers

Provide the children with assorted colors of playdough. Invite the children to create hot dogs and hamburgers. Encourage the children to discuss hot dogs and hamburgers as they create. Which do they like best? What do they like to eat on their hot dogs and hamburgers? Expand the conversation based on what the children tell you. You may wish to mention that the words *hot dog* and *hamburger* begin with the letter H.

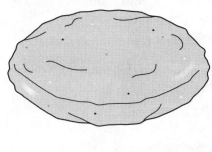

> ☆ *Learning Extension:* Challenge the children to brainstorm a list of more foods that begin with the letter H. Some examples are ham, hash browns, hush puppies, hot chocolate, etc.

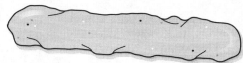

Make Handprints in Damp Sand

Add some water to a sand table or basin to make the sand slightly damp. Invite the children to press their hands into the damp sand. Encourage the children to make observations about what happens in the sand. Help the children notice that all of their handprints are slightly different! You may also wish to mention that the word *handprint* starts with the letter H.

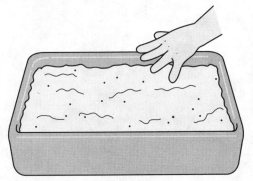

> ☆ *Learning Extension:* Invite the children that show readiness to create the letter H in the damp sand. You may need to model this for the children.

Explore Letter H Lacing Cards

Draw several block letter H's on posterboard using the pattern on page 90 and cut out. Use a hole punch to make a series of holes around each letter cutout. Vary the number of holes so that some will be easier to lace than others. Tie a length of yarn to one hole and wrap the free end with tape. Be sure the yarn can wrap around the letter twice. Set out the letter H lacing cards. Assist the children as needed as they explore the lacing cards.

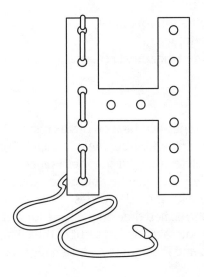

© HighReach Learning® Inc.

The Letter H

Cooking with Holly Hippo
Letter H Recipes

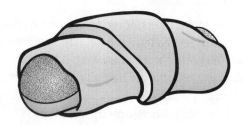

HOT DOGS AND CROISSANTS

1 package of hot dogs
1 roll of croissants

Heat oven to specified temperature on croissant package. Cut hot dogs in half. Roll halved hot dogs in croissants. Place on cookie sheet and bake.

HEAVENLY HASH

21 oz. can cherry pie filling
14 oz. can sweetened condensed milk
15 oz. can chunk pineapple, with liquid
1 small container of whipped topping
1 cup shredded coconut

Mix ingredients together and chill for at least one hour before serving.

HAPPY HAMBURGER PIZZA

pre-made pizza crust
2 Tbsp. olive oil
¼ lb ground hamburger meat
1 jar spaghetti sauce
1 bag shredded mozzarella cheese
ketchup
mustard

Turn oven to specified heat on pizza crust package. Brown hamburger meat in skillet. Drizzle olive oil on pizza crust. Put spaghetti sauce on pizza crust. Put browned hamburger on top of sauce. Cover with shredded cheese. Place in oven and cook to specified time on package for pizza crust. When you take the pizza out of the oven, use the ketchup and mustard to make a happy face.

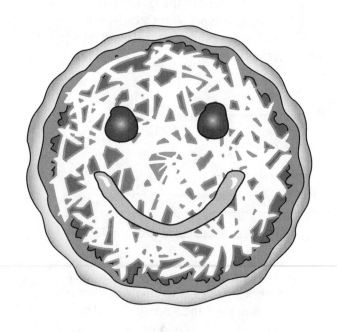

The Letter H

98

© HighReach Learning® Inc.

H is for .

H is for .

H is for that

Likes to run and play.

hand　　　　**hay**　　　　**horse**

My H Rhyme

H is for hand.

H is for horse
that likes to run and play.

H is for hay.

Name

The Letter H

100

© HighReach Learning® Inc.

© HighReach Learning® Inc.

The Letter I

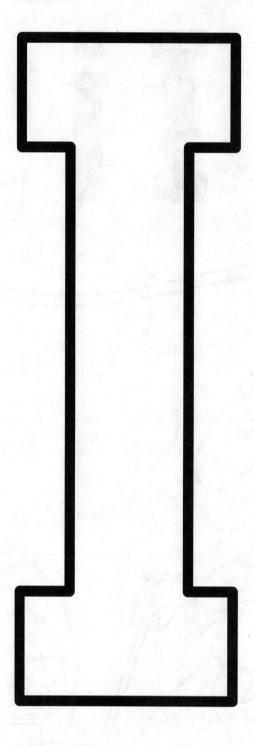

© HighReach Learning® Inc.

Language Activities

Introduce Isabel Iguana and the Letter I

Decorate a copy of the Letter I Display (page 101) as desired. Point to Isabel Iguana on the display. Invite the children to guess what type of animal Isabel is. If necessary explain that Isabel is an iguana. You may wish to share the rhyme below several times and invite the children to join in.

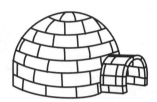

ISABEL IGUANA

Isabel the iguana
Is intelligent, I know.
She pulls around her igloo,
That's made from ice and snow.

Invite the children to discuss what they learned about Isabel in the rhyme. Invite the children to name what Isabel is pulling in the wagon. Discuss igloos. Encourage the children to share their ideas about igloos. Have they ever seen an igloo? How do they think an igloo is made?

Point to both the capital I and the lowercase i on the display. Explain that these are both ways to write the letter. Explain that Isabel likes the letter I best because it is the first letter of her name. Help the children decide if they know anyone whose name begins with I.

Talk About Letter I Words

Invite the children to talk about words they know that begin with the letter I. Write any suggestions down on sentence strips, a large sheet of paper, or chart paper. Attach the words to the wall at the children's eye level. Some familiar word suggestions are:

Short Sounds:	Long Sounds:
inch	ice
inventor	ice cream
insect	idea
igloo	ivy

Explain that all of these words begin with the letter I, but the letter I makes more than one sound. In the words *igloo* and *iguana,* the letter makes the same sound as in Isabel Iguana. In the words *ice cream* and *ice,* the sound of the letter is the same as its name.

⭐ ***Learning Extension:*** Invite the children to clap for the syllables of words that begin with the letter I (i-gua-na, inch-worm, in-sect, ice).

Language Activities

Share the Letter I Rebus Rhyme

Share the Letter I Rebus Rhyme (page 111) to develop a sense of rhythm and rhyme and to practice naming pictures. Show the display as you recite the rhyme several times. Afterwards, point to each picture on the chart and encourage the children to name it. Discuss each picture and invite the children to share times when they have seen similar items.

☆ *Learning Extension:* Talk about the letter I. Look at all of the words on the display. Help the children locate the letter I. Explain that the letter I can be written more than one way. Point to the capital I on the display and then point to the lowercase i. Help the children find all of the capital and lowercase letter I's on the display.

Create Letter I Rhyme Books

Give each child a copy of the Letter I Rhyme Book (page 112) and crayons or markers. Invite the children to point to the pictures as you read the text.

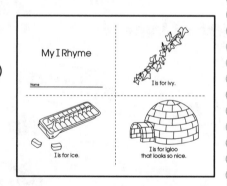

Encourage the children to decorate the pictures as desired. Cut along the dotted lines and stack the pages in order. Staple the pages together. Invite the children to write their names on the rhyme books. Assist the children as needed.

☆ *Learning Extension:* Invite a child to "read" his/her Letter I Rhyme Book to you. Encourage the child to point to the letter I in the book.

Talk About Inventors

Explain to the children that the word *invent* means to think up a new way of doing something. Challenge the children to work together to create an invention. Provide cardboard boxes and other materials such as knobs from broken appliances, large buttons, plastic tubing, duct tape, drinking straws, or any other interesting materials that you have available. ***Caution: When choosing materials to offer, keep in mind the age of the children. If you are working with younger children who may place items in their mouths, avoid buttons, knobs, or any other items that may be considered choking hazards.*** Be sure to also provide some art supplies such as crayons, markers, scissors, tape, and glue. As the children work, invite them to talk about their invention, and mention that the word *invention* begins with the letter I.

The Letter I

104

© HighReach Learning® Inc.

Science Activities

Perform an Ice Experiment

Place an ice cube on a small paper plate and lay a 6" piece of string across the top of the ice cube. Ask the children if they think that you can pick up the ice cube with the sting. Encourage the children to share their thoughts with the group. Sprinkle a little salt on the string and the ice cube. Hold both ends of the string and lift up to raise the ice cube off the plate. Invite the children to guess how they think the experiment works. After they respond, explain that the salt melts the ice around the string. The string sinks into the water and then the water freezes again, trapping the string in the ice. Help the children take turns repeating the experiment with new ice cubes, and mention that the word *ice* begins with the letter I.

Talk About Insects

Gather several nonfiction books about insects. Invite the children to explore the books and talk about any insects they recognize. Expand the conversation based on what the children tell you. You may wish to mention that the word *insect* begins with the letter I. You may also wish to talk about safety around insects. Some suggestions for discussion are listed below.

❖ Do not step on insects or touch them with your hands
❖ If an insect bites or stings you, let a grown-up know right away

> ☆ *Learning Extension:* Invite a child to show you a picture of an insect. Talk about the characteristics of the insect with the child. Does it have antennae? How many legs does it have? Does it have wings?

Measure Using Inches

Provide the children with 1" counting cubes. If you do not have counting cubes available, cut some 1" construction paper squares. Show the children a ruler or yardstick and point out how the inches are marked off. Explain to the children that each one of the cubes or paper squares is one inch long. Encourage the children to arrange the cubes or paper squares along the side of the ruler or yardstick to demonstrate. Then invite the children to measure other classroom items in inches using the ruler, yardstick, counting cubes, or paper squares. As the children explore, you may wish to mention that the word *inch* begins with the letter I.

Large Muscle Activities

Imitate Animals

Invite the children to imitate their favorite animals. Explain that imitate means to copy, and that the word *imitate* begins with the letter I. You may wish to help the children think of animals by starting with suggestions such as moving like iguanas, horses, dogs, etc.

Explore Instruments

Provide the children with various toy instruments such as bells, drums, tambourines, etc. Encourage the children to make music, and mention that the word *instument* begins with the letter I. You may suggest that the children line up parade style and march around the classroom or playground as they use the instruments.

☆ *Learning Extension:* As the children explore the instruments, invite them to talk about the different sounds they make.

Move Like Inchworms

Show the children how to move like inchworms, or have a child demonstrate. Bend at the waist and place your hands on the floor in front of your body without bending your knees. Keep your feet in place, but walk your hands forward as far as you can. Then keep your hands in place and, still keeping your knees straight, walk your feet forward as far as you can. Then keep your feet in place and walk your hands forward again. Repeat these actions as you move around the classroom or the playground. After you have demonstrated, encourage the children to imitate your actions. As the children move, you may wish to mention that the word *inchworm* begins with the letter I.

The Letter I

© HighReach Learning® Inc.

Art Activities

Make Igloo Pictures

Explain to the children that the Inuit (IN-you-it) people live where it is cold and snowy outside. These people are also called Eskimos. Explain that the Inuit word for house is *igloo,* and that the Inuit people build many types of homes and call all of them igloos. Many times when people think of igloos, they usually think of the snow homes the Inuit build. Long ago the Inuit learned to build homes from blocks of packed snow. Today, some Inuit people still build snow homes when they go on fishing and camping trips. Provide the children with large sheets of blue construction paper, small square sponges, and shallow dishes of white paint. Invite the children to use the sponges to create igloos on their papers. As the children work, you may wish to mention that the words *Inuit* and *igloo* begin with the letter I.

☆ *Learning Extension:* Provide the children with blue construction paper, old paintbrushes, glue in shallow dishes, and white packing peanuts. Invite the children to spread glue on their papers and add the packing peanuts to the glue to create igloos.

Create Insects

Provide the children with assorted clean recyclables (newspapers, paper grocery bags, paper-towel rolls, etc.), collage materials, glue, crayons, and markers. Encourage the children to use the materials to make their own insects. Invite the children to talk about the materials they are using and the insects they are making. As the children work, you may wish to mention that the word *insect* begins with the letter I.

☆ *Learning Extension:* After the children make their insects, write "I is for insect" on an index card for each child. Use a highlighter for each letter I and crayons for the other letters. Encourage the child to name each letter I, try to trace it, and then attach the card to his/her insect.

© HighReach Learning® Inc.

The Letter I

Art Activities

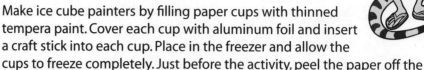

Ice Painting

Make ice cube painters by filling paper cups with thinned tempera paint. Cover each cup with aluminum foil and insert a craft stick into each cup. Place in the freezer and allow the cups to freeze completely. Just before the activity, peel the paper off the frozen painters. Place the ice cube painters in shallow dishes. Give the children sheets of white construction paper. Invite the children to hold the frozen paintbrushes by the craft sticks and rub them across their papers to create designs. As the children work, you may wish to mention that the word *ice* begins with the letter I.

Make Letter I Collages

Give a child old newspapers or magazines and scissors. Invite the child to search for the letter I in the newspapers or magazines. The child may wish to tear or cut the letters out. Give the child a sheet of paper and a glue stick. Encourage the child to attach the letter I cutouts to the paper as desired. Assist the child as needed.

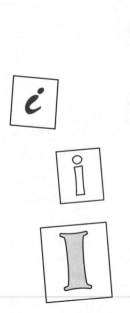

☆ **Learning Extension:** If you are working with a group of children, invite them to work together to make one big letter I collage. If you have bulletin board, butcher, or chart paper, you may even wish to cut the paper in the shape of the letter I. Help the children locate and cut or tear out large examples of the letter from captions and headlines. Have the children glue all the letter cutouts to the paper.

 © HighReach Learning® Inc.

Small Muscle Activities

Play an Ice Cream Cone Game

Make an ice cream cone game by cutting five simple ice cream cone shapes from brown construction paper. Print each numeral 1–5 on a separate ice cream cone shape. Cut 15 ice cream scoops from assorted colors of construction paper as shown.

Store the cones and scoops in a zipper-top bag. Give the children the zipper-top bag. Encourage the children to name the number on each ice cream cone and place the corresponding quantity of scoops on each cone. As the children play mention that the term *ice cream* begins with the letter I.

☆*Learning Extension:* If the children show readiness, create more cones with higher numerals and more scoops.

Invisible Tape Art

Give the children rolls of invisible tape (transparent) and white construction paper. Invite the children to tear off several pieces of invisible tape and put them on the construction paper as desired. Assist the children with the tape as needed. As the children work, you may wish to mention to the children that they are using invisible tape, and that the word *invisible* begins with the letter I. The word *invisible* means transparent or hidden from sight. After the children finish putting the tape on the construction paper, provide them with shallow dishes of paint and paintbrushes. Invite the children to paint over the tape. Encourage the children to talk about what happens when they paint over the tape.

Explore Letter I Lacing Cards

Draw several block letter I's on posterboard using the pattern on page 102 and cut out. Use a hole punch to make a series of holes around each letter cutout. Vary the number of holes so that some will be easier to lace than others. Tie a length of yarn to one hole and wrap the free end with tape. Be sure the yarn can wrap around the letter twice. Set out the letter I lacing cards. Assist the children as needed as they explore the lacing cards.

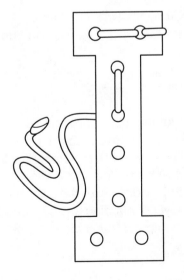

© HighReach Learning® Inc.

The Letter I

Cooking with Isabel Iguana
Letter I Recipes

INSTANT ICE CREAM

For each serving:
1 pint-sized zipper-top bag
1 gallon-sized zipper-top bag
1 Tbsp. sugar
½ cup milk
6 Tbsp. salt
¼ tsp. vanilla

Fill the gallon-sized
zipper-top bag half full
with ice. Add salt and
seal the bag. Put milk,
vanilla, and sugar into
the pint-sized zipper-top
bag and seal it. Place the small bag inside the
large one and seal again carefully. Have children
shake until the mix becomes ice cream, about 5
minutes. Take out the small bag and wipe off the
salt and ice. Open carefully, and give the children
spoons to enjoy their homemade ice cream.

INSECT SNACK

celery sticks
carrot sticks
licorice sticks
raisins
cream cheese

Give each child a piece of wax paper. Provide each
child with ingredients to create an insect. You may
need to help the children with spreading cream
cheese or assist them as needed in other ways. As
the children work, invite them to talk about their
insect creations.

INDIVIDUAL ENGLISH TRIFLES

1 lb. store-bought angel food cake or pound cake
raspberry jam
1 large can fruit cocktail in natural juice
1 (3.5 oz.) package of instant vanilla pudding mix
milk
whipped topping
decorative sprinkles

Prepare the pudding mix according to directions on the package. Cut
the cake into ½" slices. Give each child 2 slices. Help each child spread
jam on one slice. Cover with the other slice to make jam "sandwiches."
Cut each sandwich into ½" cubes and put into a cup. Help children
spoon some fruit cocktail with the juice onto the layer of cake in each
cup. Spoon a layer of pudding onto the fruit in each child's cup and
then top with whipped topping and sprinkles. Makes 8 servings.

The Letter I

110

© HighReach Learning® Inc.

I is for  .

I is for .

I is for

That looks so nice.

ivy   ice   igloo

I is for ivy.

I is for igloo
that looks so nice.

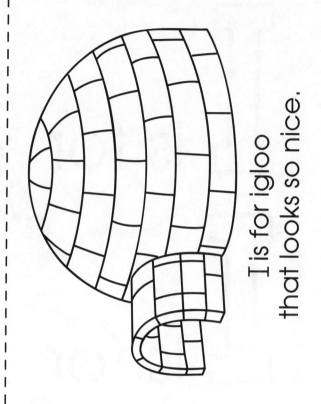

My I Rhyme

I is for ice.

© HighReach Learning® Inc.

© HighReach Learning® Inc.

113

The Letter J

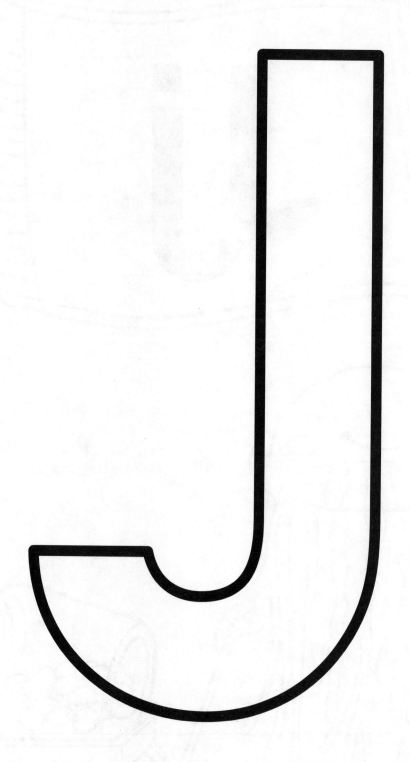

The Letter J

© HighReach Learning® Inc.

Language Activities
Introduce Jenny Jellyfish and the Letter J

Decorate a copy of the Letter J Display (page 113) as desired. Point to Jenny Jellyfish on the display. Invite the children to guess what type of animal Jenny is. If necessary explain that Jenny is a jellyfish. You may wish to share the rhyme below several times and invite the children to join in.

JENNY JELLYFISH

Jenny is a jellyfish,
Who jumps and jiggles too.
She has a jar of jelly beans,
She just might share with you.

Invite the children to discuss what they learned about Jenny in the rhyme. Invite the children to name what Jenny is pulling in the wagon. Do the children like to eat jelly beans? What else could they put in a jar? Encourage the children to share their ideas.

Point to both the capital J and the lowercase j on the display. Explain that these are both ways to write the letter. Explain that Jenny likes the letter J best because it is the first letter of her name. Help the children decide if they know anyone whose name begins with J.

Talk About Letter J Words

Invite the children to talk about words they know that begin with the letter J. Write any suggestions down on sentence strips, a large sheet of paper, or chart paper. Attach the words to the wall at the children's eye level. Some familiar word suggestions are:

jam	jellyfish	jockey
jar	jelly bean	juice
jelly	jewelry	jump

☆**Learning Extension:** Invite the children to clap for the syllables of words that begin with the letter J (jel-ly-fish, jump, jock-ey).

Dictate a Recipe for Jelly

Invite the children to dictate their ideas about how they think jelly is made. As the children watch, print the word *jelly* at the top of a sheet of chart paper. Write the children's ideas on the chart paper as they dictate them. Give suggestions as needed. You may wish to discuss different types of jellies, such as grape, strawberry, raspberry, etc. You also may wish to share that jelly is made from fruit juice. Show the children the word *jelly* on the chart. Help the children notice that the word *jelly* begins with the letter J. After the children finish sharing, read their ideas back to them.

Language Activities

Share the Letter J Rebus Rhyme

J is for ✈.

J is for 🫙.

J is for 🪼

That swims very far.

jet   jar   jellyfish

Share the Letter J Rebus Rhyme (page 123) to develop a sense of rhythm and rhyme and to practice naming pictures. Show the display as you recite the rhyme several times. Afterwards, point to each picture on the chart and encourage the children to name it. Discuss each picture and invite the children to share times when they have seen similar items.

> ☆ **Learning Extension:** Talk about the letter J. Look at all of the words on the display. Help the children locate the letter J. Explain that the letter J can be written more than one way. Point to the capital J on the display and then point to the lowercase j. Help the children find all of the capital and lowercase letter J's on the display.

Talk About Jellyfish

Invite the children to share their ideas about jellyfish. Remind the children that Jenny is a jellyfish, and the word *jellyfish* begins with the letter J. You may wish to share a nonfiction book about jellyfish with the children or use some of the suggestions below for discussion. Try to answer any questions the children may have and expand the conversation based on what the children tell you.

❖ A jellyfish is made up mostly of water (98%)
❖ Some jellyfish glow in the dark
❖ Jellyfish have soft bodies and long, stinging, poisonous tentacles
❖ Jellyfish use their tentacles to catch fish to eat
❖ If you ever see a jellyfish, stay away from it; their stings could hurt

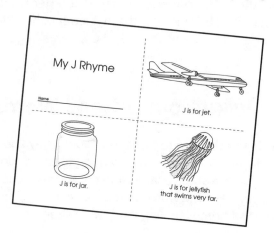

My J Rhyme

Name

J is for jet.

J is for jar.

J is for jellyfish
that swims very far.

Create Letter J Rhyme Books

Give each child a copy of the Letter J Rhyme Book (page 124) and crayons or markers. Invite the children to point to the pictures as you read the text. Encourage the children to decorate the pictures as desired. Cut along the dotted lines and stack the pages in order. Staple the pages together. Invite the children to write their names on the rhyme books. Assist the children as needed.

> ☆ **Learning Extension:** Invite a child to "read" his/her Letter J Rhyme Book to you. Encourage the child to point to the letter J in the book.

The Letter J

116

© HighReach Learning® Inc.

Science Activities

Graph Juice Preferences

Make a graph on chart paper with three columns and 15–20 rows. At the base of each column, draw a cup. Color one of the cups red, one purple, and one orange. At the top of the graph, print the question: Which juice is my favorite? Give each child three small cups of juice to taste – orange, cranberry, and grape. Show the children the graph and read the question at the top. Encourage the children to notice the letter J in the word *juice*. Give each child a coding dot or happy face sticker. Help the child put the sticker in the column above the drawing of his/her favorite type of juice. When all of the children are finished, use the graph to help the children decide which type of juice they like the best and which type they like the least.

☆ *Learning Extension:* Invite a child to count the stickers in each column with you. Which column has the most stickers? Which column has the fewest stickers?

Which juice is my favorite?		
		☺
		☺
		☺
		☺
☺		☺
☺		☺
☺	☺	☺
☺	☺	☺
☺	☺	☺
☺	☺	☺

Guess the Jelly Beans

Show the children a jar of jelly beans, and mention that the term *jelly bean* begins with the letter J. Invite each child to guess how many jelly beans are in the jar. Write down the children's guesses on a sheet of paper. After all of the children have guessed, empty the jar and count the jelly beans in front of the children. How accurate were the children's guesses?

☆ *Learning Extension:* Give each child a cup of jelly beans from the jar. Invite the children to sort the jelly beans by color. Encourage the children to count each pile of jelly beans with you. Which color has more? Which color has less?

How Far Can You Jump?

Use a strip of masking tape inside or sidewalk chalk outside to mark a starting line. Invite one child at a time to stand on the starting line and jump as far as he/she can. Mark the floor or ground where the child lands with tape or chalk. Use a measuring tape or yardstick to measure the distance. If you do not have a yardstick or measuring tape available, you may wish to use non-standard units of measurement such as string, blocks, etc. to measure how far the child jumped. As the children take turns jumping, you may wish to mention that the word *jump* begins with the letter J.

☆ *Learning Extension:* Invite the children to jump again. Challenge each child to jump farther than they did the first time. Encourage the children to help you as you measure their jumps.

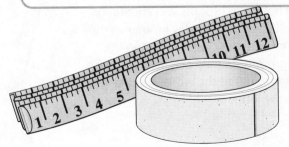

© HighReach Learning® Inc.

The Letter J

Large Muscle Activities

Explore Jump Ropes

Provide the children with jump ropes, or turn a long jump rope and encourage the children to take turns jumping. If the children are not yet ready to jump a turning rope, you may wish to lay the rope on the classroom floor or on the ground and the children can simply jump over it. As the children play mention that the word *jump* begins with the letter J.

Play Jacks

Show the children a set of jumbo plastic jacks, and mention that the word *jacks* begin with the letter J. Demonstrate how to play the game using the following rules. Toss the jumbo jacks lightly so they spread out on the floor. Next, bounce the rubber ball and try to pick up one jack, letting the ball bounce once. Catch the ball while still holding the jack. Place the caught jack aside in a separate pile. Continue, trying to pick up one jack at a time until all the jacks are collected. Use only one hand. Each turn continues until the child misses the ball, misses the jack, or drops the jack after picking it up.

Pretend to Be Jockeys

Explain to the children that a jockey is a person who rides a racehorse. Provide stick horses or brooms and encourage the children to role-play jockeys as they ride around the classroom or on the playground. As they play, you may wish to mention that the word *jockey* begins with the letter J.

Move with Jingle Bells

Give each child a large jingle bell. Challenge the children to find ways to make music with the bells. Some suggestions are jiggling or jumping with the bells. You may wish to mention that the words *jingle, jiggle,* and *jump* all begin with the letter J.

© HighReach Learning® Inc.

Art Activities

Create Tactile Letter J's

Give each child a copy of the capital letter J (page 114), an old paintbrush, and a shallow dish of glue. Invite the children to trace the letter J with their fingers. Encourage the children to spread glue on their letter J's as desired. Provide the children with small bathroom cups filled with sand, salt, or rice. Invite the children to shake the sand, salt, or rice onto the glue. Set aside to dry. After the glue dries, invite the children to trace their tactile letter J's with their fingers. How does the J feel? Use descriptive words such as bumpy, rough, etc. as you interact with the child.

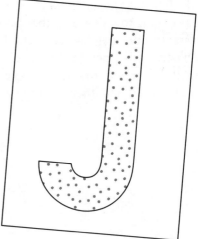

Make Jewelry

Provide the children with assorted materials such as large beads and lacing string, aluminum foil, shiny confetti, stickers, sequins, and sections of paper-towel rolls. Encourage the children to use the materials to create jewelry, such as necklaces or bracelets from the beads and lacing string, rings by rolling and twisting the aluminum foil, and bracelets from the paper-towel roll sections cut to make cuffs and decorated. As the children work, you may wish to mention that the word *jewelry* begins with the letter J.

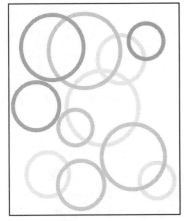

Jar Lid Prints

Locate plastic jar lids in different sizes. Provide the children with construction paper, jar lids, and shallow dishes of paint. Encourage the children to dip the jar lids in the paint and make prints on their papers. Help the children notice the differences in the prints as they work. You may also wish to remind the children that the word *jar* begins with the letter J.

> ☆ *Learning Extension:* Invite the children to sort or order (seriate) the jar lids by size. Assist the children as needed.

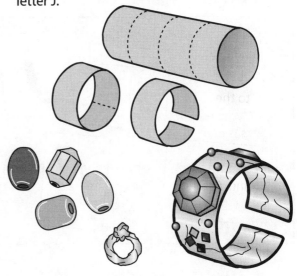

Art Activities
Create Jellyfish Puppets

Give each child a large paper plate and scissors. Help the children fold the paper plates in half and cut along the fold line. Help the children tape the two halves together leaving the bottom open to create a puppet. Give each child several crepe paper streamers. Help the children attach the crepe paper streamers to the straight edge of the plate halves to resemble jellyfish tentacles. Provide crayons and markers, as the children may wish to add details to their jellyfish puppets. As the children work, you may wish to remind them that the word *jellyfish* begins with the letter J.

Make Letter J Collages

Give a child old newspapers or magazines and scissors. Invite the child to search for the letter J in the newspapers or magazines. The child may wish to tear or cut the letters out. Give the child a sheet of paper and a glue stick. Encourage the child to attach the letter J cutouts to the paper as desired. Assist the child as needed.

☆ **Learning Extension:** If you are working with a group of children, invite them to work together to make one big letter J collage. If you have bulletin board, butcher, or chart paper, you may even wish to cut the paper in the shape of the letter J. Help the children locate and cut or tear out large examples of the letter from captions and headlines. Have the children glue all the letter cutouts to the paper.

The Letter J

© HighReach Learning® Inc.

Small Muscle Activities

Explore a Jack-in-the-Box

Show the children a jack-in-the-box toy. Invite a child to wind up the toy using the handle. As the child winds the handle, explain to the children that this toy is called a jack-in-the-box, and the word *jack* begins with the letter J. After the toy pops out, push it back down and continue, giving all of the children a turn to wind the handle.

Jigsaw Puzzles

Provide the children with assorted jigsaw puzzles. Make sure the puzzles are appropriate for the ages and abilities of the children in your group. As the children work, you may wish to mention that these are jigsaw puzzles, and the word *jigsaw* begins with the letter J.

> ☆ *Learning Extension:* Provide children that show readiness with more advanced jigsaw puzzles. Assist the children as needed.

Explore Letter J Lacing Cards

Draw several block letter J's on posterboard using the pattern on page 114 and cut out. Use a hole punch to make a series of holes around each letter cutout. Vary the number of holes so that some will be easier to lace than others. Tie a length of yarn to one hole and wrap the free end with tape. Be sure the yarn can wrap around the letter twice. Set out the letter J lacing cards. Assist the children as needed as they explore the lacing cards.

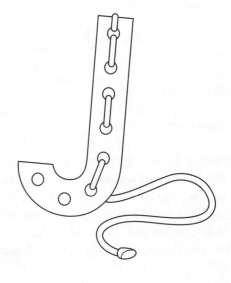

© HighReach Learning® Inc.

The Letter J

Cooking with Jenny Jellyfish
Letter J Recipes

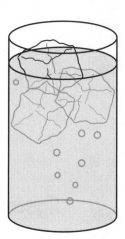

JAMMIN' JELLY JAM

1 tsp. corn syrup
2–3 drops lemon juice
1 cup thawed, drained frozen berries

Encourage the children to help mix and mash all of the ingredients together. Serve on bread or crackers.

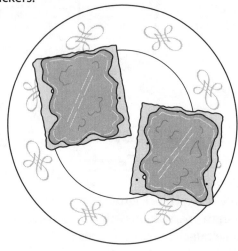

JUICE IN A JIFFY

1 (12 oz.) can pineapple juice concentrate
1 (32 oz.) bottle cranberry juice cocktail
1 liter bottle sparkling water

Pour pineapple juice concentrate into a large pitcher and add 2 cans water. Add cranberry juice and stir. Slowly pour in sparkling water. Serve over ice. Recipe makes about 3 quarts.

JELLY BEAN CAKE

2 cups flour
½ cup jelly beans, chopped (not licorice)
1 cup sugar
1 cup butter, softened
8 oz. cream cheese, softened
1 tsp. vanilla
3 eggs
1½ tsp. baking powder
¼ tsp. salt
powdered sugar

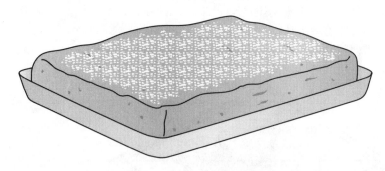

Preheat the oven to 350°. Grease and flour a 9" x 13" cake pan. Toss the chopped jelly beans with 2 Tbsp. flour in a small bowl and set aside. Beat together the sugar, butter, cream cheese, and vanilla until well blended in a large bowl. Add the eggs one at a time, beating after each addition. Add remaining flour, baking powder, and salt. Spoon half of the batter evenly into the bottom of the prepared pan. Stir the jelly beans into the remaining batter and spoon on top. Bake for 35 to 40 minutes or until a toothpick inserted into the center comes out clean. Cool pan for 10 minutes. Sprinkle with powdered sugar.

© HighReach Learning® Inc.

J is for 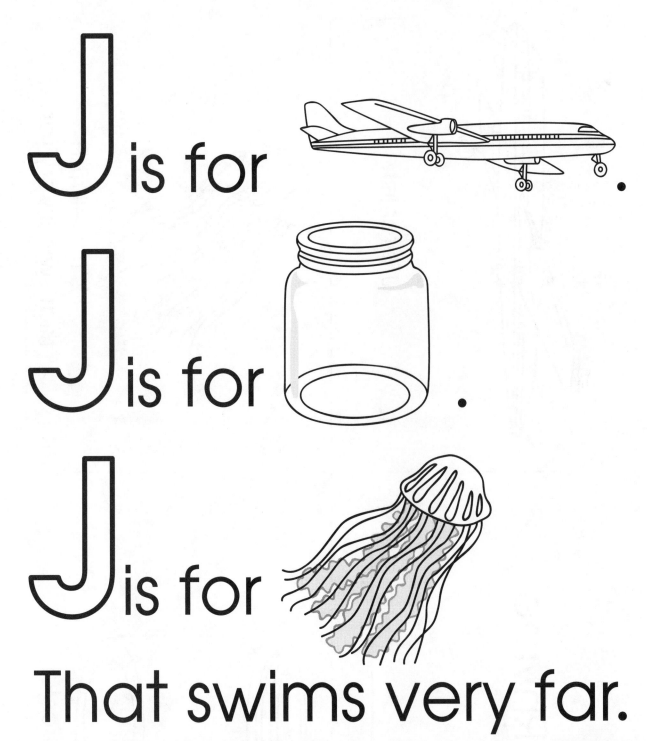.

J is for .

J is for

That swims very far.

jet jar jellyfish

© HighReach Learning® Inc.

123

The Letter J

My J Rhyme

J is for jet.

J is for jellyfish
that swims very far.

J is for jar.

Name

© HighReach Learning® Inc.

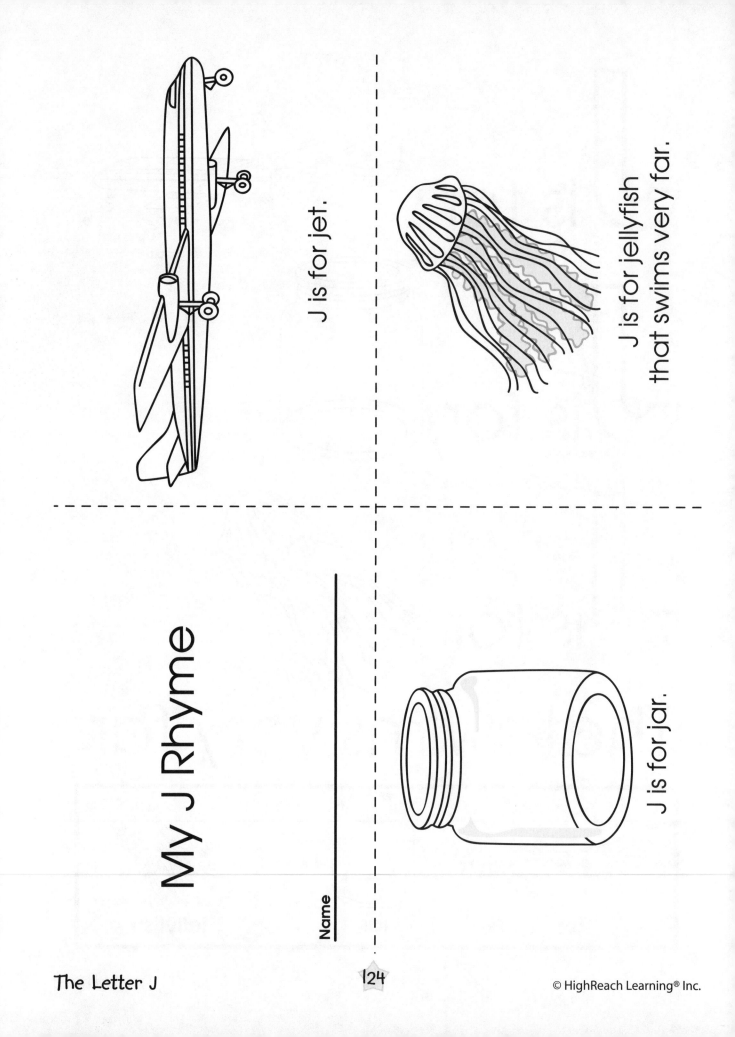

© HighReach Learning® Inc.

The Letter K

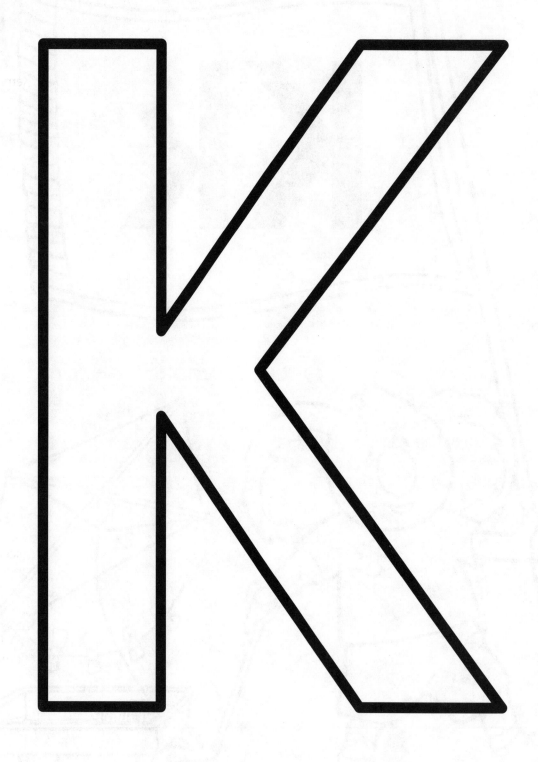

The Letter K

© HighReach Learning® Inc.

Language Activities

Introduce Kerry Koala and the Letter K

Decorate a copy of the Letter K Display (page 125) as desired. Point to Kerry Koala on the display. Invite the children to guess what type of animal Kerry is. If necessary explain that Kerry is a koala. You may wish to share the rhyme below several times and invite the children to join in.

KERRY KOALA

Kerry is a koala,
Who's always very kind.
If you want to fly her kite,
She really wouldn't mind!

Invite the children to discuss what they learned about Kerry in the rhyme. Encourage the children to name the item on the display that Kerry is pulling in the wagon. Invite the children to discuss kites. Have they ever seen or flown a kite? Encourage the children to share their ideas.

Point to both the capital K and the lowercase k on the display. Explain that these are both ways to write the letter. Explain that Kerry likes the letter K best because it is the first letter of her name. Help the children decide if they know anyone whose name begins with K.

Talk About Letter K Words

Invite the children to talk about words they know that begin with the letter K. Write any suggestions down on sentence strips, a large sheet of paper, or chart paper. Attach the words to the wall at the children's eye level. Some familiar word suggestions are:

kaleidoscope	key	kite	koala
kangaroo	king	kitten	
ketchup	kiss	kiwi	

king   key   kitten

koala   ketchup

> ☆ *Learning Extension:* Invite the children to clap for the syllables of words that begin with the letter K (kan-ga-roo, king, ki-wi).

Discuss Kindness

Discuss the value of kindness. Remind the children that Kerry Koala is kind, and explain that being kind to other people means treating them nicely. As the children watch, title a sheet of chart paper "Ways to Be Kind." Challenge the children to think of ways they can be kind. As the children make suggestions, list them on a sheet of chart paper. You may need to give some examples such as sharing toys, helping clean up, giving hugs, etc. After the children finish, read their suggestions back to them. Point to the word *kind* on the chart and help the children notice that it begins with the letter K.

Ways to Be Kind

The Letter K

Language Activities

Share the Letter K Rebus Rhyme

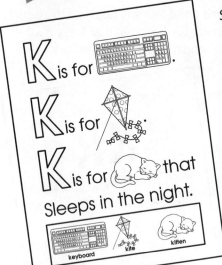

Share the Letter K Rebus Rhyme (page 135) to develop a sense of rhythm and rhyme and to practice naming pictures. Show the display as you recite the rhyme several times. Afterwards, point to each picture on the chart and encourage the children to name it. Discuss each picture and invite the children to share times when they have seen similar items.

☆ *Learning Extension:* Talk about the letter K. Look at all of the words on the display. Help the children locate the letter K. Explain that the letter K can be written more than one way. Point to the capital K on the display and then point to the lowercase k. Help the children find all of the capital and lowercase letter K's on the display.

Create Letter K Rhyme Books

Give each child a copy of the Letter K Rhyme Book (page 136) and crayons or markers. Invite the children to point to the pictures as you read the text. Encourage the children to decorate the pictures as desired. Cut along the dotted lines and stack the pages in order. Staple the pages together. Invite the children to write their names on the rhyme books. Assist the children as needed.

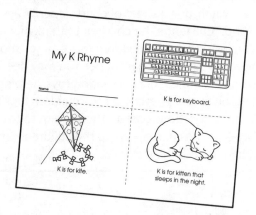

☆ *Learning Extension:* Invite a child to "read" his/her Letter K Rhyme Book to you. Encourage the child to point to the letter K in the book.

Play King, King, Who Took Your Crown?

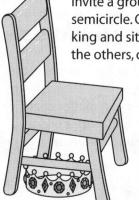

Invite a group of children to sit in a semicircle. Choose one child to be the king and sit in a chair facing away from the others, covering his/her eyes. Place a toy crown under the king's chair. Tap a child from the group to quietly come forward, pick up the crown, and return to his/her place, hiding the crown behind his/her back. Encourage all of the children to put their hands behind their backs as well. Once the child has hidden the crown, ask the group to chant, "King, king, take a look around. Someone came and took your crown!" Encourage the king to turn around to the group and use three guesses to find out who has the crown. If the king guesses correctly, the child with the crown becomes the king. If the king does not guess correctly after three guesses, choose another child to be the king and play again. As the children play the game, you may want to mention that the word *king* begins with the letter K.

The Letter K

128

© HighReach Learning® Inc.

Science Activities

Explore a Kaleidoscope

Invite the children to look through a kaleidoscope. Encourage the children to describe what they see. How do they think the kaleidoscope works? Mention that the word *kaleidoscope* begins with the letter K during your discussion,

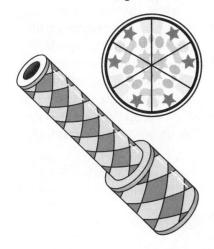

> ☆ *Learning Extension:* You may wish to share some of the following information about kaleidoscopes with the children that show readiness.
>
> ❖ The first kaleidoscope was invented in Scotland a long time ago.
>
> ❖ The interior of a kaleidoscope may have 2, 3, 4, or more mirrors.
>
> ❖ The objects inside a kaleidoscope can be pieces of dried flowers, marbles or other transparent, colored objects! The objects reflect off of the mirrors inside the kaleidoscope.

Explore Kiwifruit

Show the children some kiwifruit. Invite the children to talk about how the kiwi feels in their hands. Encourage the children to guess what they think the inside of the kiwi looks like. Have any of the children ever tasted kiwi? Invite them to share their experiences. Away from the children, cut open the kiwi. Show the children the inside of the kiwi. What color is the inside? What does it look like? Expand the conversation based on what the children tell you. During your discussion, you may wish to mention that the word *kiwi* begins with the letter K.

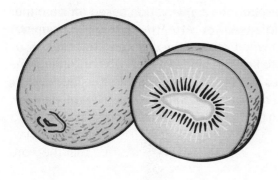

Fly a Kite

Show the children a kite (the best kind of kite to use for this activity is a small, lightweight children's kite). Invite the children to share any experiences they have had with kites. Encourage the children to share their ideas on how a kite flies. Does the kite need wind to fly? Challenge the children to make predictions about whether or not the kite will fly. Try to fly the kite outside. You may need to run to get the kite to fly. Were the children's predictions correct? Invite the children to take turns flying the kite. As the children play, you may wish to mention that the word *kite* begins with the letter K. *Caution: Closely supervise the children during this activity.*

© HighReach Learning® Inc.

The Letter K

Large Muscle Activities

Have a Kangaroo Relay

Invite a small group of children to play a game. Explain to the children that the word *kangaroo* begins with the letter K, and that they are going to pretend to be kangaroos. Mark an area of the room or playground with two long strips of tape to designate the relay area. Encourage the children to line up behind one strip. Ask the first child in line to hold his/her hands at waist level and cup them to form a "kangaroo pocket." Place a beanbag in the child's cupped hands. Ask the child to hop like a kangaroo to the other tape line, turn around, and hop back. If the beanbag is dropped, the child should pick it up and keep hopping. When the child returns to the starting point, he/she should say the letter K and drop the beanbag in the cupped hands of the next child in line. Continue until each child has had a chance to hop like a kangaroo.

Practice Kicking Balls

Show the children assorted playground balls. Invite the children to practice kicking. Help the children notice if any of the balls are easier to kick or go farther than the others. As the children play, you may wish to mention that the word *kick* begins with the letter K. Continue until all of the children have had a chance to practice kicking.

☆ **Learning Extension:** Invite a child to help you measure how far he/she kicked the ball. Challenge the child to kick the ball again even farther than the first attempt!

Find the Hidden Kitten

When the children are not present, hide a plush toy kitten in the classroom or outside. Explain to the children that you have hidden a toy kitten. You may wish to mention that the word *kitten* begins with the letter K. Invite the children to share their experiences with kittens. Make sure to expand the conversation based on what the children tell you. After the children share, explain that when you tell the children "Go!" they should try to find the hidden kitten. Give the children clues as needed. After they find the hidden kitten, you may want to hide it again. Play the game as long as the children show interest.

The Letter K

130

© HighReach Learning® Inc.

Art Activities

Create Tactile Letter K's

Give each child a copy of the capital letter K (page 126), an old paintbrush, and a shallow dish of glue. Invite the children to trace the letter K with their fingers. Encourage the children to spread glue on their letter K's as desired. Provide the children with small bathroom cups filled with sand, salt, or rice. Invite the children to shake the sand, salt, or rice onto the glue. Set aside to dry. After the glue dries, invite the children to trace their tactile letter K's with their fingers. How does the K feel? Use descriptive words such as bumpy, rough, etc. as you interact with the child.

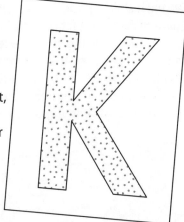

Create Kites

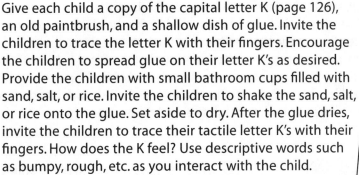

Cut several large diamond shapes from construction paper. Give each child a diamond and crayons or markers. Invite the children to decorate the diamonds as desired, and explain that they are going to make kites. Remind the children that Kerry Koala likes kites, and that the word *kite* begins with the letter K. After the children finish decorating the diamond shapes, give them two crepe paper streamers. Help each child attach a crepe paper streamer tail and a crepe paper streamer to the middle of the back of the kite as shown. Invite the children to try to fly their kites outside.

☆ *Learning Extension:* After the children make their kites, write "K is for kite" on an index card for each child. Use a highlighter for each letter K and crayons for the other letters. Encourage the child to name the letter K, try to trace it, and then attach the card to the back of his/her kite.

Make Crowns for Kings

Remind the children that sometimes kings wear crowns, and mention that the word *king* begins with the letter K. Provide the children with large sheets of construction paper. Help the children fold the paper lengthwise. Provide craft scissors that cut wavy, scalloped, or zigzag lines. Invite the children to cut a line just below the folded edge to create two strips with fancy edges. Provide crayons and markers, glue, and assorted sparkly arts and crafts materials to use to decorate the strips. When the children are finished, tape the strips end to end. Invite the children to wear their crowns and pretend to be kings.

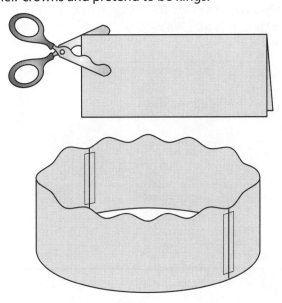

Art Activities

Make Kaleidoscopes

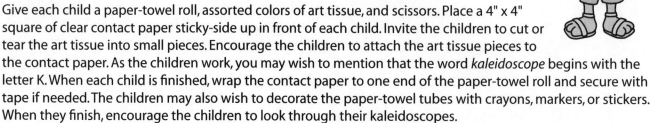

Give each child a paper-towel roll, assorted colors of art tissue, and scissors. Place a 4" x 4" square of clear contact paper sticky-side up in front of each child. Invite the children to cut or tear the art tissue into small pieces. Encourage the children to attach the art tissue pieces to the contact paper. As the children work, you may wish to mention that the word *kaleidoscope* begins with the letter K. When each child is finished, wrap the contact paper to one end of the paper-towel roll and secure with tape if needed. The children may also wish to decorate the paper-towel tubes with crayons, markers, or stickers. When they finish, encourage the children to look through their kaleidoscopes.

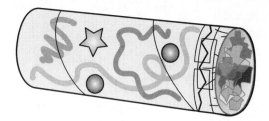

☆ *Learning Extension:* Invite the children to look into each other's kaleidoscopes. What looks different? What looks the same?

Create Key Rubbings

Give each child a sheet of plain white paper and unwrapped crayons. Show the children assorted keys and mention that the word *key* begins with the letter K. Invite each child to choose a key. Help the children fasten the keys to the table using loops of masking tape. Encourage the children to lay their papers on top of the keys and rub over the papers with the sides of unwrapped crayons. The designs from the keys will magically appear on their papers! Invite the children to discuss how they think this happens.

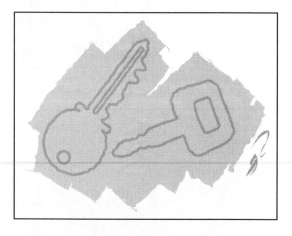

Make Letter K Collages

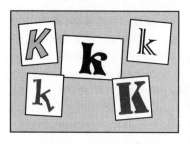

Give a child old newspapers or magazines and scissors. Invite the child to search for the letter K in the newspapers or magazines. The child may wish to tear or cut the letters out. Give the child a sheet of paper and a glue stick. Encourage the child to attach the letter K cutouts to the paper as desired. Assist the child as needed.

☆ *Learning Extension:* If you are working with a group of children, invite them to work together to make one big letter K collage. If you have bulletin board, butcher, or chart paper, you may even wish to cut the paper in the shape of the letter K. Help the children locate and cut or tear out large examples of the letter from captions and headlines. Have the children glue all the letter cutouts to the paper.

© HighReach Learning® Inc.

Small Muscle Activities

Keys and Locks

Show the children assorted keys and locks. Challenge the children to work together to find out which keys unlock the locks. Assist the children as needed. As the children work, mention that the word *key* begins with the letter K.

Match Kisses

Make matching sets of one to three kiss prints on index cards. To do so, apply lipstick and press your mouth onto index cards. Mix the index cards together. Invite a child to choose an index card. Help the child count the kiss prints on the card, and mention that the word *kiss* begins with the letter K. Next, encourage the child to find the matching card. Continue playing until the child has matched all of the kisses!

☆ **Learning Extension:** If the child shows readiness, create kiss print cards with greater numbers of kisses for the child to count and match.

Find the Kings

Provide the children with a deck of playing cards. Show the children a king playing card, and then shuffle the cards. Invite the children to search for kings in the deck. How many kings did the children find? Invite them to count the kings with you. You may wish to mention that the word *king* begins with the letter K. Shuffle the cards again and repeat the activity as long as the children show interest.

Explore Letter K Lacing Cards

Draw several block letter K's on posterboard using the pattern on page 126 and cut out. Use a hole punch to make a series of holes around each letter cutout. Vary the number of holes so that some will be easier to lace than others. Tie a length of yarn to one hole and wrap the free end with tape. Be sure the yarn can wrap around the letter twice. Set out the letter K lacing cards. Assist the children as needed as they explore the lacing cards.

© HighReach Learning® Inc.

The Letter K

Cooking with Kerry Koala
Letter K Recipes

Kool Kabobs

coffee stirrer straws
bananas
strawberries
watermelon
kiwis
apples
sponge cake

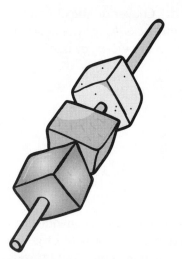

Cut the fruit and cake into cubes. Invite the children to make their own kabobs. Encourage children to try at least one new food. The children may need help putting the fruit on the straws. Make sure the children remove the fruit from the straws before they eat them.

Kidney Bean Krunch

1 can kidney beans
½ cup diced celery
¼ cup sweet pickle salad cubes
¼ cup mayonnaise
3 Tbsp. chili sauce
½ tsp. salt

Drain kidney beans in a strainer and rinse well. Combine beans with all remaining ingredients and invite the children to help you mix together. Chill before serving.

Krispy K's

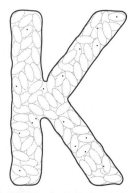

¼ cup butter
1 large package
    marshmallows
5 cups of crispy cereal
additional butter to
    grease hands

Heat marshmallows in pan until melted. Remove from heat and stir in butter and cereal. Allow to cool to warm so it is safe for the children to handle. Grease the children's hands with butter and invite them to mold the mixture into several large K shapes. Place on wax paper to cool completely and serve for snack. You may wish to add each child's initials to the wax paper by his/her letter.

Kiwi-Strawberry Smoothie

1 kiwi
1 banana
6 strawberries
½ cup vanilla
    frozen yogurt
¾ cup pineapple
    orange juice

Peel the kiwi and banana and chop into slices. Place all ingredients in a blender. Blend until smooth. If desired, place in the freezer for a few hours. Serve the children this healthy treat!

© HighReach Learning® Inc.

K is for 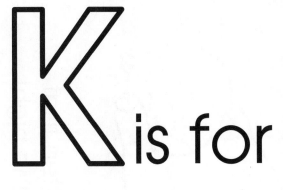 .

K is for 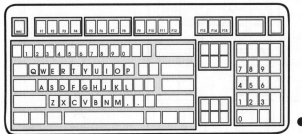 .

K is for  that

Sleeps in the night.

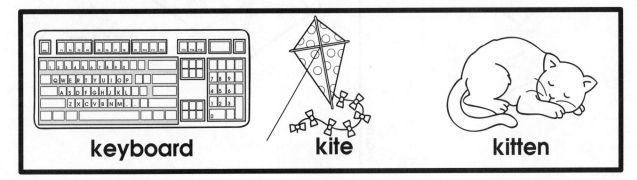

keyboard   kite   kitten

© HighReach Learning® Inc.   135   The Letter K

My K Rhyme

K is for keyboard.

K is for kitten that sleeps in the night.

K is for kite.

Name

© HighReach Learning® Inc.

137

The Letter L

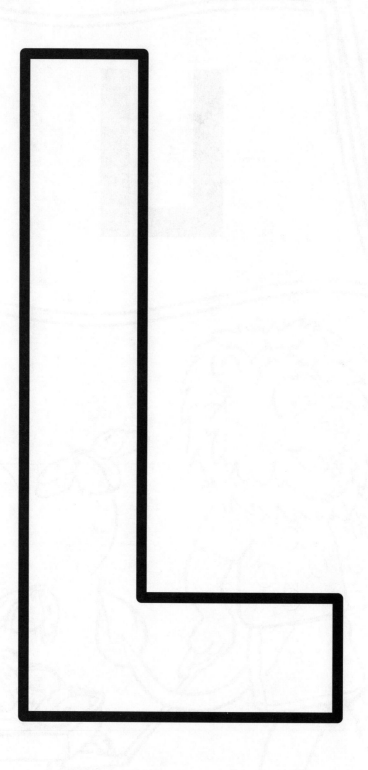

Language Activities

Introduce Lenny Lion and the Letter L

Decorate a copy of the Letter L Display (page 137) as desired. Point to Lenny Lion on the display. Invite the children to guess what type of animal Lenny is. If necessary explain that Lenny is a lion. You may wish to share the rhyme below several times and invite the children to join in.

LENNY LION

Lenny Lion loves ladybugs
Who live on leaves outside.
He pulls some in his wagon,
And they really like the ride!

Ask the children what they learned about Lenny in the rhyme. Encourage the children to name what Lenny is pulling in the wagon. What do the children know about ladybugs? Have they ever seen a ladybug? Where do they think ladybugs live?

Point to both the capital L and the lowercase l on the display. Explain that these are both ways to write the letter. Explain that Lenny likes the letter L best because it is the first letter of his name. Help the children decide if they know anyone whose name begins with L.

Talk About Letter L Words

Invite the children to talk about words they know that begin with the letter L. Write any suggestions down on sentence strips, a large sheet of paper, or chart paper. Attach the words to the wall at the children's eye level. Some familiar word suggestions are:

ladybug   lemonade   library   long
laundry   length   lion
leap   lettuce   lollipop

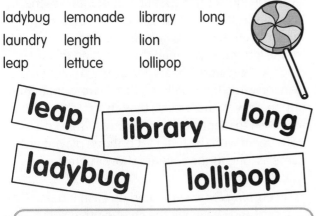

☆ **Learning Extension:** Invite the children to clap for the syllables of words that begin with the letter L (lem-on-ade, leap, li-on).

Talk About Visiting the Library

Ask the children if they have ever visited the library. Invite the children to share any experiences they may have had, and expand the conversation based on what the children tell you. Mention that the word library begins with the letter L. Explain that the library is a fun place to visit when you want to look at books and learn about things. Invite the children to collect their favorite books to create a classroom library. The children may want to pretend to check the books in and out or pretend that they are looking for books at the library.

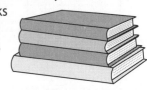

☆ **Learning Extension:** Plan a trip to the local library. Invite the children to tell you about things they would like to learn about at the library. You might even suggest that the children look for books about things that begin with the letter L, such as lions, llamas, lightning, etc.

Language Activities
Share the Letter L Rebus Rhyme

Share the Letter L Rebus Rhyme (page 147) to develop a sense of rhythm and rhyme and to practice naming pictures. Show the display as you recite the rhyme several times. Afterwards, point to each picture on the chart and encourage the children to name it. Discuss each picture and invite the children to share times when they have seen similar items.

☆**Learning Extension:** Talk about the letter L. Look at all of the words on the display. Help the children locate the letter L. Explain that the letter L can be written more than one way. Point to the capital L on the display and then point to the lowercase l. Help the children find all of the capital and lowercase letter L's on the display.

Create Letter L Rhyme Books

Give each child a copy of the Letter L Rhyme Book (page 148) and crayons or markers. Invite the children to point to the pictures as you read the text. Encourage the children to decorate the pictures as desired. Cut along the dotted lines and stack the pages in order. Staple the pages together. Invite the children to write their names on the rhyme books. Assist the children as needed.

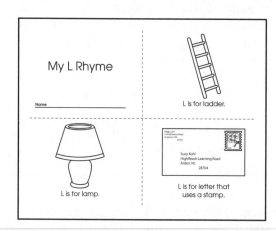

☆**Learning Extension:** Invite a child to "read" his/her Letter L Rhyme Book to you. Encourage the child to point to the letter L in the book.

Listen and Lean for the Letter L

Encourage the children to sit in a circle. Invite the children to help you think of words that begin with the letter L. Start by giving suggestions or inviting the children to look at the word wall. Write each suggestion on an index card. Write a few more words on index cards that do not begin with the letter L. Mix the index cards together. Explain to the children that you would like for them to listen for the letter L as you read the words on the index cards. If the children hear the letter L, they should lean forwards. If the children hear a word that does not begin with the letter L, they should sit still. You may wish to mention that the words *listen* and *lean* both begin with the letter L. Continue playing the game as long as the children show interest.

☆**Learning Extension:** Hold up each index card and challenge the children that show readiness to identify and lean for the words that begin with the letter L.

The Letter L

© HighReach Learning® Inc.

Science Activities

Measure Length

Invite the children to gather several items for measuring, such as books, blocks, toys, etc. Explain to the children that when we measure things, they are often checked for length, and that the word *length* begins with the letter L. Explain that the length of an object is how long it is. Show the children a ruler or a tape measure. Explain that these items are used to measure how many inches long an object is. Show the children an example by measuring your thumb. Invite the children to guess the length in inches of a few of the items they gathered. Show the children one of the items and encourage them to estimate its length in inches. Then use the ruler or tape measure to check the actual length. Repeat this procedure for several of the items you collected.

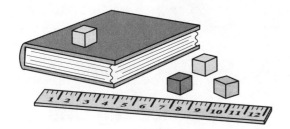

☆ *Learning Extension:* If the children show readiness, invite them to practice measuring the length of some of the items on their own.

Explore a Level

Show the children a level and name it. Explain that a level is a tool used to show if something is level or straight, and mention that the word *level* begins with the letter L. To demonstrate how the level is used, build a level wall with blocks. Show the children the bubbles in the level. When checking to see if the block wall is level, place the level horizontally on the wall. Help the children notice the bubble that is in the middle of the level. Is the bubble in the middle between the two marks? You may wish to show the children that you can use a level to see if vertical things such as doorways and walls are level. Demonstrate this by simply holding the level against a wall or doorway and look at the bubbles on either end of the level. After you finish, invite the children to practice taking turns using the level.

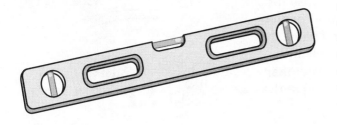

Taste Lemons and Limes

Prepare a graph by dividing a sheet of chart paper into two columns and divide the columns into several rows. At the base of one column, draw a lemon and color it yellow. At the base of the other column, draw a lime and color it green. Slice lemons and limes. Give each child a slice of lemon and lime. Invite the children to lick the lemon and lime slices. You may wish to mention that the words *lemon* and *lime* both begin with the letter L.

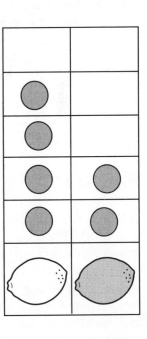

Ask the children to choose which fruit they like better and have them place a coding dot or sticker in the appropriate column of the graph. Ask the children to decide which fruit was chosen by more people. Help the children count the number of stickers in each column.

© HighReach Learning® Inc.

The Letter L

Large Muscle Activities

Roll Like Logs

Cover the area for the activity with exercise mats or blankets. Invite the children to pretend that they are logs and roll across the ground. You may wish to mention that the word *log* begins with the letter L. Encourage the children to lie down with their arms at their sides on the blankets or exercise mats and roll like logs on the covered area.

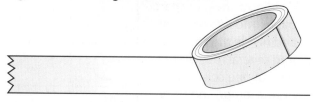

Leap Over a Long Line

Use masking tape or chalk to make a long line on the floor or outside. Encourage the children to run up to the line and then leap over it. As the children play, you may wish to mention that the words *leap, long,* and *line* all begin with the letter L.

Practice Leg Lifts

Invite the children to lie down. Demonstrate how to do leg lifts. Encourage the children to imitate your actions. Invite the children to suggest other ways to move their legs. As the children move, you may wish to mention that the words *leg* and *lift* both begin with the letter L.

☆ *Learning Extension:* Invite the children that show readiness to count as high as they can as they do leg lifts.

Play a Looking for Letter L Leaves Game

Cut several construction paper leaves and label one third of them with capital letter L's, another third with lowercase letter l's, and do not write anything at all on the remaining leaves. Draw a capital letter L and a lowercase letter l on a sheet of construction paper and attach it to a basket. Spread the leaves all over the floor or outside. Explain to the children that when you say "Go!" you want them to look for all of the leaves that have the letter L (both capital and lowercase) on them and put them in the basket. You may wish to mention that the word *leaf* begins with the letter L. As the children drop the leaves in the basket, invite them to point to and name the letter L. After they finish, spread out the leaves again. Challenge the children to try to gather the leaves with the letter L faster than they did during their first attempt! Continue playing as long as the children show interest.

The Letter L

142

© HighReach Learning® Inc.

Art Activities

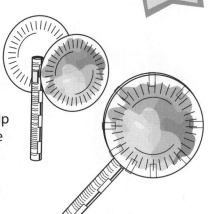

Make Large Lollipops

Explain to the children that they are going to make large lollipops. Give each child two large paper plates. Provide watercolor paints, containers of water, and paintbrushes. Encourage the children to decorate the backs of the paper plates with the watercolor paints. As the children work, you may wish to mention that the words *large* and *lollipop* both begin with the letter L. As the paint dries, help each child stack two to three sheets of old newspaper and roll tightly. Tape the edges to secure. Once the paint is dry, put the paper plates together and secure with tape around the edges, leaving a hole for the newspaper roll at the bottom. Help the children insert the end of the roll into the hole and secure with tape.

Lace Collage

Provide the children with assorted types of lace, scissors, glue, and construction paper. Invite the children to explore the lace and cut it into pieces. Encourage the children to glue the lace as desired to create designs on their papers. As the children work, you may wish to mention that the word *lace* begins with the letter L.

Create Tactile Letter L's

Give each child a copy of the capital letter L (page 138), an old paintbrush, and a shallow dish of glue. Invite the children to trace the letter L with their fingers. Encourage the children to spread glue on their letter L's as desired. Provide the children with small bathroom cups filled with sand, salt, or rice. Invite the children to shake the sand, salt, or rice onto the glue. Set aside to dry. After the glue dries, invite the children to trace their tactile letter L's with their fingers. How does the L feel? Use descriptive words such as bumpy, rough, etc. as you interact with the child.

Leaf Prints

Provide the children with a variety of fresh nontoxic or artificial leaves with raised veins. Encourage the children to explore the leaves and feel them to find the side with the raised veins. Provide the children with shallow dishes of paint, paintbrushes, and construction paper. Invite the children to coat the veined side of the leaves with paint and press them onto the construction paper to make prints. Encourage each child to make several prints. As the children work, you may wish to mention that the word *leaf* begins with the letter L.

> ☆ *Learning Extension:* After the children finish making leaf prints, write "L is for leaf" on an index card for each child. Use a highlighter for each letter L and crayons for the other letters. Encourage the children to name the letter L, try to trace it, and then attach the cards to the backs of their pictures.

Art Activities

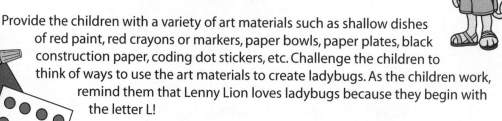

Create Ladybugs

Provide the children with a variety of art materials such as shallow dishes of red paint, red crayons or markers, paper bowls, paper plates, black construction paper, coding dot stickers, etc. Challenge the children to think of ways to use the art materials to create ladybugs. As the children work, remind them that Lenny Lion loves ladybugs because they begin with the letter L!

☆*Learning Extension:* After the children finish and the glue or paint dries, invite them to move their ladybugs as you sing the following song.

LADYBUG
(tune: "Are You Sleeping?")

Ladybug, ladybug,
In the air, in the air.
Flying all around.
Crawling on the ground.
Fly away, fly away.

Create Paper Loop Chains

Cut strips of construction paper. The strips should be at least two inches wide and eight inches long. Give each child several strips of paper and crayons and markers. Invite the children to decorate the paper strips as desired. Explain to the children that they are going to create loops with the paper strips, and mention that the word *loop* begins with the letter L. Demonstrate how to make a loop with a strip of paper. You can use either tape or glue to secure the loop. Thread another strip of paper through the loop and secure. Encourage the children to imitate your actions with their paper strips. When all of the children are finished, you may wish to attach their paper loop chains together to create one large loop chain. Look at all of those loops!

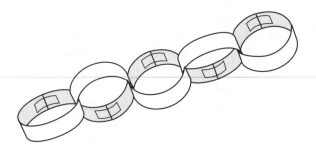

Make Letter L Collages

Give a child old newspapers or magazines and scissors. Invite the child to search for the letter L in the newspapers or magazines.

The child may wish to tear or cut the letters out. Give the child a sheet of paper and a glue stick. Encourage the child to attach the letter L cutouts to the paper as desired. Assist the child as needed.

☆*Learning Extension:* If you are working with a group of children, invite them to work together to make one big letter L collage. If you have bulletin board, butcher, or chart paper, you may even wish to cut the paper in the shape of the letter L. Help the children locate and cut or tear out large examples of the letter from captions and headlines. Have the children glue all the letter cutouts to the paper.

The Letter L

144

© HighReach Learning® Inc.

Small Muscle Activities

Draw and Cut Lines

Provide the children with paper, crayons or markers, and scissors. Encourage the children to draw straight or curved lines on their papers, and then to try to cut along the lines. As the children work, you may wish to mention that the word *line* begins with the letter L. Assist the children as needed.

Sort Laundry

Give the children a pile of clean laundry. Challenge the children to sort the laundry. They may choose to sort the laundry by color, size, or in other ways. Assist the children as needed. As the children work, you may wish to mention that the word *laundry* begins with the letter L.

☆ *Learning Extension:* Invite a child that shows readiness to practice folding the laundry. You may need to demonstrate how to do this for the child.

Explore Letter L Lacing Cards

Draw several block letter L's on posterboard using the pattern on page 138 and cut out. Use a hole punch to make a series of holes around each letter cutout. Vary the number of holes so that some will be easier to lace than others. Tie a length of yarn to one hole and wrap the free end with tape. Be sure the yarn can wrap around the letter twice. Set out the letter L lacing cards. Assist the children as needed as they explore the lacing cards.

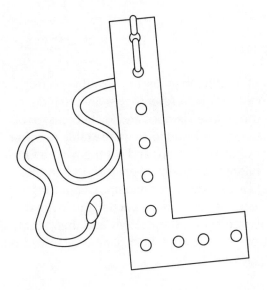

Cooking with Lenny Lion
Letter L Recipes

LAYERED CHEDDAR FRUIT SALAD

½ cup mayonnaise
½ cup sour cream
1 Tbsp. brown sugar
1½ cups shredded cheddar cheese
4 cups of shredded lettuce
3 cups fresh peaches, peeled, pitted, sliced
3 cups fresh strawberries, sliced
3 cups seedless grapes, sliced in half

In a small bowl, invite the children to help whisk mayonnaise, sour cream, and brown sugar together. In a larger bowl, toss 1 cup of cheese together with the lettuce. In a 2½ quart clear plastic bowl, layer half the lettuce, the peaches, the remaining lettuce, strawberries, grapes and remaining cheese. Spread mayonnaise mixture over the top and chill. Serve cold.

LUSCIOUS LEMON PIE

6 oz. frozen lemonade concentrate, thawed
14 oz. sweetened condensed milk
8 oz. container frozen whipped topping, thawed
graham cracker piecrust

Stir together the lemonade concentrate and sweetened condensed milk. Gently fold in whipped topping. Spread in a prepared piecrust and chill an hour or more.

HOMEMADE LEMONADE

12 lemons
2¼ cups sugar
1½ quarts cold water
ice cubes

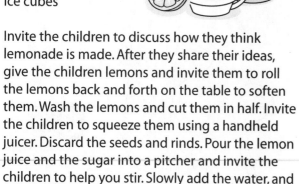

Invite the children to discuss how they think lemonade is made. After they share their ideas, give the children lemons and invite them to roll the lemons back and forth on the table to soften them. Wash the lemons and cut them in half. Invite the children to squeeze them using a handheld juicer. Discard the seeds and rinds. Pour the lemon juice and the sugar into a pitcher and invite the children to help you stir. Slowly add the water, and continue stirring until the sugar has dissolved. Add ice cubes and serve!

LOTS OF LETTUCE

heads of lettuce
assorted salad vegetables (tomatoes, onions, cucumbers, radishes, celery, mushrooms, bell peppers, carrots, cauliflower, broccoli)
salad dressing

Encourage the children to help you wash the lettuce and break it into small pieces. Put the lettuce in a large salad bowl. Then invite the children to help wash the other vegetables. Cut the vegetables and encourage the children to help add them to the salad. Top with your choice of salad dressing.

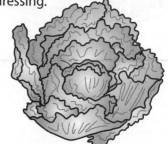

© HighReach Learning® Inc.

L is for .

L is for .

L is for .

That uses a stamp.

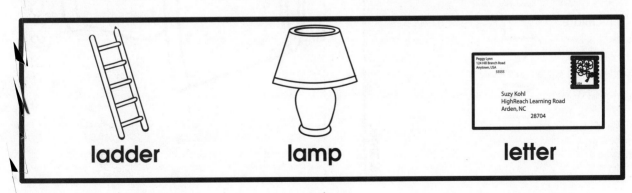

ladder   lamp   letter

L is for ladder.

Peggy Lynn
124 Hill Branch Road
Anytown, USA
55555

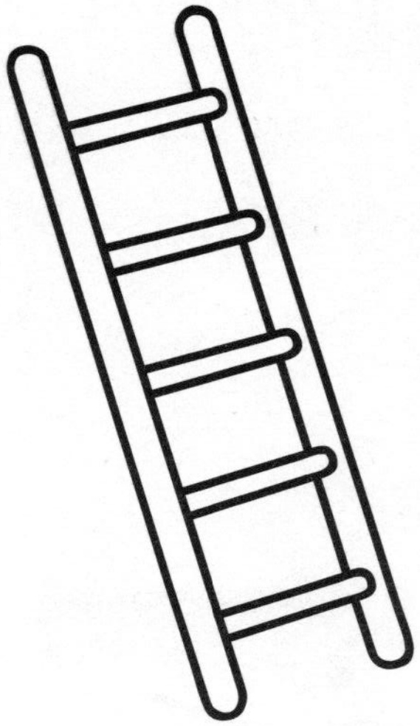

Suzy Kohl
HighReach Learning Road
Arden, NC
28704

USA

L is for letter that
uses a stamp.

My L Rhyme

Name _____

L is for lamp.

148

© HighReach Learning® Inc.

Language Activities

Introduce Mary & Marsha Mouse and the Letter M

Decorate a copy of the Letter M Display (page 149) as desired. Point to Mary and Marsha Mouse on the display. Invite the children to guess what type of animal they are. If necessary explain that Mary and Marsha are mice. You may wish to share the rhyme below several times and invite the children to join in.

MARY AND MARSHA MOUSE

Mary and Marsha Mouse
March up and down the street.
They like to give out marshmallows
To everyone they meet!

Invite the children to discuss what they learned about Mary and Marsha in the rhyme. Invite the children to name what Mary and Marsha are pulling in the wagon. Encourage the children to share their experiences with marshmallows. Have they ever seen or eaten marshmallows? Do they like or dislike them?

Point to both the capital M and the lowercase m on the display. Explain that these are both ways to write the letter. Explain that Mary and Marsha like the letter M best because it is the first letter of their names. Help the children decide if they know anyone whose name begins with M.

Talk About Letter M Words

Invite the children to talk about words they know that begin with the letter M. Write any suggestions down on sentence strips, a large sheet of paper, or chart paper. Attach the words to the wall at the children's eye level. Some familiar word suggestions are:

macaroni	maraca	minute	music
mad	mask	money	
magnet	memory	moon	

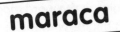

☆ **Learning Extension:** Invite the children to clap for the syllables of words that begin with the letter M (mon-ey, mad, mac-a-ro-ni).

Explore Money

Show the children assorted coins and paper money. Explain to the children that we use money to buy things, and mention that the word

money begins with the letter M. Encourage the children to notice the differences between the coins and the paper money. How do the coins feel in their hands? How does the paper feel? Invite the children to tell you what they might buy if they had a quarter, a dollar, or even one hundred dollars. *Note: Be sure to wash hands after handling money.*

☆ **Learning Extension:** Invite the children to sort the money. They may wish to sort the money by size, color, or type. Assist the children as needed.

© HighReach Learning® Inc. The Letter M

Language Activities
Share the Letter M Rebus Rhyme

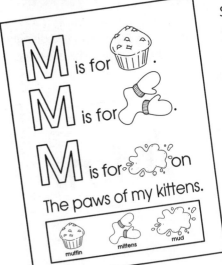

Share the Letter M Rebus Rhyme (page 159) to develop a sense of rhythm and rhyme and to practice naming pictures. Show the display as you recite the rhyme several times. Afterwards, point to each picture on the chart and encourage the children to name it. Discuss each picture and invite the children to share times when they have seen similar items.

> ☆ **Learning Extension:** Talk about the letter M. Look at all of the words on the display. Help the children locate the letter M. Explain that the letter M can be written more than one way. Point to the capital M on the display and then point to the lowercase m. Help the children find all of the capital and lowercase letter M's on the display.

Create Letter M Rhyme Books

Give each child a copy of the Letter M Rhyme Book (page 160) and crayons or markers. Invite the children to point to the pictures as you read the text. Encourage the children to decorate the pictures as desired. Cut along the dotted lines and stack the pages in order. Staple the pages together. Invite the children to write their names on the rhyme books. Assist the children as needed.

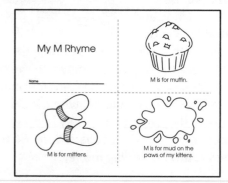

> ☆ **Learning Extension:** Invite a child to "read" his/her Letter M Rhyme Book to you. Encourage the child to point to the letter M in the book.

What Makes You Merry or Mad?

Draw two columns on a sheet of chart paper. As the children watch, write the word *merry* at the top of one of the columns with a happy face underneath the word. In the other column, write the word *mad* with a sad face underneath the word. Point to the word *merry*, and help the children notice that it begins with the letter M. Explain that to be *merry* means to be happy. Encourage the children to dictate their ideas about what makes them merry. You

may need to help the children by giving suggestions such as going outside, playing with toys, etc. Write down the children's suggestions. Next, point to the word *mad* and help the children notice that it begins with the letter M. Encourage the children to dictate their ideas about what makes them mad. Write down the children's suggestions. After the children finish, read all of their suggestions back to them.

The Letter M

152

© HighReach Learning® Inc.

Science Activities

Talk About the Moon

Show the children a picture of the moon or read a book featuring the moon. Invite the children to share their thoughts about the moon. You may wish to mention that the word *moon* begins with the letter M. Try to answer any questions that the children have. Share any of the facts below that are appropriate for the children in your group.

❖ The moon is mostly made of rocks and metal

❖ The moon orbits, or moves, around Earth

❖ When the moon orbits Earth, it appears to change into different shapes and sizes in the sky

❖ The surface of the moon is not smooth; there are craters or holes on the moon that have been caused by meteorites, which are rocks that fall from space

☆ *Learning Extension:* Invite the children to look for the moon in the sky. Encourage the children to describe what they see. Does it look like a big circle, a half circle, or a thin slice?

Explore Magnets

Show the children a magnet. Explain that a magnet attracts items that are made out of certain metals, and mention that the words *magnet* and *metal* begin with the letter M. Encourage the children to share their experiences with magnets. After the children share, show them an assortment of items that are attracted to a magnet, such as pipe cleaners, stainless steel spoons, steel wool, steel paper clips, etc. Then show the children an assortment of items that are not attracted to a magnet, such as a cork, plastic spoons, aluminum toy pot, block, etc. Invite the children to predict which items will stick to the magnet. Choose a child to hold the magnet next to each of the items to find out what happens. Place the items that are attracted to the magnet in one box and the other items in another box. When all of the objects have been sorted, encourage the children to share what they think is the same about the items that are attracted to the magnet.

Play a Memory Game

Place several items on a blanket and show the children. Without the children seeing, remove one of the items. Encourage the children to tell you which item is missing. As the children play the game, you may wish to mention that the word *missing* begins with the letter M. Repeat the game as long as the children show interest.

How Long Is a Minute?

Show the children a kitchen timer. Explain to the children that time is measured in minutes, and mention that the word *minute* begins with the letter M. Set the timer for a minute and invite the children to run in place or perform another action until the timer goes off. Repeat the activity and invite the children to perform other simple tasks for one minute.

☆ *Learning Extension:* Explain to a child that shows readiness that a minute is made up of seconds. Invite the child to explore the kitchen timer. Are there any numbers on the timer that the child recognizes?

© HighReach Learning® Inc.

The Letter M

Large Muscle Activities

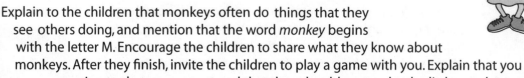

Play Monkey See, Monkey Do

Explain to the children that monkeys often do things that they see others doing, and mention that the word *monkey* begins with the letter M. Encourage the children to share what they know about monkeys. After they finish, invite the children to play a game with you. Explain that you are going to do a movement and that they should pretend to be little monkeys and imitate your actions. Recite the rhyme below and then do a movement, such as hop on one foot, touch toes, take big steps, etc. Encourage the children to do what you do, continuing the game as long as the children show interest.

MONKEY SEE, MONKEY DO

Monkey see, monkey do.
See if you can do it, too.

Toss Meteorites

Give each child a large square of aluminum foil. Invite the children to crumple the foil up into balls to create meteorites. Remind the children that meteorites are rocks or stones that sometimes fall from space onto the moon's surface. You may wish to mention that the words *moon* and *meteorite* both begin with the letter M. Put a hula hoop or basket a few feet away from where the children are standing. Encourage the children to toss the meteorites into the hula hoop or basket. You may need to give the children several turns. If the children need to be challenged more, move the hula hoop or basket a few feet farther away.

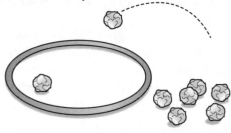

☆**Learning Extension:** If the children show readiness, encourage them to count how many meteorites land in the hula hoop or basket, and how many land outside the hoop or basket. Are there more meteorites in or out of the hula hoop or basket?

Play Musical Chairs

Encourage the children to help you arrange some chairs in a circle, facing out. Each child will need a chair. Encourage the children to march around the outside of the circle of chairs as you play some music from a cassette or CD. Stop the music from time to time. Each time the music stops, each child should quickly sit in the nearest chair. Repeat this procedure several times. Young children will enjoy this game more if you do not remove a chair after each round.

© HighReach Learning® Inc.

Art Activities

Make a Mural

M is for mural

As the children watch, write the words "M is for mural" in large bold letters on a large sheet of butcher paper. Help the children notice that the word *mural* begins with the letter M. Explain to the children that a mural is a work of art that is usually very large, such as an entire wall. Set out the butcher paper and crayons, markers, shallow dishes of paint, and paintbrushes. Encourage the children to work together to create a mural. After they finish, invite the children to describe their work.

Create Tactile Letter M's

Give each child a copy of the capital letter M (page 150), an old paintbrush, and a shallow dish of glue. Invite the children to trace the letter M with their fingers. Encourage the children to spread glue on their letter M's as desired. Provide the children with small bathroom cups filled with macaroni, salt, or rice. Invite the children to shake the macaroni, salt, or rice onto the glue. Set aside to dry. After the glue dries, invite the children to trace their tactile letter M's with their fingers. How does the M feel? Use descriptive words such as bumpy, rough, etc. as you interact with the child.

Make Maracas

Provide each child with two 16 or 20 oz. plastic soda bottles with lids, a sheet of white construction paper, and crayons or markers. Explain to the children that they are making maracas, and mention that the word *maraca* begins with the letter M. Help each child fold his/her sheet of construction paper in half. Encourage the children to cut or tear the paper along the fold line. Invite the children to decorate the construction paper strips as desired. Wrap each strip around a soda bottle and secure with tape. Show the children a plastic funnel. Give each child a small cup of rice. Help the child place the funnel in the top of each plastic bottle. Pour a small amount of rice into the funnel. Replace the lid on each plastic bottle and secure with glue. Invite the children to make music with their maracas. Shake, shake, shake!

☆ *Learning Extension:* Put rice in one of the plastic bottles and unpopped popcorn kernels in the other bottle. Invite the children to shake the bottles and compare the sounds.

Paint with Marbles

Show the children some large marbles. Invite the children to share their experiences with marbles, and mention that the word *marble* begins with the letter M. Give each child a sheet of white construction paper. Help the child place the paper inside a plastic sweater box. Have the child dip some marbles in paint, place them in the box, and put the lid on the box. Have the child tilt the box back and forth several times, then open the box to reveal the interesting creation. Continue, using the same procedure with each child.

Art Activities

Make Masks

Provide the children with large paper plates and assorted art and collage materials. Challenge the children to use the materials to create masks. As the children work, mention that the word *mask* begins with the letter M. After the children finish, use scissors to cut eyeholes, and attach elastic string to the backs of the masks or attach craft sticks to the bottoms of the masks to use as handles. Encourage the children to incorporate their masks into their play.

> ☆ *Learning Extension:* After the children finish making their masks, write "M is for mask" on an index card for each child. Use a highlighter for each letter M and crayons for the other letters. Encourage the children to name the letter M, try to trace it, and then attach the cards to the back of their masks.

Macaroni Designs

Place uncooked macaroni in a zipper-top bag in front of the children. Add several drops of food coloring and a small amount of rubbing alcohol. Shake the bag to coat the macaroni. Encourage the children to predict what will happen to the macaroni, and mention that the word *macaroni* begins with the letter M. You may wish to repeat the procedure for assorted colors of macaroni. Place the macaroni on baking sheets to dry. After the macaroni dries, show it to the children. Encourage the children to notice what happens to the macaroni; are their predictions correct? Provide the children with construction paper and glue. Invite the children to use the glue to create designs with the macaroni on their papers.

Make Letter M Collages

Give a child old newspapers or magazines and scissors. Invite the child to search for the letter M in the newspapers or magazines. The child may wish to tear or cut the letters out. Give the child a sheet of paper and a glue stick. Encourage the child to attach the letter M cutouts to the paper as desired. Assist the child as needed.

> ☆ *Learning Extension:* If you are working with a group of children, invite them to work together to make one big letter M collage. If you have bulletin board, butcher, or chart paper, you may even wish to cut the paper in the shape of the letter M. Help the children locate and cut or tear out large examples of the letter from captions and headlines. Have the children glue all the letter cutouts to the paper.

 © HighReach Learning® Inc.

Small Muscle Activities

Explore Measuring Cups

Put assorted measuring cups in a water table or basin of water. Explain to the children that these are measuring cups, and that they are used to measure different kinds of things. You may wish to mention that the word *measure* begins with the letter M. Encourage the children to explore the measuring cups. As the children explore, help them notice the differences between the measuring cups. Do some of the cups hold more water? Less water?

☆ *Learning Extension:* Put two small plastic buckets near the water table or basin of water. Give a child a small and a large measuring cup. Invite the child to use the small measuring cup to transfer water to one of the buckets. Count the number of cups of water it takes to fill the bucket. Then invite the child to use the large measuring cup to fill the other bucket. Count the number of cups it takes to fill the bucket. Which measuring cup filled the bucket faster? Challenge the child to explain why he/she thinks this happened.

Explore Mail

Provide the children with assorted junk mail. The children may wish to open the mail or sort the mail by color, size, or in other ways. As the children explore the mail, you may wish to mention that the word *mail* begins with the letter M.

☆ *Learning Extension:* Invite the children that show readiness to find and name the letter M on the mail.

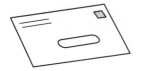

Match Mittens

Cut out several matching pairs of simple mitten shapes from wallpaper samples, colored posterboard, etc. as shown. Mix all of the mittens together and put them in a zipper-top bag. Give a child the zipper-top bag. Invite the child to remove the mittens from the bag and match them together. As the child explores, you may wish to mention that the words *matching* and *mitten* both begin with the letter M.

Explore Letter M Lacing Cards

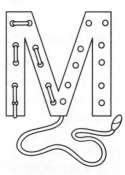

Draw several block letter M's on posterboard using the pattern on page 150 and cut out. Use a hole punch to make a series of holes around each letter cutout. Vary the number of holes so that some will be easier to lace than others. Tie a length of yarn to one hole and wrap the free end with tape. Be sure the yarn can wrap around the letter twice. Set out the letter M lacing cards. Assist the children as needed as they explore the lacing cards.

© HighReach Learning® Inc.

The Letter M

Cooking with Marsha and Mary Mouse Letter M Recipes

MARVELOUS MILKSHAKES

¾ cup milk
1 scoop ice cream (any flavor)
canned or fresh fruit (strawberries,
    bananas, etc.)

Mix the milk and ice cream in a
bowl. Beat with a spoon or use a
mixer or blender. Add fruit and serve.

MUD PUDDLES

1 cup cereal, any type
½ cup fat-free chocolate milk

Combine cereal and milk in a medium bowl
and enjoy. You may wish to mention that the
chocolate milk looks like mud!

MILK CHOCOLATE MACAROONS

1 bag (14 oz.) flaked coconut
1 can (14 oz.) sweetened condensed milk
1 cup milk chocolate baking chips
2 tsp. vanilla

Preheat the oven to 350°. Invite the children to
help you combine all of the ingredients and mix
well with a wooden spoon. Grease baking sheets
well with butter or shortening. Have the children
help drop teaspoons of coconut mixture 1" apart
on the greased sheets. Bake for 8 to 10 minutes.
Dip a spatula in water and remove the cookies
from the sheet at once. Cool on wire racks.

MONKEY BREAD

1½ cups sugar
3 Tbsp. ground cinnamon
3 (12 oz.) cans refrigerated buttermilk biscuits
½ cup butter

Preheat the oven to 350°. Mix the cinnamon and
sugar together. Cut biscuits into fourths and give
each child a fourth. Have the children roll each
piece in the cinnamon sugar mix, and layer the
biscuits in a pan. Melt the butter and stir in the
remainder of the cinnamon and sugar mixture
until dissolved. Spoon the melted butter mixture
over the biscuits. Bake for 35 minutes.

 © HighReach Learning® Inc.

M

M is for .

M is for .

M is for on

The paws of my kittens.

muffin   mittens   mud

© HighReach Learning® Inc.

The Letter M

My M Rhyme

Name _____

M is for muffin.

M is for mud on the
paws of my kittens.

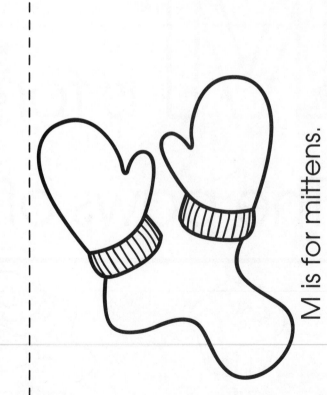

M is for mittens.

The Letter M

160

© HighReach Learning® Inc.

© HighReach Learning® Inc.

The Letter N

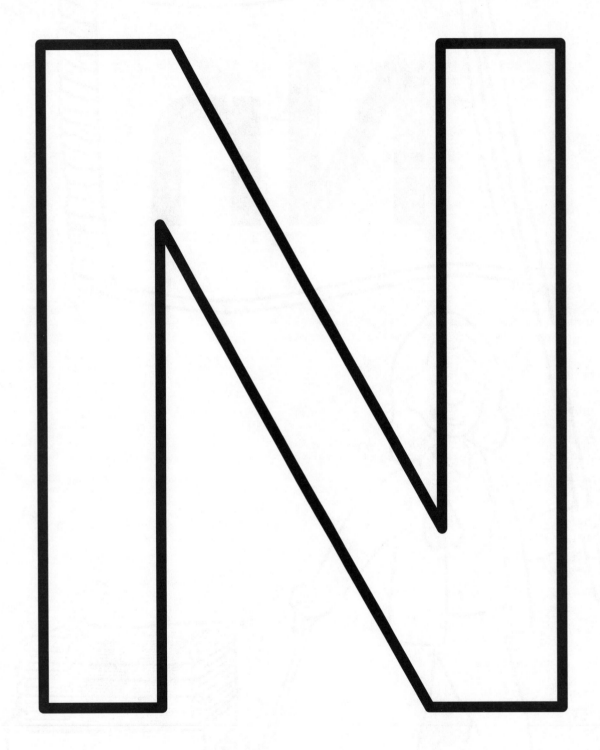

The Letter N

© HighReach Learning® Inc.

Language Activities
Introduce Nora Nurse and the Letter N

Decorate a copy of the Letter N Display (page 161) as desired. Point to Nora Nurse on the display. Invite the children to guess what type of job Nora does. If necessary explain that Nora is a nurse. You may wish to share the rhyme below several times and invite the children to join in.

NORA NURSE

Nora is a nurse,
Who takes good care of you.
And when she isn't working,
She likes to read the news.

Invite the children to discuss what they learned about Nora in the rhyme. Invite the children to name what Nora is pulling in the wagon. Have the children ever seen a nurse before? Where does a nurse work? Encourage the children to share their ideas and experiences. Try to answer any questions that the children may have about nurses.

Point to both the capital N and the lowercase n on the display. Explain that these are both ways to write the letter. Explain that Nora likes the letter N best because it is the first letter of her name. Help the children decide if they know anyone whose name begins with N.

Talk About Letter N Words

Invite the children to talk about words they know that begin with the letter N. Write any suggestions down on sentence strips, a large sheet of paper, or chart paper. Attach the words to the wall at the children's eye level. Some familiar word suggestions are:

nachos	necklace	night	nurse
nail	nest	north	
napkin	newspaper	number	

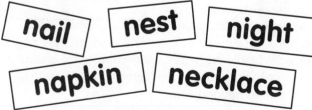

☆ **Learning Extension:** Invite the children to clap for the syllables of words that begin with the letter N (news-pa-per, num-ber, nail).

Name Numbers

Encourage the children to sit in a circle. Give one child a tennis ball or beanbag. Begin playing music and have the children pass the ball or beanbag around the circle. When you stop the music, invite the child that is holding the ball or beanbag to name a number. You may wish to lead the children in clapping their hands as many times as the number that has been named. As the children play the game, you may wish to mention that the word *number* begins with the letter N.

☆ **Learning Extension:** Invite the first child with the ball to start by saying "One!" then the next child with the ball should say "Two!" and so on. Challenge the children to continue as high as they can count.

Language Activities

Share the Letter N Rebus Rhyme

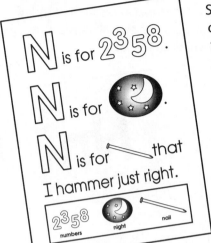

N is for 2358.

N is for ☽ (moon).

N is for ⟋ that I hammer just right.

2358 numbers   night   nail

Share the Letter N Rebus Rhyme (page 171) to develop a sense of rhythm and rhyme and to practice naming pictures. Show the display as you recite the rhyme several times. Afterwards, point to each picture on the chart and encourage the children to name it. Discuss each picture and invite the children to share times when they have seen similar items.

> ☆ *Learning Extension:* Talk about the letter N. Look at all of the words on the display. Help the children locate the letter N. Explain that the letter N can be written more than one way. Point to the capital N on the display and then point to the lowercase n. Help the children find all of the capital and lowercase letter N's on the display.

Talk About Neighborhood Noises

Use a tape recorder to record several sounds in your neighborhood. For example, you could record the sound of sanitation workers collecting the trash, a bird singing, a car honking, children playing, a dog barking, someone knocking on the door, or the sound of an ice cream truck. Talk to the children about noises that they may hear in the neighborhood. Play the recording of neighborhood noises and help the children identify each sound. Make sure to mention that the words *noise* and *neighborhood* both begin with the letter N.

Play a Name Game

Invite the children to play a game with you. Say the following rhyme using your name to begin. Repeat the game several times, using the name of each child in your group. You may wish to mention that the word *name* begins with the letter N.

THE NAME RHYME

Ms. Heather, Ms. Heather, shout her name!
(*Shout name.*)

Now very softly say the same.
(*Whisper name.*)

Say her name and clap and shout.
(*Shout name and clap on each syllable.*)

Then close your lips and clap it out.
(*Close mouth and clap each syllable of name.*)

Create Letter N Rhyme Books

Give each child a copy of the Letter N Rhyme Book (page 172) and crayons or markers. Invite the children to point to the pictures as you read the text. Encourage the children to decorate the pictures as

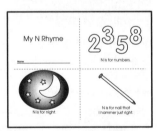

My N Rhyme   2358
Name   N is for numbers.
              N is for night.   N is for nail that I hammer just right.

desired. Cut along the dotted lines and stack the pages in order. Staple the pages together. Invite the children to write their names on the rhyme books. Assist the children as needed.

> ☆ *Learning Extension:* Invite a child to "read" his/her Letter N Rhyme Book to you. Encourage the child to point to the letter N in the book.

The Letter N

164

© HighReach Learning® Inc.

Science Activities

Talk About Nests

Show the children a picture of a nest or read a nonfiction book featuring nests. Encourage the children to share their ideas and experiences with nests. Where have they seen a nest? What goes in a nest? What do they think a nest is made of? During the discussion, you may wish to mention that the word *nest* begins with the letter N. Share any of the following information that is appropriate for the children in your group.

❖ A nest is normally built by birds to hold their eggs and provide a home for their babies

❖ Nests can be built in a tree, on the ground, or in other places

❖ Nests can be made of many materials including twigs, grass, leaves, mud, and sand

☆ *Learning Extension:* After the discussion, take the children outside. Encourage the children to collect items that can be used to make nests. They may find dried leaves, pine needles, pinecones, grass, or other items. When you return to the classroom, have the children use the items they found to make nests. They may need to use glue or tape to join the materials together. Encourage the children to talk about their nests as they work.

Explore a Compass

Show the children a compass. Explain to the children that a compass is used to help people find their way around, by helping them find directions. Help the children notice the parts of the compass, including the letters inside. Tell the children what the letters inside the compass mean. Help the children find the letter N, and explain that it stands for north. Then show the children the needle inside the compass. Encourage the children to walk around the playground or classroom while holding the compass. As they move around, invite the children to describe what happens to the needle in the compass. Challenge the children to try to keep the needle pointing towards the letter N.

Who Knows the Nose?

Locate pictures of animals with prominent noses. Some examples of animals you may want to use are elephant, toucan, horse, dolphin, etc. Enlarge and make two copies of each picture. From one of each set, cut out the animal's nose. Attach the pictures of the noses to large index cards. Show the children the picture of each animal's nose. Challenge the children to guess what the animal is. Give clues as needed. Once the children guess, show them the picture of the animal. As the children play the game, you may wish to mention that the word *nose* begins with the letter N.

☆ *Learning Extension:* Use the pictures to create the Animal Nose Game. Attach the picture of each animal to one side of a large index card. Attach the picture of the animal's nose to the other side. Put the cards nose-side up on the table. Invite a child to guess that name of the animal by looking at the picture of the nose on the card. Invite the child to turn the card over to see if he/she is correct.

Large Muscle Activities

Toss Newspaper

Give each child a sheet of newspaper. Remind the children that Nora Nurse likes newspapers, and mention that the word *newspaper* begins with the letter N. Encourage the children to crush their newspapers into balls. Show the children a large box or basket and encourage them to toss the newspaper balls into it. Help the children count how many newspaper balls land inside the box/basket and how many land outside.

Move Along a Number Path

Draw several large bold numerals on construction paper or posterboard pieces. Secure the numbers to the classroom floor or to the ground outside in order, forming a number path. Show the children the numbers. Invite the children to count the numbers along the path with you. Then invite the children to move along the path in different ways. You may wish to suggest that they move backwards, walk slowly, or hop along the path. As the children move, you may wish to mention that the word *number* begins with the letter N.

☆ **Learning Extension:** Invite the children that show readiness to name the numbers they recognize on their own as they move along the path.

Go on a Name Hunt

Write each child's name on an index card. Hide the index cards around the classroom or outside. Explain to the children that you have hidden their names. You may wish to mention that the word *name* begins with the letter N. When you say "Go!" the children should try to find their names. Assist the children as needed. Continue playing the game as long as the children show interest.

☆ **Learning Extension:** Distribute the name cards to the children, making sure that each child does not get his/her own name. When you say "Go!" challenge each child to find who has his/her name card.

© HighReach Learning® Inc.

Art Activities

Napkin Art

Give each child a paper napkin. Invite the children to share what they think napkins are used for, and mention that the word *napkin* begins with the letter N. Provide the children with markers. Invite the children to draw on the napkins. Encourage the children to talk about what happens to the colors on their napkins as they create.

☆ **Learning Extension:** Add several drops of food coloring to water in small paper cups. Provide the children with the cups of colored water and plastic droppers. Invite the children to use the droppers to drop colored water onto the napkins. Encourage the children to describe what happens to the colored water as it soaks into the napkins.

Create Tactile Letter N's

Give each child a copy of the capital letter N (page 162), an old paintbrush, and a shallow dish of glue. Invite the children to trace the letter N with their fingers. Encourage the children to spread glue on their letter N's as desired. Provide the children with small bathroom cups filled with an assortment of small noodles, salt, or rice. Invite the children to shake the noodles, salt, or rice onto the glue. Set aside to dry. After the glue dries, invite the children to trace their tactile letter N's with their fingers. How does the N feel? Use descriptive words such as bumpy, rough, etc. as you interact with the child.

Make Nachos

Lead a discussion about nachos with the children, and mention that the word *nachos* begins with the letter N. Have they ever eaten nachos? Do they like nachos? After the discussion, provide the children with paper plates, yellow construction paper, scissors, and glue. Invite the children to cut or tear triangles from the construction paper to create tortilla chips. Assist the children as needed. Encourage the children to glue their chips to their paper plates. Then provide the children with thick orange paint in squeeze bottles. Encourage the children to squeeze the orange paint onto their paper plates and pretend that it is cheese sauce. As the children work, encourage them to talk about their creations.

© HighReach Learning® Inc.

The Letter N

Art Activities
Create Nighttime Pictures

Provide the children with large sheets of black construction paper, sticky stars, and assorted colors of chalk. Encourage the children to talk about things that they do or see at night. You may wish to give examples such as eat dinner, read stories, brush teeth, sleep, moon and stars, etc.

During the discussion, mention that the word *night* begins with the letter N. After the discussion, invite the children to use the materials to create nighttime pictures. Encourage the children to talk about their creations as they work.

☆ *Learning Extension:* As the children watch, use a pencil to print a capital N and a lowercase n on the back of each child's paper. Invite the children to use the chalk to trace the letters on their papers.

Newspaper Sculptures

Give the children old newspapers and masking tape. Challenge the children to think of what they could make with the masking tape and newspapers. You may wish to mention that the word *newspaper* begins with the letter N. During the discussion, you may want to suggest that the children make sculptures. Demonstrate for the children how to tear, roll, crush, twist, and turn the newspaper to make a sculpture. Attach the pieces together with masking tape. Encourage the children to talk about their creations as they work.

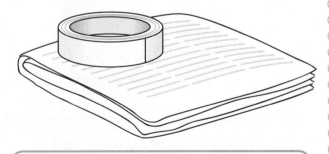

☆ *Learning Extension:* Challenge the children to work together to create a sculpture. Invite the children to talk together to create a plan for what they want to make. Give the children assistance as needed.

Make Letter N Collages

Give a child old newspapers or magazines and scissors. Invite the child to search for the letter N in the newspapers or magazines. The child may wish to tear or cut the letters out. Give the child a sheet of paper and a glue stick. Encourage the child to attach the letter N cutouts to the paper as desired. Assist the child as needed.

☆ *Learning Extension:* If you are working with a group of children, invite them to work together to make one big letter N collage. If you have bulletin board, butcher, or chart paper, you may even wish to cut the paper in the shape of the letter N. Help the children locate and cut or tear out large examples of the letter from captions and headlines. Have the children glue all the letter cutouts to the paper.

The Letter N

© HighReach Learning® Inc.

Small Muscle Activities

Practice Hammering Nails

Invite one child at a time to practice hammering nails. Provide the child with safety goggles, a small lightweight hammer, wood scraps, and nails. *Caution: Make sure to use wood scraps that are sanded to avoid splinters.* Sit in an area where the children can safely hammer nails, making sure that the surface on which they hammer will not be harmed if a nail comes through the underside of the wood. Make sure that you provide constant supervision, and that you wear safety goggles along with the child during this activity. Have the child put on the safety goggles. Get a few nails started in a piece of wood. Demonstrate for the child how to use the hammer. Invite the child to try to hammer the nails into the wood. As the child works, talk to the child about the way to safely use these items. You may also wish to mention that the word *nail* begins with the letter N.

☆ *Learning Extension:* Draw a capital letter N on a wood scrap. Challenge the child to practice hammering nails along the letter N.

Create Necklaces

Give each child a length of yarn to make a necklace. Provide assorted materials that could be laced onto the string such as large noodles, large beads, dry round cereal, or any other items you have available. Encourage the children to lace the materials onto the yarn however they would like. As the children work, mention that the word *necklace* begins with the letter N, and give assistance as needed. When the children finish, help them tie the ends of the yarn together. Encourage the children to wear their necklaces.

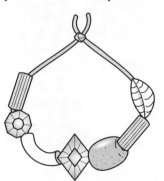

☆ *Learning Extension:* Invite the children to create patterns on their necklaces as they work. You may wish to give an example such as red bead, yellow bead, red bead, yellow bead or macaroni, bead, macaroni, bead. When they finish, encourage the children to talk about the patterns they created.

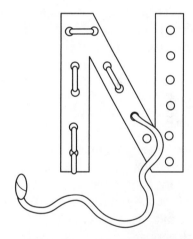

Explore Letter N Lacing Cards

Draw several block letter N's on posterboard using the pattern on page 162 and cut out. Use a hole punch to make a series of holes around each letter cutout. Vary the number of holes so that some will be easier to lace than others. Tie a length of yarn to one hole and wrap the free end with tape. Be sure the yarn can wrap around the letter twice. Set out the letter N lacing cards. Assist the children as needed as they explore the lacing cards.

© HighReach Learning® Inc.

The Letter N

Cooking with Nora Nurse
Letter N Recipes

No-Drip Yogurt Pops

1 cup boiling water
1 package fruit-flavored
    gelatin mix
1 banana
1 cup plain yogurt

Combine boiling water and
gelatin in a blender and pulse
until gelatin is dissolved. Blend in banana and
then yogurt until smooth. Pour mixture into
popsicle molds and freeze.

Nacho Pie

1 (30 oz.) can chili with beans
1 (10.7 oz.) can condensed cheddar cheese soup
½ (14 oz.) can sweetened condensed milk
1 package tortilla chips

Heat chili in a medium saucepan. Heat cheese
soup and milk in a small saucepan until creamy.
Give each child several tortilla chips in a bowl.
Invite the children to crush the tortilla chips.
Spoon slightly warmed chili over the chips and
then drizzle with cheese sauce.

Nifty Noodles

1 (16 oz.) package egg noodles
2 (5 oz.) cans chunk chicken, drained
2 (10.7 oz.) cans condensed
    cream of mushroom soup
½ tsp. garlic salt
½ tsp. black pepper

Bring a large pot of water to a boil, add pasta,
and cook until noodles are slightly soft, about
8-10 minutes; drain. Return pasta to pot and add
the rest of the ingredients. Stir until blended and
cook 5 more minutes on low heat. Serve warm.

Noisy Nibble Mix

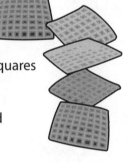

7 cups rice or corn cereal squares
1 cup mini pretzels
¼ cup butter
¾ cup brown sugar, packed
⅛ cup water
1 tsp. vanilla

Preheat the oven to 250°. Combine cereal and
pretzels on a greased baking sheet. Heat the
butter, brown sugar, and water in a saucepan.
Bring to a boil and continue boiling for 5
minutes; do not stir. Remove from heat and stir
in vanilla. Pour syrup over cereal and heat for
one hour, stirring every 15 minutes. Allow to cool
completely before serving.

N is for 2³5⁸.

N is for .

N is for that I hammer just right.

numbers   night   nail

© HighReach Learning® Inc.

171

The Letter N

My N Rhyme

N is for numbers.

2 3 5 8

N is for nail that
I hammer just right.

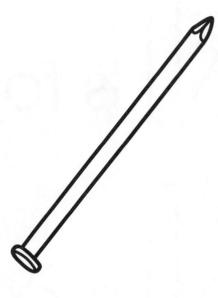

N is for night.

Name _____

© HighReach Learning® Inc.

© HighReach Learning® Inc.

173

The Letter O

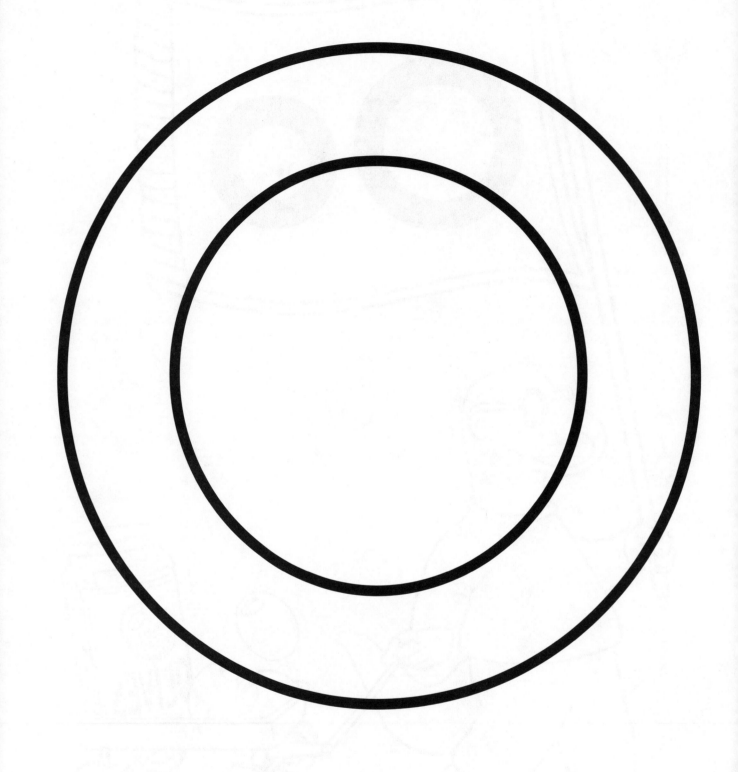

Language Activities

Introduce Ollie Otter and the Letter O

Decorate a copy of the Letter O Display (page 173) as desired. Point to Ollie Otter on the display. Invite the children to guess what type of animal Ollie is. If necessary explain that Ollie is an otter. You may wish to share the rhyme below several times and invite the children to join in.

OLLIE OTTER

Ollie is an otter,
Who eats olives every day.
And if you'd like to try one,
"Please" is all you have to say.

Invite the children to discuss what they learned about Ollie in the rhyme. Invite the children to name what Ollie is pulling in the wagon. Invite the children to share their experiences with olives. Have they ever tried an olive? Do they like or dislike olives? Where do they think an otter lives? Have they ever seen an otter? Encourage the children to share their ideas.

Point to both the capital O and the lowercase o on the display. Explain that these are both ways to write the letter. Explain that Ollie likes the letter O best because it is the first letter of his name. Help the children decide if they know anyone whose name begins with O.

Talk About Letter O Words

Invite the children to talk about words they know that begin with the letter O. Write any suggestions down on sentence strips, a large sheet of paper, or chart paper. Attach the words to the wall at the children's eye level. Some familiar word suggestions are:

Short Sounds:	Long Sounds:
octopus	ocean
olive	old
on	open
opera	over
otter	oatmeal

olive   on   octopus

otter   opera

Explain that all of these words begin with the letter O, but the letter O makes more than one sound. In the words *olive* and *octopus,* the letter makes the same sound as in Ollie. In the words *oatmeal* and *open,* the sound of the letter is the same as its name.

☆ *Learning Extension:* Invite the children to clap for the syllables of words that begin with the letter O (oc-to-pus, on, oat-meal).

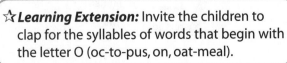

© HighReach Learning® Inc.

The Letter O

Language Activities

Share the Letter O Rebus Rhyme

Share the Letter O Rebus Rhyme (page 183) to develop a sense of rhythm and rhyme and to practice naming pictures. Show the display as you recite the rhyme several times. Afterwards, point to each picture on the chart and encourage the children to name it. Discuss each picture and invite the children to share times when they have seen similar items.

☆ **Learning Extension:** Talk about the letter O. Look at all of the words on the display. Help the children locate the letter O. Explain that the letter O can be written more than one way. Point to the capital O on the display and then point to the lowercase o. Help the children find all of the capital and lowercase letter O's on the display.

Create Letter O Rhyme Books

Give each child a copy of the Letter O Rhyme Book (page 184) and crayons or markers. Invite the children to point to the pictures as you read the text. Encourage the children to decorate the pictures as desired. Cut along the dotted lines and stack the pages in order. Staple the pages together. Invite the children to write their names on the rhyme books. Assist the children as needed.

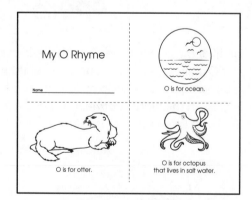

☆ **Learning Extension:** Invite a child to "read" his/her Letter O Rhyme Book to you. Encourage the child to point to the letter O in the book.

Talk About Opposites That Begin with the Letter O

As the children watch, title a sheet of chart paper "O Is for Opposites." Explain to the children that you are going to list opposites that begin with the letter O. Point to and name the letter O's in the title. Make a list of the following words underneath the title: *on, old, out, over, open,* and *outdoors.* Point to and name each of the words. Then challenge the children to think of the opposites that go along with each word. Give the children clues as needed. After the children name the correct opposite, list it next to the first word as shown. After you finish, invite the children to point to and name any letter O's that they see on the chart.

O Is for Opposites	
on	off
old	new
out	in
over	under
open	closed
outdoors	indoors

© HighReach Learning® Inc.

Science Activities

O

Explore Orchids

Show the children a few nontoxic real or artificial orchids. Explain to the children that the beautiful flowers are called orchids, and mention that the word *orchid* begins with the letter O. You may also wish to share that orchids come in all colors and can be speckled or streaked. Provide the children with unbreakable magnifying glasses and invite them to explore the flowers. As they explore the orchids, encourage the children to describe what they see.

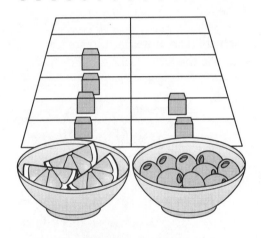

Taste Oranges and Olives

Attach a sheet of chart paper to the table. Prepare a table graph by dividing the paper into two columns and dividing the columns into several rows. Place a bowl of orange slices at the base of one column. Place a bowl of olives at the base of the other column. Give each child an orange slice and an olive. Invite the children to taste the olives and oranges. You may wish to mention that the words *olive* and *orange* both begin with the letter O. Ask the children to choose which food they like better and have them place a small block in the appropriate column of the graph. Ask the children to decide which food was chosen by more people. Help the children count the number of blocks in each column.

What Lives in the Ocean?

Read the children a nonfiction book about the ocean. Encourage the children to share their ideas and any experiences they have had with the ocean. Make sure to expand the conversation based on what the children tell you, and try to answer any questions they may have. Invite the children to talk about what they think lives in the ocean. Help the children notice that the word ocean begins with the letter O. Brainstorm a list of things that live in the ocean, and write down exactly what the children say. You may need to give suggestions such as jellyfish, sharks, whales, dolphins, and plants. The children may be familiar with octopuses. You may wish to share that an octopus is an animal that lives in the ocean, and mention that the word *octopus* begins with the letter O.

☆ **Learning Extension:** Share any of the following facts about the octopus that are appropriate for the children in your group:

❖ An octopus has a soft body and eight arms
❖ Each arm has two rows of suction cups
❖ If an octopus loses an arm, it will grow another one
❖ Octopuses live in dens, spaces under rocks, crevices on the ocean floor, or holes they dig under large rocks

© HighReach Learning® Inc.

177

The Letter O

Large Muscle Activities

Complete an Obstacle Course

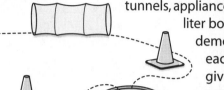

Set up an obstacle course using any available materials that you have. Some examples are play tunnels, appliance boxes, hula hoops, plastic cones, or even two-liter bottles. Show the children the obstacle course and demonstrate how the children should move around, over, or through each obstacle. Invite each child to move through the obstacle course, giving assistance as needed. As the children play, you may wish to mention that the word *obstacle* begins with the letter O.

Move with the Letter O

Write a large bold capital letter O on an index card for each child. Give each child an index card. Invite the children to name the letter on their index cards. Encourage the children to use the letter O index cards to follow directions using the words *on, off,* and *over.* Some examples are listed below. As the children move, you may wish to mention that the words *on, off,* and *over* all begin with the letter O.

❖ Hold the O *over* your head
❖ Balance the O *on* your head
❖ Put the O *on* the floor and jump over it
❖ Put your elbow *on* the O
❖ Take your elbow *off* the O

Use Bodies to Make the Letter O

Invite the children to use their bodies to make the letter O. Challenge them to find several different ways to do this. For example, they could use their arms, hands, fingers, legs, or even their whole bodies.

☆ *Learning Extension:* Invite the children to break off into pairs. Challenge each pair of children to work together to make even bigger letter O's.

Play an Over/Under Game

Encourage the children to line up single file. Give the child standing in the front of the line a playground ball. Have the child pass the ball overhead to the next child in line. Then have that child pass the ball between his/her legs to the next child in line. Have the children alternate passing the ball over their heads and under their legs all the way down the line. Help the children realize that they can hear the name of the letter O at the beginning of the word *over.* After the children gain skill at passing the ball, encourage them to pass it more quickly to see how fast they can move the ball down the line.

The Letter O

178

© HighReach Learning® Inc.

Art Activities

Create Tactile Letter O's

Give each child a copy of the capital letter O (page 174), an old paintbrush, and a shallow dish of glue. Invite the children to trace the letter O with their fingers. Encourage the children to spread glue on their letter O's as desired. Provide the children with small bathroom cups filled with oats, round cereal, or rice. Invite the children to shake the oats, cereal, or rice onto the glue. Set aside to dry. After the glue dries, invite the children to trace their tactile letter O's with their fingers. How does the O feel? Use descriptive words such as bumpy, rough, etc. as you interact with the child.

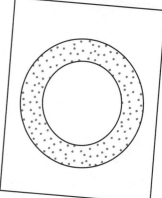

Paint While Listening to Opera Music

Provide the children with paint in shallow dishes, paintbrushes, and paper. Play some opera music as the children create. As the children work, explain that they are listening to opera music, and mention that the word *opera* begins with the letter O. Encourage the children to tell you how the music makes them feel. Does it make them want to paint fast or slow? Do they want to paint something happy or sad?

☆ **Learning Extension:** Title each child's paper "O is for opera music." Invite the children to point to and name the letter O's. The child may wish to trace the letter O's or create more letter O's with the paint.

Create Ocean Pictures

Give each child a sheet of finger-paint paper. Have each child rub a damp sponge over the paper to moisten it. Spoon some blue finger paint onto the children's papers. Invite the children to use their hands to swirl the paint across the paper to create ocean pictures. As the children work, you may wish to mention that the word *ocean* begins with the letter O. Provide the children with sand or nonmetallic glitter in shakers. The children may wish to add the sand or glitter to their ocean pictures, as well as other details using assorted art materials.

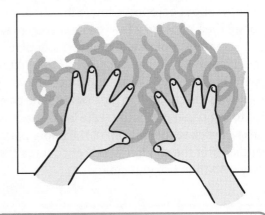

☆ **Learning Extension:** Invite the children that show readiness to make a capital O and a lowercase o in the finger paint on their ocean pictures.

© HighReach Learning® Inc.

The Letter O

Art Activities

Sponge Print Orange Ovals

Provide the children with oval sponges, shallow dishes of orange paint, and paper. Invite the children to use the oval sponges to make prints on their papers. As the children work, help them notice that the sponges are shaped like ovals, and that the paint is the color orange. You may wish to mention that the words *oval* and *orange* both begin with the letter O.

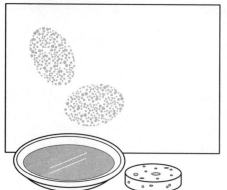

Make Octopus Props

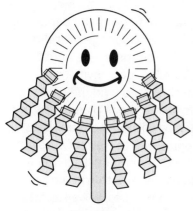

Give each child a paper plate, crayons and markers, glue or tape, and eight 2" x 9" construction paper strips. Explain to the children that they are going to make octopuses, and mention that the word *octopus* begins with the letter O. Encourage the children to share what they know about octopuses. Invite the children to decorate their paper plates as desired. They may wish to create octopus faces on the paper plates. Remind the children that an octopus has eight legs. Help the children fanfold the construction paper strips. Invite the children to glue or tape the paper strips to the paper plates to create legs. Attach a large craft stick to the bottom of the paper plate for a handle. After the children finish, encourage them to play with their octopus creations.

> ☆ *Learning Extension:* Encourage the children to think of what type of home an octopus may live in. Challenge the children to create an octopus home from blocks or any other materials you have available.

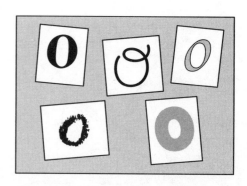

Make Letter O Collages

Give a child old newspapers or magazines and scissors. Invite the child to search for the letter O in the newspapers or magazines. The child may wish to tear or cut the letters out. Give the child a sheet of paper and a glue stick. Encourage the child to attach the letter O cutouts to the paper as desired. Assist the child as needed.

> ☆ *Learning Extension:* If you are working with a group of children, invite them to work together to make one big letter O collage. If you have bulletin board, butcher, or chart paper, you may even wish to cut the paper in the shape of the letter O. Help the children locate and cut or tear out large examples of the letter from captions and headlines. Have the children glue all the letter cutouts to the paper.

The Letter O

© HighReach Learning® Inc.

Small Muscle Activities

Practice Putting On and Taking Off Clothing

Provide assorted clothing with different types of fasteners, such as buttons, zippers, and snaps. The children can practice putting the clothes on and taking them off. As the children explore the clothing, mention that the words *on* and *off* both begin with the letter O.

Oatmeal Dough

Encourage the children to help you create oatmeal dough using the recipe below.

2 cups rolled oats (quick or regular)
1 cup flour
¾ cup water

Place all ingredients in a large mixing bowl. Stir with a wooden spoon to moisten all ingredients. Turn out on a floured surface and knead well. If too sticky, work in a small amount of flour. If dry and crumbly, add a small amount of water. After you finish making the dough, invite the children to use it to shape the letter O or make other objects as desired. As the children explore the dough, mention that the word *oatmeal* begins with the letter O.

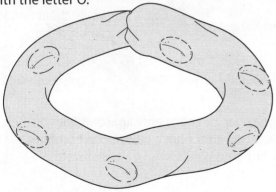

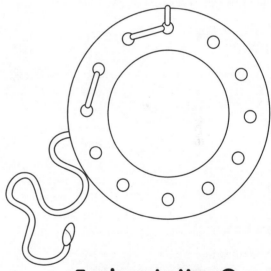

Explore Letter O Lacing Cards

Draw several block letter O's on posterboard using the pattern on page 174 and cut out. Use a hole punch to make a series of holes around each letter cutout. Vary the number of holes so that some will be easier to lace than others. Tie a length of yarn to one hole and wrap the free end with tape. Be sure the yarn can wrap around the letter twice. Set out the letter O lacing cards. Assist the children as needed as they explore the lacing cards.

© HighReach Learning® Inc.

The Letter O

Cooking with Ollie Otter
Letter O Recipes

OUTRAGEOUS ORANGE OMELETS

eggs
milk
red and yellow food coloring
butter
shredded cheddar cheese
salt

Beat together 2 eggs and ¼ cup milk for each omelet. Add some red and yellow food coloring to the egg mixture. Melt some butter into a heated skillet pan. After the egg is almost cooked, add shredded cheddar cheese to the center, fold over, and flip. Cook for a few more minutes to melt cheese, and thoroughly cook the egg. Sprinkle with salt and serve warm.

OPEN-FACED OVAL OWL SNACKS

sliced bread
apple butter
raisins or grapes

Cut bread slices into oval shapes. Give each child an oval. Invite the children to use plastic spoons or knives to spread apple butter on the ovals. The children may wish to design an owl face using grapes, raisins, or shapes cut from the leftover bread.

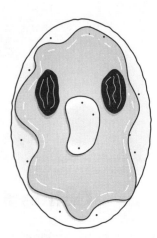

OATMEAL COOKIES

1 cup shortening
1½ cups brown sugar
2 eggs
½ cup milk
¼ tsp. baking soda
2 tsp. baking powder
1 tsp. salt
1 tsp. cinnamon
¼ tsp. nutmeg
3 cups quick-cooking rolled oats

Preheat the oven to 400°. Cream together the shortening, brown sugar, and eggs until light and fluffy. Stir in milk. Sift dry ingredients together and add to creamed mixture. Drop batter from a tablespoon two inches apart onto a greased cookie sheet. Bake for 8 minutes. Cool slightly before removing from pan.

© HighReach Learning® Inc.

O is for .

O is for .

O is for  that

Lives in salt water.

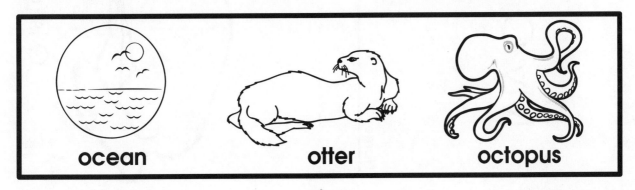

ocean   otter   octopus

O is for ocean.

O is for octopus
that lives in salt water.

My O Rhyme

Name _____

O is for otter.

© HighReach Learning® Inc.

The Letter P

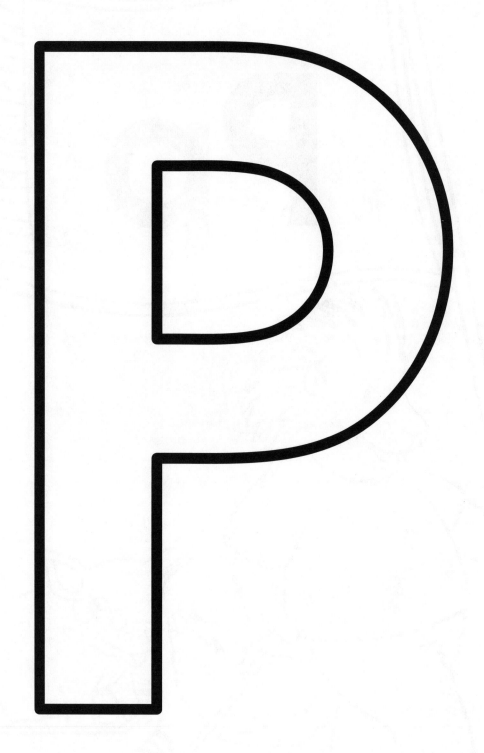

The Letter P

© HighReach Learning® Inc.

Language Activities

Introduce Petey Porcupine and the Letter P

Decorate a copy of the Letter P Display (page 185) as desired. Point to Petey Porcupine on the display. Invite the children to guess what type of animal Petey is. If necessary explain that Petey is a porcupine. You may wish to share the rhyme below several times and invite the children to join in.

PETEY PORCUPINE

Petey is a porcupine.
He loves his pet pig, Pat.
He pulls Pat everywhere he goes.
What do you think of that?

Invite the children to discuss what they learned about Petey in the rhyme. Invite the children to name the item on the display that Petey is pulling in the wagon. Invite the children to share what they know about porcupines and pigs. Have they ever seen a porcupine or a pig? Do they think a pig would make a good pet? Why or why not? Encourage the children to share their ideas and experiences.

Point to both the capital P and the lowercase p on the display. Explain that these are both ways to write the letter. Explain that Petey likes the letter P best because it is the first letter of his name. Help the children decide if they know anyone whose name begins with P.

Talk About Letter P Words

Invite the children to talk about words they know that begin with the letter P. Write any suggestions down on sentence strips, a large sheet of paper, or chart paper. Attach the words to the wall at the children's eye level. Some familiar word suggestions are:

pig	pickle	parachute	puzzle
pet	push	pizza	
puppet	parade	picnic	

☆ **Learning Extension:** Invite the children to clap for the syllables of words that begin with the letter p (pig, par-a-chute, pa-rade).

Play Pass the Porcupine

Encourage the children to sit in a circle. Show the children a Koosh ball or a similar type ball. Explain to the children that they should pretend that the ball is a porcupine like Petey from the display, and mention that the word *porcupine* begins with the letter P. Encourage the children to pass the ball around the circle as you play music. When you stop the music, the child holding the ball should try to name a word that begins with the letter P. Give assistance as needed.

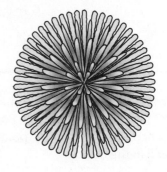

© HighReach Learning® Inc.

The Letter P

Language Activities
Share the Letter P Rebus Rhyme

Share the Letter P Rebus Rhyme (page 195) to develop a sense of rhythm and rhyme and to practice naming pictures. Show the display as you recite the rhyme several times. Afterwards, point to each picture on the chart and encourage the children to name it. Discuss each picture and invite the children to share times when they have seen similar items.

☆ *Learning Extension:* Talk about the letter P. Look at all of the words on the display. Help the children locate the letter P. Explain that the letter P can be written more than one way. Point to the capital P on the display and then point to the lowercase p. Help the children find all of the capital and lowercase letter P's on the display.

Create Letter P Rhyme Books

Give each child a copy of the Letter P Rhyme Book (page 196) and crayons or markers. Invite the children to point to the pictures as you read the text. Encourage the children to decorate the pictures as desired. Cut along the dotted lines and stack the pages in order. Staple the pages together. Invite the children to write their names on the rhyme books. Assist the children as needed.

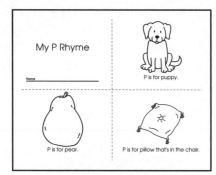

☆ *Learning Extension:* Invite a child to "read" his/her Letter P Rhyme Book to you. Encourage the child to point to the letter P in the book.

Talk About Pets

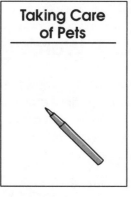

Read a book about pets to the children. Invite the children to talk about their experiences with pets. What types of pets do they have? If they do not have a pet, what type of pet would they like to have? After the children share their ideas and experiences, title a sheet of chart paper "Taking Care of Pets." Invite the children to suggest ways to care for pets. As the children share their ideas, write their suggestions on the chart paper. During the discussion, you may wish to explain to the children that there are some needs that are shared by all pets, but some pets have needs that are different from others. For example, all pets need food, water, room to exercise, and a clean place to live. Some pets, such as cats and dogs, need their owners to pet them and hold them. Other pets, such as goldfish, do not need to be handled. After all of the children share their ideas, read what you wrote back to them.

The Letter P

188

© HighReach Learning® Inc.

Science Activities

Taste Pickles

Prepare a pickle tasting graph by cutting a long narrow strip of posterboard and dividing it into two columns, and then dividing the columns into several rows. At the top of the graph, label the columns "sweet" and "sour." Show the children a jar of sweet pickles and a jar of sour (dill) pickles. Invite the children to share their experiences with pickles and predict which type they will like best. After the children share, mention that the word *pickle* begins with the letter P. Give each child a sweet and a sour pickle to taste. Give each child a large paper clip. Help the children slide the paper clips onto the edge of the appropriate column on the graph to show which type of pickle they like best as shown. You may also want to mention that the term *paper clip* begins with the letter P. When the graph is finished, have the children help you decide which type of pickle is preferred by the class.

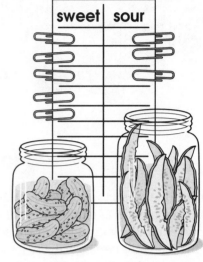

☆ *Learning Extension:* Invite a child to count the paper clips on each side of the graph with you. Which side has more? Which side has less?

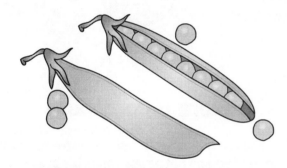

Explore Peas in Pods

Give the children fresh sugar snap peas. Invite the children to explore the pods, and invite them to guess what might be inside. Explain to the children that there are peas inside the pods, and mention that the words *pea* and *pod* both begin with the letter P. Invite the children to share their experiences with peas. Have they ever eaten peas? Do they like or dislike peas? After the children share their ideas, invite them to remove the peas from the pods.

☆ *Learning Extension:* Help the children count the peas inside each pod. Are there the same number of peas in each pod?

Explore and Measure Pints

Show the children a pint container. Explain to the children that the container holds a pint, and mention that the word *pint* begins with the letter P. Invite the children to predict how many cups of water it will take to fill the pint. After the children share their ideas, place the container in a shallow baking pan. Let the children take turns filling a one-cup measuring cup with water and pouring it into the container. If the container has a narrow opening, have the children use a funnel. They will find that the container holds two cups. Show the children another pint container that is a different shape than the first one. Ask the children if they think the container will hold more than a pint, less than a pint, or exactly a pint. After they share their ideas, have them fill the second container with the water from the first container. The children may be surprised to find that even though it is a different shape, the container still holds the same amount of water.

© HighReach Learning® Inc.   189   The Letter P

Large Muscle Activities

Push and Pull Wagons

As the children watch, print the words *push* and *pull* in large bold letters on each side of a sheet of construction paper. Show the children the words and help them identify the letter P at the beginning. Show the children a wagon and invite them to take turns pushing or pulling each other (or plush toys, dolls, etc.). As the children play, encourage them to share which action is easier to do, pushing or pulling. *Caution: Make sure to closely supervise this activity.*

Have a Pink Pedaling Parade

Decorate riding toys with pink streamers. Show the children one of the riding toys with pedals. Point to the pedals and invite the children to identify this part. Print the word *pedal* on a sheet of paper and help the children discover that this word begins with the letter P. Print the words *pink* and *parade* on the same sheet of paper. Encourage the children to identify the letter P in these words as well. Explain to the children that you would like for them to participate in a pink pedaling parade! Encourage the children to ride the pink decorated toys as they have a parade.

Pretend to Be Popcorn

As the children watch, print the words *popping* and *popcorn* on a sheet of paper. Point to and name the words and help the children realize that the words *popping* and *popcorn* both begin with the letter P. Then use the following directions to lead the children in a creative movement activity about popping popcorn. Feel free to add your own ideas and suggestions to the directions!

❖ Let's pretend that we are tiny kernels of corn in the bottom of the popcorn popper. *(Curl body into a ball.)*

❖ Here comes some oil. That tickles! Now the popper is getting warmer and warmer. In fact it is getting really hot! That makes me want to wiggle and jiggle! *(Wiggle body all around.)*

❖ Oh, my goodness! It is getting very hot now. Let's wiggle even faster! It's so hot now that I think I'm ready to pop! Pop! Pop! Pop! *(Hop and pop all around.)*

Explore a Parachute

Encourage the children to stand in a circle around a parachute, if you do not have a parachute available, use a large sheet. Have each child grab the edge of the parachute and pull it taut. Invite the children to move in a circle, move the parachute up and down, or any other movements they desire. As the children move, you may wish to mention that the word *parachute* begins with the letter P.

The Letter P

190

© HighReach Learning® Inc.

Art Activities

Create Tactile Letter P's

Give each child a copy of the capital letter P (page 186), an old paintbrush, and a shallow dish of glue. Invite the children to trace the letter P with their fingers. Encourage the children to spread glue on their letter P's as desired. Provide the children with small bathroom cups filled with potato flakes, salt, or rice. Invite the children to shake the potato flakes, salt, or rice onto the glue. Set aside to dry. After the glue dries, invite the children to trace their tactile letter P's with their fingers. How does the P feel? Use descriptive words such as bumpy, rough, etc. as you interact with the child.

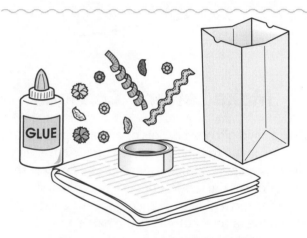

Make Paper Bag Pets

Provide the children with small paper lunch bags, old newspapers, glue, tape, and assorted art materials. Help the children stuff the lunch bags with old newspapers, fold the end closed, and tape to secure. Invite the children to use the art materials to decorate the bags to create the pets of their choice. As the children work, mention that the word *pet* begins with the letter P. After the children finish, invite them to tell you about their pets.

☆ *Learning Extension:* Invite the children that show readiness to dictate a sentence or sentences about their pets. Write exactly what the children say on index cards. Attach the index cards to the paper bag pets.

Make Paper Plate Pizzas

Give each child a large paper plate, crayons and markers, red coding dot stickers, red paint in shallow dishes, paintbrushes, crumpled brown construction paper, and other art materials for making pizzas. As the children watch, write "P is for pizza" on the back of each paper plate. Invite the children to share their experiences with pizza. Do they like or dislike pizza? What kinds of toppings do they like on pizza? After the children share, point to the word *pizza* and mention that it begins with the letter P. Invite the children to decorate their paper plates like pizzas using the materials. Assist the children as needed.

© HighReach Learning® Inc.

The Letter P

Art Activities
Create Pictures with Potato Printers

Away from the children, create potato printers by cutting several large, clean potatoes in half and carving shapes or designs in the potato halves as shown. Provide the children with large sheets of construction paper, potato printers, and shallow dishes of paint. Demonstrate how to use the potato printers and paint. Encourage the children to dip the potato printers design-side down in shallow dishes of paint and make designs on their papers. Assist the children as needed. As the children work, you may wish to mention that the words *potato, print,* and *paint* all begin with the letter P.

Create Picnic Plates

Give each child a large paper plate, scissors, glue, and food magazines or grocery store circulars. Talk to the children about going on a picnic. Invite the children to share their experiences with picnics. Where have they gone on a picnic? What did they pack for their picnic? After the children share, invite the children to look for foods in the magazines or grocery store circulars that they might pack for a picnic. Encourage the children to cut or tear out the pictures and glue them to their paper plates. As the children work, you may wish to mention that the word *picnic* begins with the letter P.

☆ *Learning Extension:* Invite the children that show readiness to dictate a sentence about what they might pack for a picnic. Write exactly what the children say on the backs of their paper plates.

Make Letter P Collages

Give a child old newspapers or magazines and scissors. Invite the child to search for the letter P in the newspapers or magazines. The child may wish to tear or cut the letters out. Give the child a sheet of paper and a glue stick. Encourage the child to attach the letter P cutouts to the paper as desired. Assist the child as needed.

☆ *Learning Extension:* If you are working with a group of children, invite them to work together to make one big letter P collage. If you have bulletin board, butcher, or chart paper, you may even wish to cut the paper in the shape of the letter P. Help the children locate and cut or tear out large examples of the letter from captions and headlines. Have the children glue all the letter cutouts to the paper.

The Letter P

192

© HighReach Learning® Inc.

Small Muscle Activities

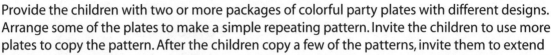

P

Pattern Party Plates

Provide the children with two or more packages of colorful party plates with different designs. Arrange some of the plates to make a simple repeating pattern. Invite the children to use more plates to copy the pattern. After the children copy a few of the patterns, invite them to extend the patterns by adding more plates to the end. As the children work, you may wish to mention that the words *party, plate,* and *pattern* begin with the letter P.

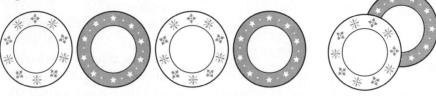

Explore Picture Puzzles

Cut pictures of items of interest to the children in your class from magazines or newspapers or print them from the Internet if you have access. Some examples of pictures may be animals, toys, community helpers, or transportation vehicles. Glue the pictures to old file folders or posterboard. After the glue dries, cut around the pictures. Cut the pictures into simple three to five piece puzzles and place them in zipper-top bags. Provide the children with the picture puzzles. As the children work to complete the puzzles, you may wish to mention that the words *picture* and *puzzle* both begin with the letter P.

Create and Explore Homemade Putty

Pour 2 tablespoons white glue into a small paper cup for each child. Add a few drops of food coloring to the glue and invite the child to mix the glue and food coloring with a plastic spoon. Pour 1 tablespoon liquid starch into a small bowl for each child. Help the child pour the glue mixture on top of the liquid starch. Allow the mixture to stand for five minutes or until the glue absorbs into the liquid starch. Have the children remove the putty from the bowls and knead. The more the children knead the putty, the better the consistency will be. Encourage the children to play with the putty. When the children finish, store the putty in plastic eggs or small zipper-top bags.

Explore Letter P Lacing Cards

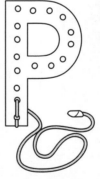

Draw several block letter P's on posterboard using the pattern on page 186 and cut out. Use a hole punch to make a series of holes around each letter cutout. Vary the number of holes so that some will be easier to lace than others. Tie a length of yarn to one hole and wrap the free end with tape. Be sure the yarn can wrap around the letter twice. Set out the letter P lacing cards. Assist the children as needed as they explore the lacing cards.

© HighReach Learning® Inc.

The Letter P

Cooking with Petey Porcupine
Letter P Recipes

Pepperoni Pizzas

refrigerator biscuits
tomato or pizza sauce
pepperoni
grated mozzarella cheese

Roll the biscuits flat to create mini pizza crusts and invite the children to add sauce, pepperoni, and cheese to their individual pizzas. Cook the pizzas in the oven using the temperature and time recommended on the biscuit container.

Purple Cows

grape juice
vanilla ice cream

Give each child a cup of grape juice and add a scoop of vanilla ice cream. Encourage the children to stir the juice and ice cream to create purple cow treats!

Pigs in a Blanket

pancake mix
pre-cooked link sausage
syrup

Make pancakes according to the instructions on the package. Heat the sausage links according to the instructions on the package. Give each child a pancake and a sausage link. Encourage the children to wrap the sausages in the pancakes. Provide syrup to the children who want to add it to their "pig in a blanket."

Positively Perfect Popcorn

microwave popcorn
½ stick butter
2 tsp. cinnamon
2 tsp. sugar

Microwave the popcorn according to directions on the package. Melt the butter in the microwave, and then add the cinnamon and sugar and stir. Put the popcorn in a big bowl. Pour the butter mixture over the popcorn and mix well. Serve immediately.

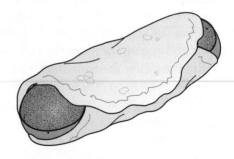

The Letter P

© HighReach Learning® Inc.

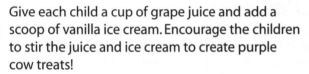

P  is for ☐ .

P is for ☐ .

P is for ☐

That's in the chair.

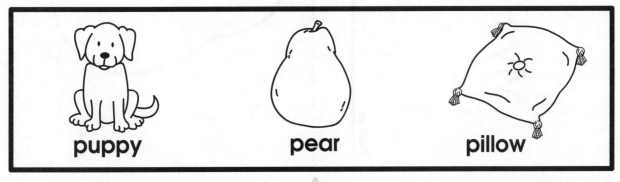

puppy   pear   pillow

© HighReach Learning® Inc.

The Letter P

P is for puppy.

P is for pillow that's in the chair.

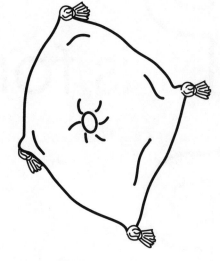

My P Rhyme

Name

P is for pear.

© HighReach Learning® Inc.

© HighReach Learning® Inc.

The Letter Q

© HighReach Learning® Inc.

Language Activities

Introduce Queen Quintella and the Letter Q

Decorate a copy of the Letter Q Display (page197) as desired. Point to Queen Quintella on the display. Invite the children to guess what her job is. If necessary explain that Quintella is a queen. You may wish to share the rhyme below several times and invite the children to join in.

QUEEN QUINTELLA

Queen Quintella loves her quilt.
She takes it everywhere.
And if you catch a little chill,
I'm sure she'd like to share!

Invite the children to discuss what they learned about Quintella in the rhyme. Encourage the children to name what Quintella is pulling in the wagon. Invite the children to share their thoughts about queens. What do they think a queen does? What does a queen wear? Help the children notice the quilt. Have they ever seen a quilt before? Encourage the children to share their ideas.

Point to both the capital Q and the lowercase q on the display. Explain that these are both ways to write the letter. Explain that Quintella likes the letter Q best because it is the first letter of her name. Help the children decide if they know anyone whose name begins with Q.

Talk About Letter Q Words

Invite the children to talk about words they know that begin with the letter Q. Write any suggestions down on sentence strips, a large sheet of paper, or chart paper. Attach the words to the wall at the children's eye level. Some familiar word suggestions are:

quack	quartz	quick	quilt
quart	queen	quiet	
quarter	question	quill	

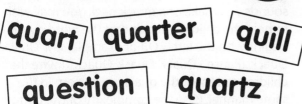

> ☆ *Learning Extension:* Invite the children to clap for the syllables of words that begin with the letter Q (ques-tion, quart, qui-et).

Play a Questioning Game

Explain to the children that a question is something a person asks when they want to know something, and mention that the word *question* begins with the letter Q. Encourage the children to play a questioning game with you. Choose a child to think of an item in the room. Help the other children ask questions to see if they can guess the item. Help the children phrase the questions so they can be answered with "yes" or "no." Some examples are "Does it have wheels?" or "Is it small?" Continue the game until the children guess the item. Invite another child to think of an item and ask questions again.

Language Activities

Share the Letter Q Rebus Rhyme

Share the Letter Q Rebus Rhyme (page 207) to develop a sense of rhythm and rhyme and to practice naming pictures. Show the display as you recite the rhyme several times. Afterwards, point to each picture on the chart and encourage the children to name it. Discuss each picture and invite the children to share times when they have seen similar items.

> ☆ **Learning Extension:** Talk about the letter Q. Look at all of the words on the display. Help the children locate the letter Q. Explain that the letter Q can be written more than one way. Point to the capital Q on the display and then point to the lowercase Q. Help the children find all of the capital and lowercase letter Q's on the display.

Create Letter Q Rhyme Books

Give each child a copy of the Letter Q Rhyme Book (page 208) and crayons or markers. Invite the children to point to the pictures as you read the text. Encourage the children to decorate the pictures as desired. Cut along the dotted lines and stack the pages in order. Staple the pages together. Invite the children to write their names on the rhyme books. Assist the children as needed.

> ☆ **Learning Extension:** Invite a child to "read" his/her Letter Q Rhyme Book to you. Encourage the child to point to the letter Q in the book.

"Quack. Quack. Quack. Quack. Quack!"

Quack! Quack! Quack!

Explain to the children that you are going to make quacking noises, and you want them to copy the sounds you make and quack back. You may wish to help the children notice that the word *quack* begins with the letter Q. For example, say, "Quack. Quack. (Pause.) Quack. Quack. Quack." Invite the children to repeat the quacking pattern in the same manner. Base the complexity of the pattern on the developmental level of the children in your group. Once the children understand the concept, they can take turns leading quacking patterns for everyone (including you!) to repeat.

© HighReach Learning® Inc.

Science Activities

Explore and Measure Quarts

Show the children a one-quart container. Explain to the children that the container holds a quart, and mention that the word *quart* begins with the letter Q. Invite the children to predict how many cups of sand it will take to fill the quart. After the children share their ideas, place the container in the sand table or a basin of sand. Let the children take turns filling a one-cup measuring cup with sand and pouring it into the container. If the container has a narrow opening, have the children use a funnel. They will find that the container holds four cups. Show the children another one-quart container that is a different shape than the first one. Ask the children if they think the container will hold more than a quart, less than a quart, or exactly a quart. After they share their ideas, have them fill the second container with the sand from the first container. The children may be surprised to find that even though it is a different shape, the container still holds the same amount of sand.

Explore Quarters

Show the children magnifying glasses and an assortment of quarters. Invite the children to look at the quarters with the magnifying glasses. Encourage the children to describe what they see. Help the children notice that each quarter has one side that is the same as all the other quarters. What do the pictures look like on the quarters?

Explore Quartz

Show the children assorted pieces or pictures of quartz. Explain to the children that quartz is an interesting and sometimes beautiful rock that is found in many different places. You may want to share that sometimes people make jewelry with quartz. You may also wish to mention that the word *quartz* begins with the letter Q. Provide the children with magnifying glasses and invite them to explore the quartz. What do they see? Invite the children to hold the quartz and describe how it feels in their hands.

© HighReach Learning® Inc.

The Letter Q

Large Muscle Activities

Drop Quarters in a Can

Set a large metal coffee can without sharp edges or clean metal trash can on the floor in front of the children. Provide each child with a few quarters, and mention that the word *quarter* begins with the letter Q. Help each child stand in turn at arm's length from the can and try to drop the quarters into it from shoulder height. When all of the quarters have been dropped, help the children count how may went into the can and how many missed.

☆ *Learning Extension:* Encourage the children that show readiness to stand a few feet away from the can. Invite the children to try to toss the quarters into the can. If the distance is too easy, have the children move a few steps back until it becomes challenging. After they finish, invite the children to decide if more quarters went into the can or onto the floor.

Play The Queen Says

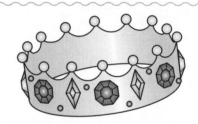

Encourage the children to form a circle. Wear a toy crown and explain to the children that you are the queen. You may wish to mention that the word *queen* begins with the letter Q. This game is played like the traditional Simon Says. Instead of saying, "Simon says," you will say, "The queen says." For example if you say, "The queen says clap your hands," everyone should do so. But if you say, "Stomp your feet," no one should follow the command because you didn't say, "The queen says." The object of the game is to listen very closely and perform only the actions the queen says to do.

☆ *Learning Extension:* Allow the children that show readiness to take turns being the queen and leading the group.

Bounce a Ball on a Quilt

Spread a small quilt on the floor and place a small playground ball in the middle. Have the children stand around the quilt, lift it by the edges, and pull it taut. Have the children lift and lower the quilt to make the ball bounce. As the children play, you may wish to mention that the word *quilt* begins with the letter Q.

Play a Quiet Game

Invite the children to talk about times when they are very quiet, such as when they sleep at night, take a nap, etc. You may wish to mention that the word *quiet* begins with the letter Q. Explain to the children that you are going to play a game. When the lights go off, the children should tiptoe around the room and move very quietly. Shhh! When the lights come back on, the children can move around as usual. Play the game as long as the children show interest.

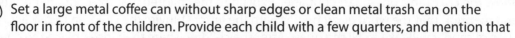

The Letter Q

© HighReach Learning® Inc.

Art Activities

Create Tactile Letter Q's

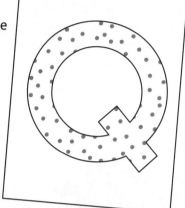

Give each child a copy of the capital letter Q (page 198), an old paintbrush, and a shallow dish of glue. Invite the children to trace the letter Q with their fingers. Encourage the children to spread glue on their letter Q's as desired. Provide the children with small bathroom cups filled with sand, salt, or rice. Invite the children to shake the sand, salt, or rice onto the glue. Set aside to dry. After the glue dries, invite the children to trace their tactile letter Q's with their fingers. How does the Q feel? Use descriptive words such as bumpy, rough, etc. as you interact with the child.

Create Pictures with a Quill Pen

Show the children some long craft feathers. Explain to the children that a long time ago, people did not have pencils, pens, or markers. Instead they made quill pens from feathers. Explain that they would dip the tip of the pen in an inkwell and then write on paper. You may also wish to mention that the word *quill* begins with the letter Q. Next, set out the feathers, paint in shallow dishes, and paper. Demonstrate for the children how to dip a feather into paint and make designs or write on the paper. Invite the children to try to write or draw using the same procedure. As the children work, encourage them to discuss the results of their efforts. Is it easy or hard to write with a quill pen?

Create a Quilt

Provide each child with a sheet of construction paper, scissors, wallpaper samples or fabric scraps, and glue. Invite the children to cut shapes from the wallpaper or fabric and glue the shapes on their papers to create quilts. Assist the children as needed, and as the children work you may wish to mention that the word *quilt* begins with the letter Q.

☆ *Learning Extension:* Give the children construction paper and crayons or markers. Help the children print their names in the middle of their papers. Then invite the children to decorate their papers as desired. When all of the children have finished, arrange their creations facedown on the floor and tape together to make a quilt. When finished, display the quilt at the children's eye level.

© HighReach Learning® Inc.

The Letter Q

Art Activities

Make Quarter Rubbings

Help the children arrange several quarters on the table and secure them with loops of tape or poster putty. Have the children place sheets of paper over the quarters and rub over them with the sides of unwrapped crayons. As the children work, you may wish to mention that the word *quarter* begins with the letter Q. The design of the quarters will appear on the paper. Invite the children to discuss why they think this happens.

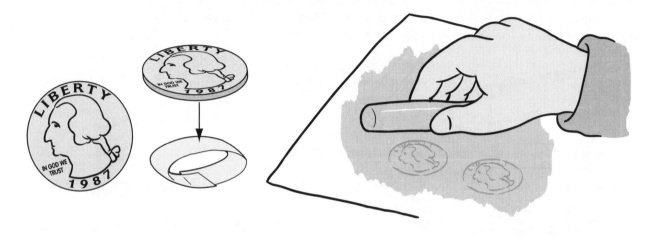

Make Letter Q Collages

Give a child old newspapers or magazines and scissors. Invite the child to search for the letter Q in the newspapers or magazines. The child may wish to tear or cut the letters out. Give the child a sheet of paper and a glue stick. Encourage the child to attach the letter Q cutouts to the paper as desired. Assist the child as needed.

☆**Learning Extension:** If you are working with a group of children, invite them to work together to make one big letter Q collage. If you have bulletin board, butcher, or chart paper, you may even wish to cut the paper in the shape of the letter Q. Help the children locate and cut or tear out large examples of the letter from captions and headlines. Have the children glue all the letter cutouts to the paper.

© HighReach Learning® Inc.

Small Muscle Activities

Letter Q Stencils

Trace the letter Q onto several old file folders using the pattern on page 198 as a guide. Use a utility knife or sharp scissors to carefully cut out the letter Q. Provide the children with letter Q stencils, paper, and colored pencils. Invite the children to use the stencils to practice making the letter Q. Assist the children as needed.

Find the Queens

Provide the children with a deck of playing cards. Show the children a queen playing card, and then shuffle the cards. Invite the children to search for queens in the deck. How many queens did the children find? Invite them to count the queens with you. You may wish to mention that the word *queen* begins with the letter Q. Shuffle the cards again and repeat the activity as long as the children show interest.

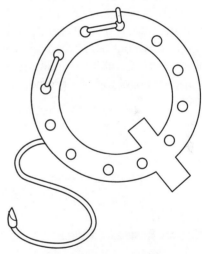

Explore Letter Q Lacing Cards

Draw several block letter Q's on posterboard using the pattern on page 198 and cut out. Use a hole punch to make a series of holes around each letter cutout. Vary the number of holes so that some will be easier to lace than others. Tie a length of yarn to one hole and wrap the free end with tape. Be sure the yarn can wrap around the letter twice. Set out the letter Q lacing cards. Assist the children as needed as they explore the lacing cards.

Cooking with Queen Quintella
Letter Q Recipes

Queen's Bread Pudding

1 cup brown sugar, packed
4 slices buttered bread
2 eggs
2⅓ cup milk
1 tsp. vanilla
½ cup raisins
½ tsp. cinnamon
½ tsp. nutmeg

Preheat the oven to 350°. Spread brown sugar in the bottom of a greased baking dish. Break the buttered bread into pieces and spread in the pan. Beat the eggs, milk, and vanilla, and then add half of the raisins. Pour over bread and top with remaining raisins. Combine cinnamon and nutmeg and sprinkle over top of ingredients. Bake for 1 hour.

Quick Quiche Squares

6 slices whole wheat bread
¼ tsp. garlic powder
1 (26 oz.) carton frozen quiche filling
   with ham, thawed

Preheat the oven to 400°. Lightly grease a 11" x 17" baking pan. Tear bread into small pieces and arrange in the bottom of dish. Stir garlic powder into quiche filling and pour over bread. Bake for 20-25 minutes or until set. Let stand five minutes. Then cut in squares and serve warm. Serves 6-8 children.

Quenching Creamy Raspberry Punch

2 (64 oz.) bottles of raspberry cream soda, chilled
1 (12 oz.) can frozen concentrated raspberry juice
½ gallon vanilla ice cream

Combine raspberry cream soda and raspberry juice concentrate in a large bowl. Stir until concentrate is dissolved. Carefully add ice cream. Stir briefly. Serve chilled.

© HighReach Learning® Inc.

Q is for ?.

Q is for [queen].

Q is for [quilt].

That's puffy and green.

question	queen	quilt

My Q Rhyme

Name _____

Q is for question mark.

Q is for quilt that's puffy and green.

Q is for queen.

© HighReach Learning® Inc.

© HighReach Learning® Inc.

The Letter R

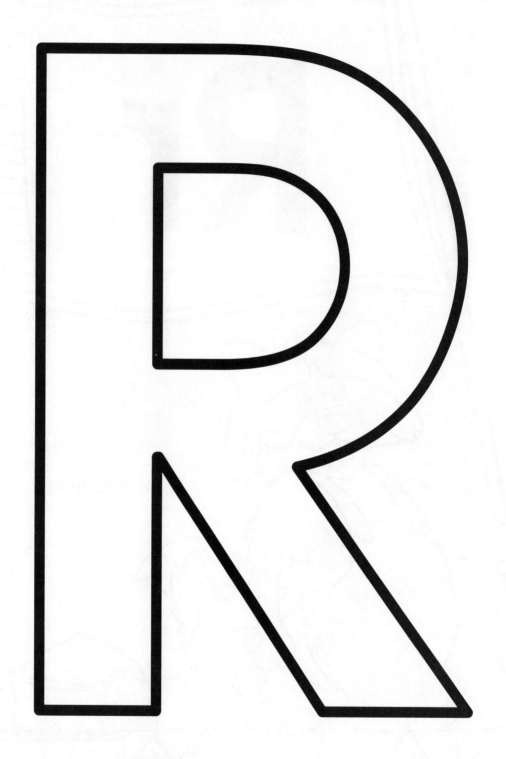

The Letter R

© HighReach Learning® Inc.

Language Activities

Introduce Rodney Raccoon and the Letter R

Decorate a copy of the Letter R Display (page 209) as desired. Point to Rodney Raccoon on the display. Invite the children to guess what type of animal Rodney is. If necessary explain that Rodney is a raccoon. You may wish to share the rhyme below several times and invite the children to join in.

RODNEY RACCOON

Rodney Raccoon
Roams along the road
Picking up some rocks
To add to his load.

Ask the children what they learned about Rodney in the rhyme. What is Rodney pulling in the wagon? Have the children ever seen a raccoon before? Where do they think raccoons live? What do they think raccoons eat? Encourage the children to share their ideas and thoughts about raccoons.

Point to both the capital R and the lowercase r on the display. Explain that these are both ways to write the letter. Explain that Rodney likes the letter R best because it is the first letter of his name. Help the children decide if they know anyone whose name begins with R.

Talk About Letter R Words

Invite the children to talk about words they know that begin with the letter R. Write any suggestions down on sentence strips, a large sheet of paper, or chart paper. Attach the words to the wall at the children's eye level. Some familiar word suggestions are:

raccoon	rainbow	rice	ruler
radio	raisin	road	
rain	ribbon	rooster	

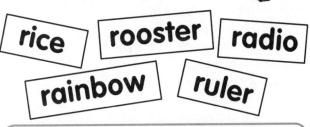

☆ **Learning Extension:** Invite the children to clap for the syllables of words that begin with the letter R (ra-di-o, rul-er, rain).

Discuss Recycling

Encourage the children to share what they know about recycling, and mention that the word *recycle* begins with the letter R. After the children share, show them the recycling symbol on a package. Explain that packages with this symbol can be recycled. Help the children understand that to recycle means to take an old product and make it into a new product. Explain that recycling is a way to show respect for the environment by not wasting products and making more room in landfills.

☆ **Learning Extension:** Encourage the children to look at a variety of recyclable packages and try to find the symbol.

Language Activities
Share the Letter R Rebus Rhyme

Share the Letter R Rebus Rhyme (page 219) to develop a sense of rhythm and rhyme and to practice naming pictures. Show the display as you recite the rhyme several times. Afterwards, point to each picture on the chart and encourage the children to name it. Discuss each picture and invite the children to share times when they have seen similar items.

☆ *Learning Extension:* Talk about the letter R. Look at all of the words on the display. Help the children locate the letter R. Explain that the letter R can be written more than one way. Point to the capital R on the display and then point to the lowercase r. Help the children find all of the capital and lowercase letter R's on the display.

Create Letter R Rhyme Books

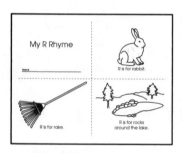

Give each child a copy of the Letter R Rhyme Book (page 220) and crayons or markers. Invite the children to point to the pictures as you read the text. Encourage the children to decorate the pictures as desired. Cut along the dotted lines and stack the pages in order. Staple the pages together. Invite the children to write their names on the rhyme books. Assist the children as needed.

☆ *Learning Extension:* Invite a child to "read" his/her Letter R Rhyme Book to you. Encourage the child to point to the letter R in the book.

Talk About Rain

Encourage the children to share their thoughts and ideas about rain. During the discussion, mention that the word *rain* begins with the letter R. After they share, explain that little drops of water gather together and form the clouds in the sky. When the clouds get very full of water drops, the water falls from the clouds, and that is rain. The rain creates puddles on the ground and helps keep the rivers, lakes, and oceans full. After the rain, the sunshine comes out and some of the water that fell to the ground evaporates back into the clouds. Then the whole cycle repeats again.

WATER DROPS MAKE ALL THE CLOUDS
(tune: "Twinkle, Twinkle, Little Star")

Water drops make all the clouds,
All the clouds, all the clouds.
(Hold arms above head to form a big circle.)
When the clouds become too full,
Raindrops will begin to fall.
(Spread out fingers and wiggle them as arms are lowered.)
First, the clouds form way up high.
(Hold arms above head to form a big circle.)
Then the rain falls from the sky.
(Spread out fingers and wiggle them as arms are lowered.)

© HighReach Learning® Inc.

Science Activities

Perform a Raisin Experiment

Pour club soda into a clear plastic container. Drop several raisins into the soda and encourage the children to watch closely and describe what happens. They will see the raisins rise to the top and then sink again. Encourage the children to share their ideas about why they think the raisins go up in the soda. During the discussion, mention that the word *raisin* begins with the letter R. Help the children notice that bubbles collect on the raisins. As the raisins become covered in bubbles, they begin to float. When the raisins reach the top, the bubbles pop and the raisins sink to the bottom again until more bubbles attach to them.

Explore Rulers

Show the children a ruler and mention that the word *ruler* begins with the letter R. Ask the children if they know what a ruler is used for, and encourage them to share their ideas. Explain that rulers are used to measure things or to see how long something is. Show the children how to measure an item, such as a book, with the ruler. Invite several children to choose something in the classroom they would like to measure using rulers. Ask the children to predict how long they think the items are. Invite them to use the rulers to measure the items. Help the children discover if their predictions were accurate. Continue measuring classroom items until all of the children have had turns using the rulers.

> ☆ *Learning Extension:* Invite a child that shows readiness to point to and name any numbers that he/she recognizes on the ruler. Then invite the child to help you count the number of inches of each item that is measured.

Make Ripples with Rocks

Tell the children that the word *ripple* begins with the letter R. Ask the children if they know what a ripple is. Demonstrate making ripples by dropping small rocks into the water table or a basin of water. Point out the ripples that spread out across the water. Invite the children to share their ideas about how they think ripples are made when a rock is dropped in the water. Encourage each child to drop a small rock in the water table to create ripples. ***Caution: Provide close supervision. Invite the children to discuss their observations.***

Make Rainbows

Explain to the children that rainbows are created when sunlight hits raindrops or water, and separates all of the colors in the light. On a sunny day, use one or more of the suggested techniques below to make rainbows. Mention that the word *rainbow* begins with the letter R.

❖ Garden hose: Attach the hose to a faucet, spray a light mist of water, and let the sun shine through it.

❖ Prism: Hold a prism so the sun shines through it. Turn it until a rainbow can be seen.

❖ Water and mirror: Place a small unbreakable mirror in a clear plastic glass of water so the sun can shine on the mirror. Turn the glass until a rainbow is reflected against the wall or ceiling.

© HighReach Learning® Inc.

The Letter R

Large Muscle Activities

Play Rooster, Rooster Will You Crow?

Choose one child to be the rooster. Invite the rest of the children to pretend to sleep on the ground. Chant the words, "Rooster, rooster will you crow? Wake up, children, it's time to go!" When the rooster crows, the other children should get up and move around quickly. Then choose another child to be the rooster. Repeat the chant and have the new rooster crow as the others pretend to sleep. Repeat until all the children have a chance to participate.

Cock-a doodle doo!

Dance to Radio Music

Turn on a radio to an appropriate station and encourage the children to dance to the music. As they dance, mention that the word *radio* starts with the letter R, and encourage the children to talk about their favorite radio music.

Race the Clock with Rakes

Invite the children to help you crumple sheets of newspaper and scatter them on the ground. Put a few baskets nearby. Explain to the children that they are going to race the clock and attempt to rake up all the newspapers before a timer goes off. Set a timer for a few minutes. Provide a few of the children with toy rakes. Have those children rake the newspapers into piles and others transfer the piles into the baskets. Repeat the activity several times so everyone gets a chance to both rake and pick up paper. As the children work, mention that the words *rake* and *race* start with the letter R. Continue until each child has had a chance to rake the leaves.

Rock and Roll

Spread out several large blankets or exercise mats. Encourage the children to sit on the blankets or mats, bend their knees up close to their chests, and wrap their arms around their knees. Suggest the children rock back and forth in this position or try to roll around. Mention that the words *rock* and *roll* begin with the letter R.

© HighReach Learning® Inc.

Art Activities
Create Tactile Letter R's

Give each child a copy of the capital letter R (page 210), an old paintbrush, and a shallow dish of glue. Invite the children to trace the letter R with their fingers. Encourage the children to spread glue on their letter R's as desired. Provide the children with small bathroom cups filled with an assortment of ribbon snips, rickrack snips, or rice. Invite the children to shake the ribbon snips, rickrack snips, or rice onto the glue. Set aside to dry. After the glue dries, invite the children to trace their tactile letter R's with their fingers. How does the R feel? Use descriptive words such as bumpy, rough, etc. as you interact with the child.

Explore Rose Dough

Make rose dough by chopping 3 cups of fresh or dried rose petals finely in a food processor or with a knife. Add 1¾ cups flour and ¼ cup salt to the chopped rose petals. Add a little bit of water at a time, blending well, until you have a soft, pliable dough. The amount of water will depend on whether the petals are dry or fresh. If the dough gets too sticky, add a little more flour. Repeat as desired to make enough dough for your group. Store the dough in a zipper-top bag.

Provide each child with a small amount of rose dough. Invite the children to shape the dough as desired or use a cookie cutter with the dough. As the children work, you may wish to mention that the dough was made with rose petals, and mention that the word *rose* begins with the letter R. After the children finish, place the rose dough creations on wax paper and allow them to air dry.

Create Raindrop Art

Provide the children with large sheets of blue construction paper and crayons and markers. Encourage the children to decorate their papers as desired. Have the children squeeze drops of white school glue randomly on their pictures to represent raindrops. After the pictures dry, help the children notice what happened to the glue, and encourage them to run their fingers over the surface of the pictures to feel the raindrops.

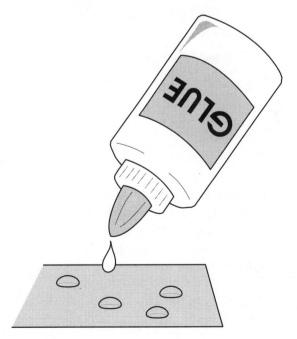

© HighReach Learning® Inc.

The Letter R

Art Activities

Create Railroad Pictures

Give each child a sheet of construction paper and a roll of masking tape. Invite the children to talk about railroad tracks. What do they think railroad tracks look like? What type of vehicle travels on railroad tracks? Encourage the children to tear the masking tape into strips to create railroad tracks on their papers. Assist the children as needed as they create, and mention that the word *railroad* begins with the letter R.

Make a Ribbon Collage

Provide the children with construction paper, glue, scissors, and assorted types of ribbon. Encourage the children to cut snips of ribbon and glue them onto their papers to create interesting ribbon art designs. As the children work, mention that the word *ribbon* begins with the letter R. After the glue dries, encourage the children to feel the interesting texture on their papers.

☆ *Learning Extension:* After the children finish, write "R is for ribbon" on an index card for each child. Use a highlighter for each letter R and crayons for the other letters. Encourage the child to name each letter R, try to trace it, and then attach the card to the back of his/her collage.

Make Letter R Collages

Give a child old newspapers or magazines and scissors. Invite the child to search for the letter R in the newspapers or magazines. The child may wish to tear or cut the letters out. Give the child a sheet of paper and a glue stick. Encourage the child to attach the letter R cutouts to the paper as desired. Assist the child as needed.

☆ *Learning Extension:* If you are working with a group of children, invite them to work together to make one big letter R collage. If you have bulletin board, butcher, or chart paper, you may even wish to cut the paper in the shape of the letter R. Help the children locate and cut or tear out large examples of the letter from captions and headlines. Have the children glue all the letter cutouts to the paper.

The Letter R

© HighReach Learning® Inc.

Small Muscle Activities

Explore Large Rubber Bands

Provide the children with pegboards and several large rubber bands. Encourage the children to use the rubber bands and the pegs in the pegboards to form different shapes. You may suggest that they make a triangle, square, star, or rectangle. As the children work, you may wish to point out that the term *rubber band* begins with the letter R.

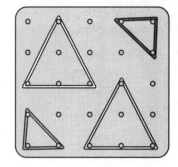

Explore Letter R Lacing Cards

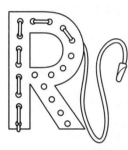

Draw several block letter R's on posterboard using the pattern on page 210 and cut out. Use a hole punch to make a series of holes around each letter cutout. Vary the number of holes so that some will be easier to lace than others. Tie a length of yarn to one hole and wrap the free end with tape. Be sure the yarn can wrap around the letter twice. Set out the letter R lacing cards. Assist the children as needed as they explore the lacing cards.

Race Cars Down Ramps

Provide the children with assorted blocks, a sheet of posterboard or cardboard, and toy cars. Challenge the children to work together to create a ramp for the cars using the materials. Assist the children as needed as they try to make a ramp. They will need to stack blocks under one end of the posterboard or cardboard. Invite the children to race cars down the ramps. As they play, suggest they add or take away blocks to change the height of the ramp, and mention that the word *ramp* begins with the letter R. How does the height of the ramp affect the way the race cars roll? Encourage the children to share their ideas.

Create Rice Rainbows

Make different colors of rice by putting approximately two cups of rice into a large zipper-top bag for each color used. Add a teaspoon of rubbing alcohol and several drops of food coloring to each bag. The more food coloring added, the deeper the color will be. Close the bags and shake them until the rice is evenly coated with the food coloring. Spread each color of rice evenly on a separate baking sheet or some paper towels and let dry. Store each color in a separate container. Provide the children with construction paper and have each child squeeze a line of glue to create a large arc. Have the child sprinkle a color of rice onto the glue. Let the rice set in the glue for a moment before gently shaking the excess rice back into the container. Have the child squeeze a second line of glue under the first arc to create a smaller arc under it. Then have the child choose a different color of rice to sprinkle over the glue. Continue until the child has made several colored arcs. As the child works, mention that the words *rice* and *rainbow* begin with the letter R.

© HighReach Learning® Inc.

The Letter R

Cooking with Rodney Raccoon
Letter R Recipes

ROOT BEER FLOAT CAKE

1 box white cake mix
1¼ cups root beer
¼ cup vegetable oil
2 eggs

Glaze
½ cup powdered sugar
3 Tbsp. root beer

Preheat the oven to 350°. Grease a baking pan. Combine cake mix, 1¼ cups root beer, oil, and eggs in a large bowl. Beat on low speed until blended. Pour batter into prepared pan. Bake 30 to 35 minutes and then allow it to cool. Use a toothpick to poke holes two inches apart along the entire cake. To make the glaze, combine powdered sugar and 3 tablespoons root beer in a bowl. Beat until the mixture is smooth and then pour over the cooled cake.

REALLY NICE RICE

1 cup long grain rice
1 (10.5 oz.) can beef consommé
1 cup water

Preheat the oven to 350°. Grease a 2-quart casserole dish. Mix all ingredients and pour into dish. Bake for about an hour or until the rice has absorbed the liquid. This recipe serves about 8 children.

RADICAL RAISIN SALAD

grated carrots
raisins
mayonnaise
vanilla yogurt

Give each child a small bowl and a plastic spoon. Cover the bottom of each child's bowl with grated carrots. Add 3 tablespoons of raisins, 1 tablespoon of mayonnaise, and 1 tablespoon of yogurt to each child's bowl. Invite the children to mix the ingredients together, then eat.

RASPBERRY FIZZLERS

1½ cups raspberry juice
3 scoops raspberry sherbet
½ cup carbonated water

Combine all ingredients in a blender and blend until smooth. Pour into small cups and serve.

© HighReach Learning® Inc.

R

R is for  .

R is for _____ .

R is for _____

Around the lake.

rabbit   rake   rocks

© HighReach Learning® Inc.

The Letter R

R is for rabbit.

R is for rocks
around the lake.

My R Rhyme

Name

R is for rake.

© HighReach Learning® Inc.

Ss

© HighReach Learning® Inc.

The Letter S

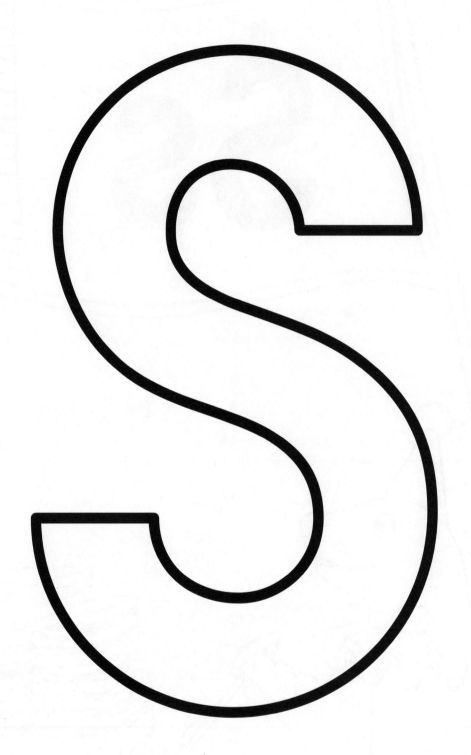

Language Activities

Introduce Sally Seal and the Letter S

Decorate a copy of the Letter S Display (page 221) as desired. Point to Sally Seal on the display. Invite the children to guess what type of animal Sally is. If necessary explain that Sally is a seal. You may wish to share the rhyme below several times and invite the children to join in.

SALLY SEAL

Sally is a seal,
Who eats sandwiches for lunch.
She likes salami best,
And she sure can eat a bunch.

Invite the children to discuss what they learned about Sally in the rhyme. Invite the children to name what Sally is pulling in the wagon. Have the children ever seen a seal? What do they think seals eat? Do real seals eat sandwiches? Encourage the children to share their thoughts and ideas.

Point to both the capital S and the lowercase s on the display. Explain that these are both ways to write the letter. Explain that Sally likes the letter S best because it is the first letter of her name. Help the children decide if they know anyone whose name begins with S.

Talk About Letter S Words

Invite the children to talk about words they know that begin with the letter S. Write any suggestions down on sentence strips, a large sheet of paper, or chart paper. Attach the words to the wall at the children's eye level. Some familiar word suggestions are:

sailboat	seed	sink	sunflower
salt	silly	sock	
sandwich	silver	song	

☆ **Learning Extension:** Invite the children to clap for the syllables of words that begin with the letter S (sink, sun-flow-er, sail-boat).

Play Guess What's in the Sock

Place a familiar item, such as a small toy car or a crayon, inside a sock and loosely tie the end. Gather a group of children to play a game. Pass the sock around and invite the children to feel it and try to guess what is inside. After several guesses, untie the end of the sock, remove the item, and show it to the children. Repeat with several different items. You may wish to mention that the word *sock* begins with S.

© HighReach Learning® Inc.

The Letter S

Language Activities

Share the Letter S Rebus Rhyme

Share the Letter S Rebus Rhyme (page 231) to develop a sense of rhythm and rhyme and to practice naming pictures. Show the display as you recite the rhyme several times. Afterwards, point to each picture on the chart and encourage the children to name it. Discuss each picture and invite the children to share times when they have seen similar items.

☆ **Learning Extension:** Talk about the letter S. Look at all of the words on the display. Help the children locate the letter S. Explain that the letter S can be written more than one way. Point to the capital S on the display and then point to the lowercase s. Help the children find all of the capital and lowercase letter S's on the display.

Create Letter S Rhyme Books

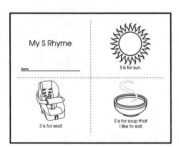

Give each child a copy of the Letter S Rhyme Book (page 232) and crayons or markers. Invite the children to point to the pictures as you read the text. Encourage the children to decorate the pictures as desired. Cut along the dotted lines and stack the pages in order. Staple the pages together. Invite the children to write their names on the rhyme books. Assist the children as needed.

☆ **Learning Extension:** Invite a child to "read" his/her Letter S Rhyme Book to you. Encourage the child to point to the letter S in the book.

Talk About the Five Senses

Explain to the children that we use our senses to learn about the world around us, and mention that the word *senses* begins with the letter S. Explain that the five senses are seeing, touching, smelling, tasting, and hearing. Encourage the children to share their thoughts and ideas about the five senses. Sing the following song and invite the children to sing with you.

MY FIVE SENSES
(tune: "Mary Had a Little Lamb")

I have two eyes that blink, blink, blink,
Blink, blink, blink,
Blink, blink, blink.
I have two eyes that blink, blink, blink,
I use my eyes to see.
(Blink eyes.)

I have two ears that listen, listen,
Listen, listen,
Listen, listen.
I have two ears that listen, listen,
I use my ears to hear.
(Whisper the word listen.)

I have one nose to sniff, sniff, sniff,
Sniff, sniff, sniff,
Sniff, sniff, sniff.
I have one nose to sniff, sniff, sniff,
I use my nose to smell.
(Make sniffing sounds.)

I have one tongue to lick, lick, lick,
Lick, lick, lick,
Lick, lick, lick.
I have one tongue to lick, lick, lick,
I use my tongue to taste.
(Lick lips with tongue.)

I have two hands that clap, clap, clap,
Clap, clap, clap,
Clap, clap, clap.
I have two hands that clap, clap, clap,
I use my hands to touch.
(Clap hands.)

The Letter S

224

© HighReach Learning® Inc.

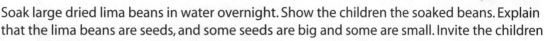

Science Activities

Examine Seeds

Soak large dried lima beans in water overnight. Show the children the soaked beans. Explain that the lima beans are seeds, and some seeds are big and some are small. Invite the children to examine the seeds closely with unbreakable magnifying glasses. Encourage the children to talk about their observations. Gently remove the seed coat and separate the halves. Help the children find the baby plant inside. Explain to the children that the baby plant gets food from the seed at first, and as it grows bigger, it sends roots down into the soil to find food and water. Then the seed grows leaves that reach up towards the sunshine, and the seed grows into a plant. Invite each child to use a magnifying glass to examine the seed and find the little plant, and mention that the words *seed, soil,* and *sunshine* begin with the letter S.

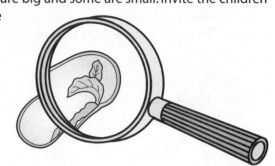

Explore Scents

Make scent canisters by gathering cotton balls and empty film canisters or other small containers with lids. Poke several holes in the lids of the film canisters. Put a few drops of a scent such as vanilla extract on a cotton ball. Place the cotton ball in a film canister and close the lid. Do this with several film canisters, using different scents such as orange, peppermint, cinnamon, and others. Show the children the film canisters or containers and explain that each one contains a different scent or smell, and mention that the words *scent* and *smell* begin with the letter S. Invite each child to smell a scent and tell what he/she thinks the scent is. As each child shares his/her opinion, remember that there is no right or wrong answer. For example, the children may not name the scent specifically but rather something that it reminds them of, such as vanilla that smells like grandmother's house or cinnamon that smells like gum that mom chews. Continue exploring the containers until all of the children have smelled the scents.

Explore Items That Sink

Fill a water table or basin with several inches of water. Print the words *sink* and *float* on index cards and tape them to plastic bins. Gather a variety of water-safe items that sink and float. Invite a child to choose one of the items and predict if it will sink or float. Suggest the child place the item in the water and watch what happens. Ask the child to decide if the prediction was correct or not. Point to the labels on the bins and read them aloud. Help the children notice that the word *sink* begins with the letter S. Then help the child place the item in the appropriate bin. Give each child a turn to choose an item, make a prediction, test the prediction, and place the item in the appropriate bin. Once all the items have been tested, review which ones floated and which ones sank.

☆ ***Learning Extension:*** Invite the children to suggest some ideas about why they think some items sink and some items float.

Large Muscle Activities

Play Simon Says

Invite the children to stand facing you. Ask the children to listen carefully to some directions. Explain that they should listen carefully and carry out only the directions that begin with the words "Simon says." Give a series of directions. Begin most directions with the words "Simon says," but from time to time, omit the phrase. Some examples follow.

❖ Simon says to hop on one foot.
❖ Jump five times and sit down.
❖ Simon says to clap your hands twice and then pat your head.

Simon says...

Make the Letter S

Challenge the children to think of ways they can make a letter S using their bodies. Encourage the children to try their ideas. Have each child work with a partner to make a letter S using their bodies. Invite the children to talk about how hard or easy it is to make an S with their bodies.

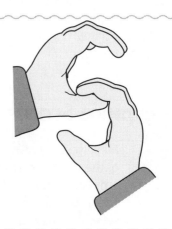

Sun Fun

Tape strips or triangles of yellow construction paper around a hula hoop to make a sun with rays. Hang the decorated hula hoop from a tree branch or on a piece of playground equipment. Encourage the children to take turns throwing beanbags through the center of the hula hoop sun. As the children play, mention that the word *sun* begins with the letter S.

☆ **Learning Extension:** Invite the children that show readiness to count the number of beanbags that go through the hula hoop sun.

The Letter S

© HighReach Learning® Inc.

Art Activities

Create Tactile Letter S's

Give each child a copy of the capital letter S (page 222), an old paintbrush, and a shallow dish of glue. Invite the children to trace the letter S with their fingers. Encourage the children to spread glue on their letter S's as desired. Provide the children with small bathroom cups filled with sand, salt, or rice. Invite the children to shake the sand, salt, or rice onto the glue. As the children work, mention that the words *sand* and *salt* both begin with the letter S. Set aside to dry. After the glue dries, invite the children to trace their tactile letter S's with their fingers. How does the S feel? Use descriptive words such as bumpy, rough, etc. as you interact with the child.

Make Suitcases

Provide each child with two small paper plate rim halves and a 9" x 12" sheet of construction paper. Help each child attach a rim to each short end of the construction paper and fold the sheet in half as shown. Provide old magazines, tape, and scissors. Invite the children to cut or tear out pictures of things that they would like to pack in their suitcases. Encourage the children to tape the items to the inside of their suitcases. As the children work, mention that the word *suitcase* begins with the letter S.

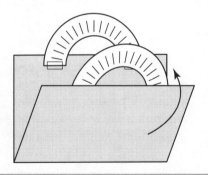

Create with Colored Salt

Pour salt into several small bowls. Give the children assorted colors of sidewalk chalk. Invite the children to stir the salt with the chalk. Encourage the children to talk about what happens to the salt. The salt should turn the color of the chalk. Give the children construction paper and glue. Invite the children to create designs with the glue and the salt on their papers. As the children work, encourage them to talk about their pictures, and mention that the word *salt* begins with the letter S.

☆ *Learning Extension:* After the children finish, write "S is for suitcase" on an index card for each child. Use a highlighter for each letter S and crayons for the other letters. Encourage the child to name each letter S, try to trace it, and then attach the card to the back of his/her suitcase.

© HighReach Learning® Inc.

The Letter S

Art Activities

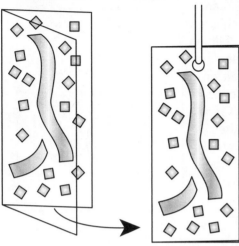

Make Silver Sun Catchers

Provide the children with 12" squares of clear contact paper, silver foil, silver nonmetallic glitter, or any other silver collage materials you have available. Peel the backing from the sheets of contact paper and place sticky-side up in front of the children. Invite the children to name the color of the art materials, and explain that you are going to make silver sun catchers. Help the children notice that the words *silver* and *sun* begin with the letter S. Encourage the children to tear and arrange bits of foil, sprinkle glitter, or use any other silver collage materials on the sticky side of the contact paper as desired. When the children finish, fold the contact paper in half. Punch a hole in each child's creation and attach a length of ribbon or string for hanging. Hang the creations in a window or in an area where the sun shines.

Create Pictures with Soap

Give each child a sheet of dark-colored construction paper and a travel-sized bar of white soap. Encourage the children to use the soap to draw pictures on the construction paper. As the children work, mention that the word *soap* begins with the letter S. When the children finish, encourage them to talk about their creations.

Make Letter S Collages

Give a child old newspapers or magazines and scissors. Invite the child to search for the letter S in the newspapers or magazines. The child may wish to tear or cut the letters out. Give the child a sheet of paper and a glue stick. Encourage the child to attach the letter S cutouts to the paper as desired. Assist the child as needed.

☆ *Learning Extension:* If you are working with a group of children, invite them to work together to make one big letter S collage. If you have bulletin board, butcher, or chart paper, you may even wish to cut the paper in the shape of the letter S. Help the children locate and cut or tear out large examples of the letter from captions and headlines. Have the children glue all the letter cutouts to the paper.

Small Muscle Activities

Pluck Seeds From Sunflowers

Set out a bowl, some blunt plastic tweezers, and some large sunflower blossoms that still have the seeds in the center. Invite interested children to use unbreakable magnifying glasses to closely examine the sunflowers. Encourage them to share their observations. Help them notice the seeds in the center of the flowers. Encourage the children to use the tweezers to pull the seeds from the sunflower and drop them into a bowl. *Caution: Closely supervise this activity and make sure the children use the materials safely.*

Make Sailboats

Locate items to make sailboats. A yogurt/ice cream shop may be able to provide plastic dishes for banana splits. Other options include foam bowls or margarine tubs. Gather enough materials to offer the children a choice. Have each child choose a dish and follow the steps below.

1. Roll a small ball of modeling clay and press lightly into the center of a dish.
2. Insert a plastic drinking straw in the clay to make the mast.
3. Cut a sail from a sample of vinyl wallpaper and tape to the mast.

After the children finish, invite them to play with their sailboats in a water table or basin of water.

Sort Socks

Mix together assorted pairs of clean colorful socks. Challenge the children to work together to sort the socks into like pairs. As the children sort the socks, mention that the words *sort* and *sock* begin with the letter S.

☆ *Learning Extension:* Give each child in the group one of the socks (make sure that another child has the match). Encourage the children to put the socks on one of their hands and hold them behind their backs. Explain to the children that when you say "Go!" they should show each other their socks and try to find the child with the matching sock.

Explore Letter S Lacing Cards

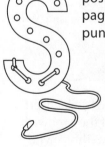

Draw several block letter S's on posterboard using the pattern on page 222 and cut out. Use a hole punch to make a series of holes around each letter cutout. Vary the number of holes so that some will be easier to lace than others. Tie a length of yarn to one hole and wrap the free end with tape. Be sure the yarn can wrap around the letter twice. Set out the letter S lacing cards. Assist the children as needed as they explore the lacing cards.

Cooking with Sally Seal
Letter S Recipes

SILLY SANDWICHES

2 slices bread per child
simple sandwich fillings
    such as cheese or jelly
cream cheese
small food items cut up
    for decorations, such
    as raisins, seeds, fruits,
    or vegetables

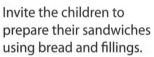

Invite the children to
prepare their sandwiches
using bread and fillings.
Help the children spread cream cheese on
top and decorate with raisins, seeds, fruits, or
vegetable pieces.

SUPER SAUCE FOR SALTINES

1 lb. bologna, cut into pieces
½ cup mayonnaise
¼ cup dill pickle relish
saltine crackers

Place the bologna in a food processor and pulse
until smooth. Put bologna mixture in a medium-
sized bowl. Invite the children to help stir in the
mayonnaise and pickle relish. Serve the super sauce
on saltine crackers.

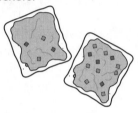

SAILBOATS

hot dog buns
cheese slices
tuna salad
pretzel sticks

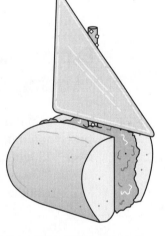

Cut the hot dog buns
in half crosswise and
cut the cheese slices
in half diagonally. Give
each child half a hot
dog bun on a small
paper plate. Help each
child use a plastic
spoon to spread tuna
salad in the middle of
the bun and lay on its side. Have each child insert
a pretzel stick between the layers of the sandwich
and prop a cheese triangle against it. Then invite
the children to eat their sailboat creations.

SAFARI PUNCH

1 envelope cherry-flavored
    unsweetened drink mix
1 envelope orange-flavored
    unsweetened drink mix
1 envelope tropical punch-flavored
    unsweetened drink mix
2¾ cups sugar
4 quarts water

Invite the children to help pour the unsweetened
drink mixes and sugar in a large pitcher. Add the
water and encourage the children to help stir until
the mixture has dissolved. Serve over ice.

The Letter S

© HighReach Learning® Inc.

S is for  .

S is for  .

S is for

That I like to eat.

sun

seat

soup

© HighReach Learning® Inc.

The Letter S

S is for sun.

S is for soup that
I like to eat.

My S Rhyme

S is for seat.

Name

© HighReach Learning® Inc.

© HighReach Learning® Inc.

The Letter T

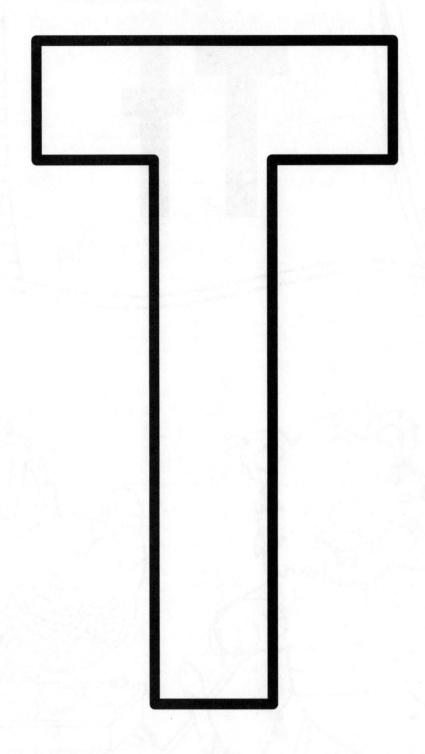

The Letter T

© HighReach Learning® Inc.

Language Activities

Introduce Tad Tiger and the Letter T

Decorate a copy of the Letter T Display (page 233) as desired. Point to Tad Tiger on the display. Invite the children to guess what type of animal Tad is. If necessary explain that Tad is a tiger. You may wish to share the rhyme below several times and invite the children to join in.

TAD TIGER

Tad Tiger totes his turkey,
Everywhere he goes.
And if you'd like to take a turn,
You just have to tell him so.

What did the children learn about Tad in the rhyme? Invite the children to name what Tad is pulling in the wagon. Have the children ever seen a tiger or a turkey? What does a tiger sound like? What does a turkey sound like? Encourage the children to share their thoughts and ideas.

Point to both the capital T and the lowercase t on the display. Explain that these are both ways to write the letter. Explain that Tad likes the letter T best because it is the first letter of his name. Help the children decide if they know anyone whose name begins with T.

Talk About Letter T Words

Invite the children to talk about words they know that begin with the letter T. Write any suggestions down on sentence strips, a large sheet of paper, or chart paper. Attach the words to the wall at the children's eye level. Some familiar word suggestions are:

teapot	tissue	towel	turkey
telephone	tongue	tower	
tiger	tool	toy	

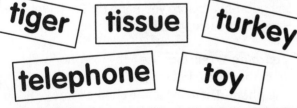

☆ *Learning Extension:* Invite the children to clap for the syllables of words that begin with the letter T (tur-key, tool, te-le-phone).

Tell Tongue Twisters

Invite the children to tell you what they know about tongue twisters. Help the children realize that the words *tongue* and *twister* begin with the letter T. Explain that a tongue twister is a saying with many words that begin with the same sound. It takes practice to say a tongue twister without making a mistake. You may want to share some familiar tongue twisters as examples. "Peter Piper" and "She Sells Seashells" are both popular. Share the tongue twister below or create your own, then encourage the children to say it with you.

TINY TAD TIGER

Tiny Tad Tiger took ten tools to town.
He tripped on his tail and his tools tumbled down.

Language Activities

Share the Letter T Rebus Rhyme

T is for [table].
T is for [tent].
T is for [toast] that
Has a nice scent.

table   tent   toast

Share the Letter T Rebus Rhyme (page 243) to develop a sense of rhythm and rhyme and to practice naming pictures. Show the display as you recite the rhyme several times. Afterwards, point to each picture on the chart and encourage the children to name it. Discuss each picture and invite the children to share times when they have seen similar items.

☆ *Learning Extension:* Talk about the letter T. Look at all of the words on the display. Help the children locate the letter T. Explain that the letter T can be written more than one way. Point to the capital T on the display and then point to the lowercase t. Help the children find all of the capital and lowercase letter T's on the display.

Create Letter T Rhyme Books

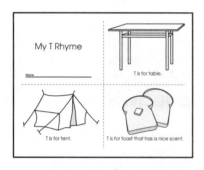

My T Rhyme

Name

T is for table.

T is for tent.   T is for toast that has a nice scent.

Give each child a copy of the Letter T Rhyme Book (page 244) and crayons or markers. Invite the children to point to the pictures as you read the text. Encourage the children to decorate the pictures as desired. Cut along the dotted lines and stack the pages in order. Staple the pages together. Invite the children to write their names on the rhyme books. Assist the children as needed.

☆ *Learning Extension:* Invite a child to "read" his/her Letter T Rhyme Book to you. Encourage the child to point to the letter T in the book.

Talk About Telephone Manners

Lead a discussion about using good manners on the telephone. Encourage the children to share their thoughts and ideas, and mention that the word *telephone* begins with the letter T. Share any of the following tips that are appropriate for the age and developmental level of the children in your group.

❖ Only answer the phone if you have permission to do so.
❖ Say hello when you pick up the phone.
❖ Speak clearly in a regular tone of voice, not too loud or too soft.
❖ If the caller does not tell you his or her name, ask, "Who is calling, please?"
❖ If you need to call someone to the phone, first lay the phone down gently. Don't shout. Instead, go and tell the person to come to the phone.

❖ Say good-bye before you hang up the telephone.
❖ Hang up the telephone gently.

☆ *Learning Extension:* Use a toy telephone to demonstrate how to politely answer the phone. Then divide the children into pairs and give each child a toy telephone. Have the children practice using good telephone manners as they pretend to call each other.

The Letter T

© HighReach Learning® Inc.

Science Activities

Tool Prints

Have the children lay dark-colored construction paper outdoors in a sunny spot and arrange plastic toy tools on top of the paper. Mention that the word *tool* begins with the letter T. Leave the paper and tools in the sun for several hours so the paper around the tools will fade. The amount of time this will take will vary depending on the brightness of the sun and the paper used. The less expensive construction paper works best as it fades more quickly. Once the paper has faded, the children can lift the tools to see the outlines on the paper.

Count Toes

Encourage the children to take off their shoes and socks and help them count their toes. When they have counted all ten, mention that the words *ten* and *toes* begin with the letter T.

> ☆ *Learning Extension:*
> After they finish counting toes, invite the children to practice tying their shoes. Assist the children as needed, and mention that the word *tie* begins with the letter T.

Pick Up Toys to a Timer

When it's time to clean up, show the children a kitchen timer. Invite the children to predict how long they think it will take them to clean up. Set the timer for the children's choice and encourage them to put away the toys before it goes off. If the timer goes off before they finish, ask them to choose another time and try again. Continue until the toys are put away, and help the children realize that the words *toy* and *timer* begin with the letter T.

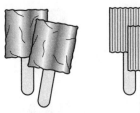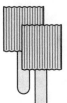

Match Textures by Touch

Glue matching squares of textured material to pairs of wide craft sticks. Some suggested materials are sandpaper, corrugated paper, burlap, corduroy, netting, etc. Be sure to create two identical sticks for each textured item. Mix all of the sticks together. Encourage the children to explore the texture sticks and try to sort them by touch. Help the children decide which pairs feel the same. As the children explore, mention that the words *texture* and *touch* both begin with the letter T.

> ☆ *Learning Extension:* Challenge a child that shows readiness to try to match the pairs of texture sticks with his/her eyes closed.

Large Muscle Activities

Jump Over Tape

Attach several strips of masking tape to the floor or a hard outdoor surface. Show the children the tape lines, and mention that the word *tape* begins with the letter T. Encourage the children to practice jumping over the tape lines.

> ☆ *Learning Extension:* Create ten tape lines. Invite the children that show readiness to jump over and count the ten tape lines with you. Help the children realize that the words *tape* and *ten* both begin with the letter T.

Practice Tiptoeing

Encourage the children to practice tiptoeing around the room. Do the children think it is easy or hard to tiptoe? Invite the children to share their ideas, and help them realize that the word *tiptoe* begins with the letter T.

Dance with Towels

Provide each child with a towel. Play some lively music and encourage the children to move and groove with their towels. You may suggest that they turn around in circles, tap their toes, or move in other ways. As they dance with the towels, mention that the word *towel* begins with the letter T.

Perform Ten Toe Touches

Lead the children in various toe touches and with each variation do repetitions of ten. As you exercise, mention that the words *toe, touch,* and *ten* all begin with the letter T. Encourage the children to count aloud with you as they touch their toes.

    © HighReach Learning® Inc.

Art Activities

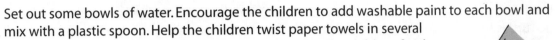

Create Tie-Dyed Towels

Set out some bowls of water. Encourage the children to add washable paint to each bowl and mix with a plastic spoon. Help the children twist paper towels in several places as shown. Then dip each twist into a bowl of colored water. After the children finish, carefully smooth out the tie-dyed creations and hang to dry.

Create Tactile Letter T's

Give each child a copy of the capital letter T (page 234), an old paintbrush, and a shallow dish of glue. Invite the children to trace the letter T with their fingers. Encourage the children to spread glue on their letter T's as desired. Provide the children with small bathroom cups filled with sand, salt, or rice. Invite the children to shake the sand, salt, or rice onto the glue. Set aside to dry. After the glue dries, invite the children to trace their tactile letter T's with their fingers. How does the T feel? Use descriptive words such as bumpy, rough, etc. as you interact with the child.

Make Toe-Tapping Pictures

Fold paper towels, place them in shallow dishes, and soak them with paint. Cover the area where you plan to work with old newspapers. Have the children take off their shoes and socks and sit in low chairs. Help them press their toes on the paint-soaked paper towels. Place a 12" x 18" sheet of construction paper on the floor at the base of each chair. Play some music and encourage the children to tap their toes on the sheets to the music. As the children work, mention that the words *tap* and *toe* begin with the letter T. After they finish, help the children wash off their feet in basins of soapy water. Encourage the children to dry their feet using paper towels. Then have the children put their socks and shoes back on, giving help as needed.

© HighReach Learning® Inc.

The Letter T

Art Activities

Make Turtle Shells

Lead a discussion about turtles with the children. Have the children ever seen a turtle? What do turtles have on their backs? Explain to the children that you are going to make turtle shells, and mention that the word *turtle* begins with the letter T. Provide each child with a sturdy oval-shaped paper plate. Encourage the children to dip sponges in shallow dishes of brown, green, orange, and yellow paint and dab them on the paper plates to make turtle shells. After the paint dries, tape the children's creations to their backs, and invite them to pretend to creep and crawl like turtles.

Create Pictures with Torn Tissue

Provide the children with construction paper and several colors of art tissue. Encourage the children to tear off pieces of tissue and glue them onto their papers as desired. As the children work, mention that the words *tear* and *tissue* both begin with the letter T.

Make Letter T Collages

Give a child old newspapers or magazines and scissors. Invite the child to search for the letter T in the newspapers or magazines. The child may wish to tear or cut the letters out. Give the child a sheet of paper and a glue stick. Encourage the child to attach the letter T cutouts to the paper as desired. Assist the child as needed.

☆ **Learning Extension:** If you are working with a group of children, invite them to work together to make one big letter T collage. If you have bulletin board, butcher, or chart paper, you may even wish to cut the paper in the shape of the letter T. Help the children locate and cut or tear out large examples of the letter from captions and headlines. Have the children glue all the letter cutouts to the paper.

© HighReach Learning® Inc.

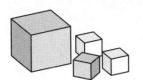

Small Muscle Activities

Create Tall Towers

Provide the children with assorted blocks. Challenge the children to use the blocks to create tall towers. As the children work, mention that the words *tall* and *tower* both begin with the letter T. After the children finish, encourage them to describe their block creations to you.

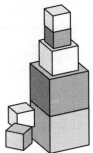

> ☆ *Learning Extension:* Give each child ten blocks. Invite the children to count the blocks with you, and then challenge the children to create tall towers using ten blocks.

Explore Tongs

Show the children some tongs, a bowl of cotton balls, and an empty bowl. Invite the children to explore the materials, and mention that the word *tongs* begins with the letter T. Ask the children which bowl is full. Which bowl is empty? Encourage the children to try to use the tongs to move the cotton balls from the full bowl to the empty one. Now which bowl is full?

Explore a Teapot and Teacups

Fill an unbreakable toy teapot with water. Set the teapot and some unbreakable toy teacups in a large shallow dish to catch any spills. Explain to the children that the teapot is full but the teacups are empty. Encourage the children to practice pouring water into the teacups. Once all the cups are full, the children can pour the water back into the teapot and try again.

> ☆ *Learning Extension:* Challenge the children to find out how many teacups of water the teapot holds. Encourage the children to work together to find the answer.

Explore Letter T Lacing Cards

Draw several block letter T's on posterboard using the pattern on page 234 and cut out. Use a hole punch to make a series of holes around each letter cutout. Vary the number of holes so that some will be easier to lace than others. Tie a length of yarn to one hole and wrap the free end with tape. Be sure the yarn can wrap around the letter twice. Set out the letter T lacing cards. Assist the children as needed as they explore the lacing cards.

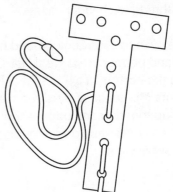

© HighReach Learning® Inc.

The Letter T

Cooking with Tad Tiger
Letter T Recipes

TONGUE TICKLERS

1 (12 oz.) bottle cranberry juice
1 (12 oz.) bottle lemon-lime carbonated beverage

In a large pitcher, mix the two liquids. Pour over ice and serve.

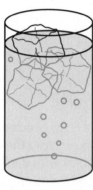

TERRIFIC TARTAR SAUCE

1 cup mayonnaise
1 Tbsp. sweet pickle relish
1 Tbsp. minced onion
2 Tbsp. lemon juice
salt and pepper to taste

Invite the children help you mix mayonnaise, relish, and onion in a small bowl. Stir in lemon juice. Season it with salt and pepper to taste. Serve with fish sticks.

TATER TOT CASSEROLE

1½ lb. lean ground beef
1 onion, chopped
¾ tsp. salt
1 pinch ground black pepper
1 (32 oz.) package tater tots, thawed
1 (10.7 oz.) can condensed cream of
    mushroom soup
1 (10.7 oz.) can condensed cream of celery soup
1 (6 oz.) can french-fried onion toppers
1 package shredded cheddar cheese

Preheat the oven to 350°. Cook ground beef, onion, salt, and pepper in a large skillet. Drain and spread into the bottom of a 9" x 13" baking dish. Add tater tots. Mix cream of mushroom and cream of celery soup together and pour over dish. Top with shredded cheese and onion toppers. Bake for 1 hour and serve warm.

TASTY TORTILLAS

2 packages cream cheese, softened
1 envelope ranch-style dressing mix
2 Tbsp. freeze-dried chives
sliced ham
6 flour tortillas (8")

Blend cream cheese, dressing mix, and chives with a wooden spoon. Spread evenly over tortillas, add ham slices, and roll up. Wrap each in plastic wrap and chill 3 hours. Slice each roll diagonally into 10 pieces. Makes 60 bite-sized pieces.

© HighReach Learning® Inc.

T is for .

T is for .

T is for that

Has a nice scent.

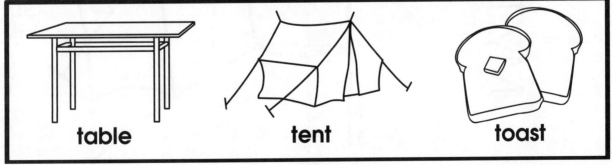

table   tent   toast

© HighReach Learning® Inc.

The Letter T

T is for table.

T is for toast that has a nice scent.

My T Rhyme

Name

T is for tent.

244

© HighReach Learning® Inc.

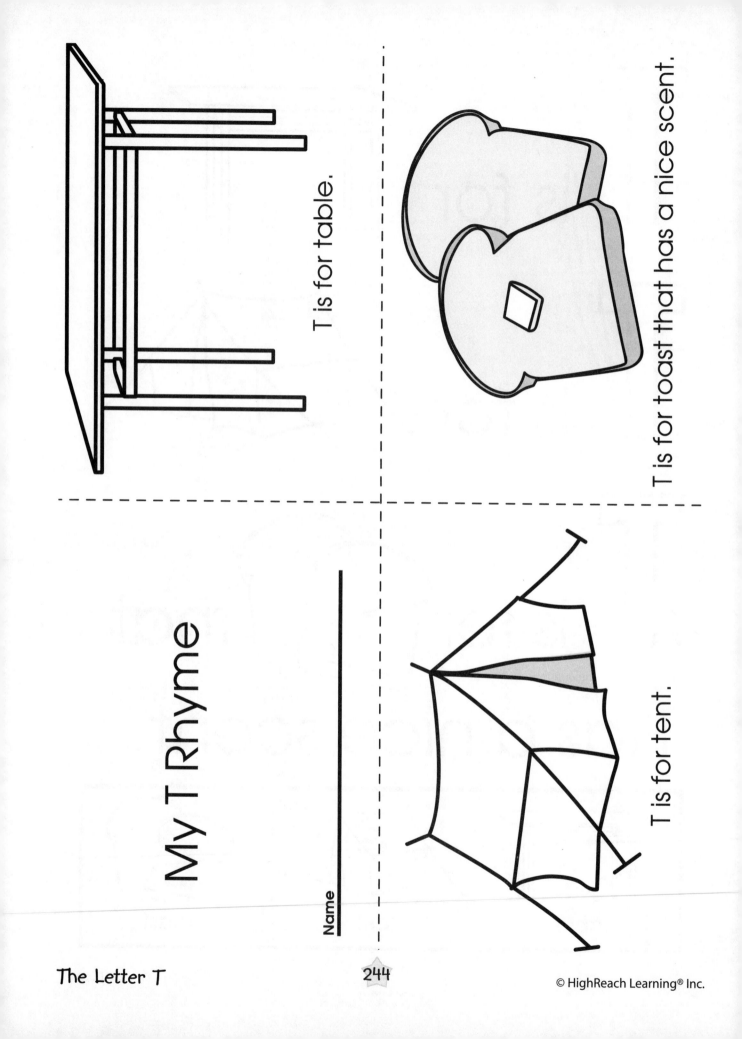

© HighReach Learning® Inc.

245

The Letter U

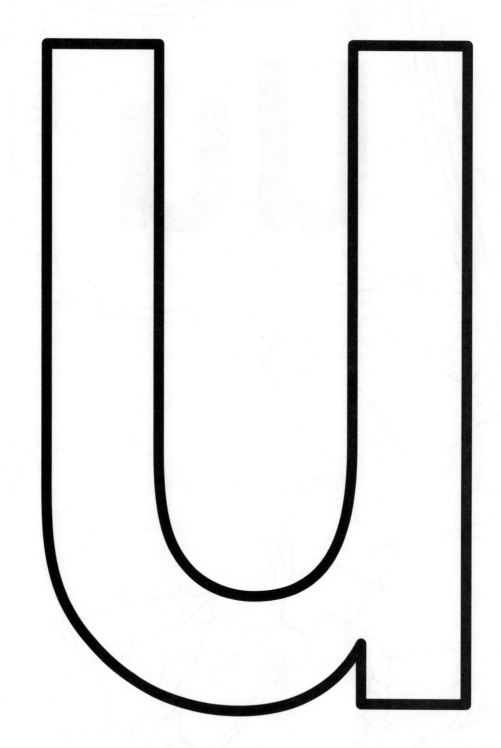

Language Activities

Introduce Unger Unicorn and the Letter U

Decorate a copy of the Letter U Display (page 245) as desired. Point to Unger Unicorn on the display. Invite the children to guess what type of animal Unger is. If necessary explain that Unger is a unicorn. You may wish to share the rhyme below several times and invite the children to join in.

UNGER UNICORN

Unger Unicorn takes his umbrella
Everywhere he goes.
If it rains he'll get really wet,
'Cause it's upside down, you know!

Invite the children to discuss what they learned about Unger in the rhyme. Invite the children to name what Unger is pulling in the wagon. Have the children ever used an umbrella? Why did they need to use it? Would an umbrella keep you dry if it were upside down? Encourage the children to share their thoughts and ideas.

Point to both the capital U and the lowercase u on the display. Explain that these are both ways to write the letter. Explain that Unger likes the letter U best because it is the first letter of his name. Help the children decide if they know anyone whose name begins with U.

Talk About Letter U Words

Invite the children to talk about words they know that begin with the letter U. Write any suggestions down on sentence strips, a large sheet of paper, or chart paper. Attach the words to the wall at the children's eye level. Some familiar word suggestions are:

Short Sounds:	Long Sounds:
umbrella	uniform
upside down	use
under	unicorn
unusual	
underground	

Explain that all of these words begin with the letter U, but the letter U makes more than one sound. In the words *umbrella* and *unusual,* the letter makes the same sound as in Unger. In the words *unicorn* and *uniform*, the sound of the letter is the same as its name.

☆ **Learning Extension:** Invite the children to clap for the syllables of words that begin with the letter U (um-brel-la, un-der, u-ni-corn).

© HighReach Learning® Inc.

247

The Letter U

Language Activities

Share the Letter U Rebus Rhyme

U is for ☂.
U is for ⬆.
U is for 🦄
That's on my red cup.

umbrella   up   unicorn

Share the Letter U Rebus Rhyme (page 255) to develop a sense of rhythm and rhyme and to practice naming pictures. Show the display as you recite the rhyme several times. Afterwards, point to each picture on the chart and encourage the children to name it. Discuss each picture and invite the children to share times when they have seen similar items.

☆ *Learning Extension:* Talk about the letter U. Look at all of the words on the display. Help the children locate the letter U. Explain that the letter U can be written more than one way. Point to the capital U on the display and then point to the lowercase u. Help the children find all of the capital and lowercase letter U's on the display.

Create Letter U Rhyme Books

Give each child a copy of the Letter U Rhyme Book (page 256) and crayons or markers. Invite the children to point to the pictures as you read the text. Encourage the children to decorate the pictures as desired. Cut along the dotted lines and stack the pages in order. Staple the pages together. Invite the children to write their names on the rhyme books. Assist the children as needed.

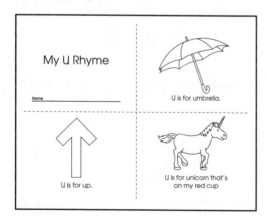

My U Rhyme

Name _____

U is for umbrella.

U is for up.

U is for unicorn that's on my red cup

☆ *Learning Extension:* Invite a child to "read" his/her Letter U Rhyme Book to you. Encourage the child to point to the letter U in the book.

Explore a Map of the United States

Show the children a large map or floor puzzle of the United States. If you live in the United States, explain that this is a map or picture of the country that you live in, and mention that the word *United* begins with the letter

United States of America

U. Explain to the children that the United States is made up of many states. Share any appropriate information with the group about the state where you live. If you live in another country, show the children a globe. Point to and name the country where you live, and then show the children where the United States is located.

☆ *Learning Extension:* If you live in the United States, help the child explore the map to find the state in which you live.

Science Activities

What Lives Underground?

Lead a discussion with the children about animals that live underground. Explain to the children that many different types of animals make their homes underground, and mention that the word *underground* begins with the letter U. Share any of the information below that is appropriate for the age and developmental level of the children in your group.

❖ Some animals live underground for all or most of the time

❖ Living underground protects animals from predators and from extreme temperatures (hot or cold)

❖ Many animals look for food underground

❖ Some animals, such as earthworms, spend their entire lives underground

❖ Some animals, such as groundhogs, chipmunks, moles, and armadillos, make their homes underground but also spend some time above the ground

Give examples of some of the different animals that make underground homes, such as foxes, rabbits, tortoises, prairie dogs, tarantulas, ants, etc.

☆ *Learning Extension:* Find out more information about the animals that interest the children. You may wish to plan a trip to the library or look for information online about the animals. Try to answer any questions the children may have.

Look at Things Upside Down

Lead the children in the song below. After singing the song several times, have the children spread their feet apart, put their hands on the floor, and look at things upside down. Encourage them to describe how things look from this perspective.

UPSIDE DOWN
(tune: "Twinkle Twinkle, Little Star")

Let's all play a silly game.
Upside down, yes that's the name
Looking at things upside down,
I turn my body all around.
Let's all play a silly game.
Upside down, yes that's
the name!

Throw Balls Underhand

Show the children how to toss a small ball underhand. Have the children line up next to you. Encourage the children to practice tossing balls underhand. After the children get the hang of the technique, measure the children's underhand tosses. Then invite the children to toss the balls overhand. Measure the distance. Do the children's balls go farther when tossed underhand or overhand? Encourage the children to help you find out, and to tell you which technique is easier and why.

Large Muscle Activities

Toss U Shapes

Provide the children with a set of toy horseshoes. Help the children notice that the horseshoes are shaped like the letter U. Draw a large letter U on posterboard or on the sidewalk. Invite the children to practice tossing the horseshoes onto the U target. Help the children count the number of horseshoes that land on the letter U and the number that do not. This may take some practice, so give each child several tries.

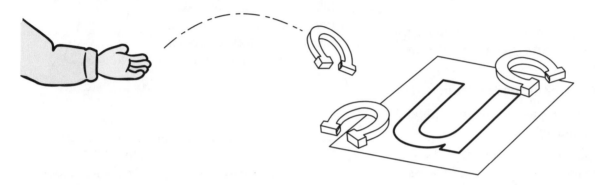

How High Up?

Give the children assorted balls to toss up into the air, such as lightweight playground balls, hollow plastic balls, and clean sock balls. Invite the children to stand several feet away from each other and practice tossing the balls up in the air. How high up do the balls go? Help the children notice if some of the balls go up higher than others. Encourage the children to share their ideas about why this happens. During the discussion, you may wish to mention that the word *up* starts with the letter U.

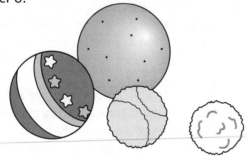

Toss Beanbags in an Upside-Down Umbrella

Open an umbrella outside and place it upside down on the ground. Provide the children with beanbags and encourage them to toss the beanbags into the upside-down umbrella. After the children toss the beanbags, have them count how many land in the umbrella and how many do not. Continue giving the children tries and mention that the words *upside-down* and *umbrella* both start with the letter U.

The Letter U

250

© HighReach Learning® Inc.

Art Activities

Make Umbrellas

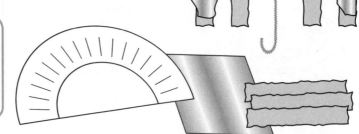

Give each child a paper plate half. Encourage the children to decorate the paper plate halves as desired with crayons or markers. Help each child tape a chenille stem to the flat side of the plate half to create an umbrella handle. The children can leave the stems straight or bend the ends to make a hook. Invite each child to tear off a few blue crepe paper streamers and tape them to the flat side of the umbrella. Encourage the children to tear scraps of aluminum foil and glue them to the streamers to create raindrops. Talk with the children about umbrellas, and help the children realize that the word *umbrella* begins with the letter U.

☆*Learning Extension:* Use a highlighter to print a capital U and a lowercase u on each child's plate half. Ask the children to name and trace the letters as they show readiness.

Create Tactile Letter U's

Give each child a copy of the capital letter U (page 246), an old paintbrush, and a shallow dish of glue. Invite the children to trace the letter U with their fingers. Encourage the children to spread glue on their letter U's as desired. Provide the children with small bathroom cups filled with sand, salt, or rice. Invite the children to shake the sand, salt, or rice onto the glue. Set aside to dry. After the glue dries, invite the children to trace their tactile letter U's with their fingers. How does the U feel? Use descriptive words such as bumpy, rough, etc. as you interact with the child.

© HighReach Learning® Inc.

The Letter U

Art Activities

Letter U Prints

Provide the children with construction paper. Set out shallow dishes of paint and horseshoe-shaped cookie cutters or vinyl horseshoes from a child's game. Encourage the children to press the cookie cutters or horseshoes into the paint and then onto the paper to make prints or to decorate their papers in another way as they wish. As the children work, help them notice that the shape of the horseshoe prints resembles the letter U.

Draw Under a Table

Tape large sheets of paper to the underside of a tabletop. Invite the children to take turns lying on their backs under the table and drawing on the paper. As they work, mention that the word *under* begins with the letter U. As each child finishes, give the child his/her artwork and replace it with a clean sheet for the next child.

Make Letter U Collages

Give a child old newspapers or magazines and scissors. Invite the child to search for the letter U in the newspapers or magazines. The child may wish to tear or cut the letters out. Give the child a sheet of paper and a glue stick. Encourage the child to attach the letter U cutouts to the paper as desired. Assist the child as needed.

☆ *Learning Extension:* If you are working with a group of children, invite them to work together to make one big letter U collage. If you have bulletin board, butcher, or chart paper, you may even wish to cut the paper in the shape of the letter U. Help the children locate and cut or tear out large examples of the letter from captions and headlines. Have the children glue all the letter cutouts to the paper.

The Letter U

252

© HighReach Learning® Inc.

Small Muscle Activities

Practice Unzipping Zippers

Provide the children with assorted clothing items with zippers, including jackets, pants, and shoes. Invite the children to practice zipping and unzipping the zippers. Give assistance as needed, and mention that the word *unzip* begins with the letter U.

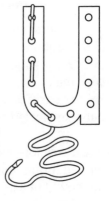

> ☆ *Learning Extension:* Invite a child that shows readiness to practice zipping up and unzipping a jacket on his/her own.

Put the Horn on the Unicorn

Draw a simple horse shape on posterboard or butcher paper as shown and attach to the wall at the children's eye level. Cut a construction paper horn shape for each child as shown. Put a piece of rolled-up masking tape on the back of each horn. Show the children the unicorn on the wall. Encourage the children to notice what's missing on the unicorn. Explain to the children that the unicorn is missing its horn. Have each child stand in front of you one at a time. Encourage the child to shut his/her eyes, and lead the child towards the unicorn. Invite the child to put the horn on the unicorn. Where did the horn land? Continue the game until each child has had a turn.

Which Is Under?

Stack several assorted colors and shapes of blocks and ask the children questions using the word *under*. Help the children notice that the word *under* begins with the letter U. For example, you might ask, "Which block is under the yellow one?" or "Which block is under the rectangular block?" Restack the blocks several times and repeat the activity using different questions.

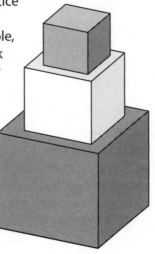

Explore Letter U Lacing Cards

Draw several block letter U's on posterboard using the pattern on page 246 and cut out. Use a hole punch to make a series of holes around each letter cutout. Vary the number of holes so that some will be easier to lace than others. Tie a length of yarn to one hole and wrap the free end with tape. Be sure the yarn can wrap around the letter twice. Set out the letter U lacing cards. Assist the children as needed as they explore the lacing cards.

Cooking with Unger Unicorn
Letter U Recipes

UGLY COOKIES

large round flat cookies
raisins
tubes of decorator frosting

Give each child a cookie, some raisins, and a tube of frosting. Allow the children to decorate the cookies, making them as "ugly" as possible. Then sit back, eat, and enjoy.

ULTIMATE CHEESE SPREAD

1 (5 oz.) jar cheese spread
1 (3 oz.) package cream cheese, softened
½ cup butter
chips, crackers, or vegetables of your choice

Put the first three ingredients in a large mixing bowl. Blend with an electric mixer until smooth and creamy. Chill. Serve with chips, crackers or vegetables.

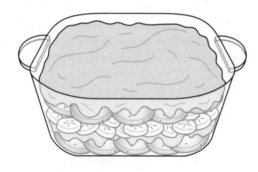

UNCOOKED BANANA PUDDING

1 (8 oz.) container sour cream
1 (8 oz) container frozen whipped topping, thawed
1 (5.2 oz) package instant vanilla pudding mix
2 cups milk
1 (16 oz.) package vanilla wafer cookies
4 bananas, peeled and sliced

Invite the children to help you combine sour cream, whipped topping, instant pudding, and milk in a large bowl. Put a layer of vanilla wafer cookies, then layer of pudding mix, and a layer of bananas in a glass dish. Repeat until all of the ingredients are used. Chill.

UPSIDE-DOWN BISCUITS

refrigerated biscuit dough
melted butter
brown sugar
crushed pineapple

For each serving, measure ½ teaspoon melted butter into a muffin tin section. Top with 1 teaspoon brown sugar and stir. Add 2 teaspoons crushed pineapple to the section and top with a refrigerated biscuit. Bake at 425° for 15-18 minutes or until brown. Let stand for 30 seconds, then turn onto wax paper (teacher only). Cool five minutes.

© HighReach Learning® Inc.

U is for .

U is for .

U is for

That's on my red cup.

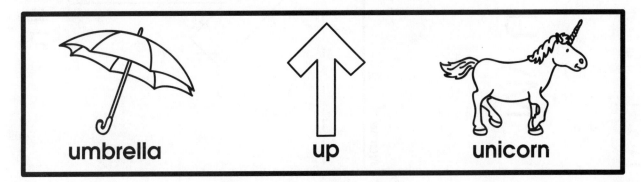

umbrella up unicorn

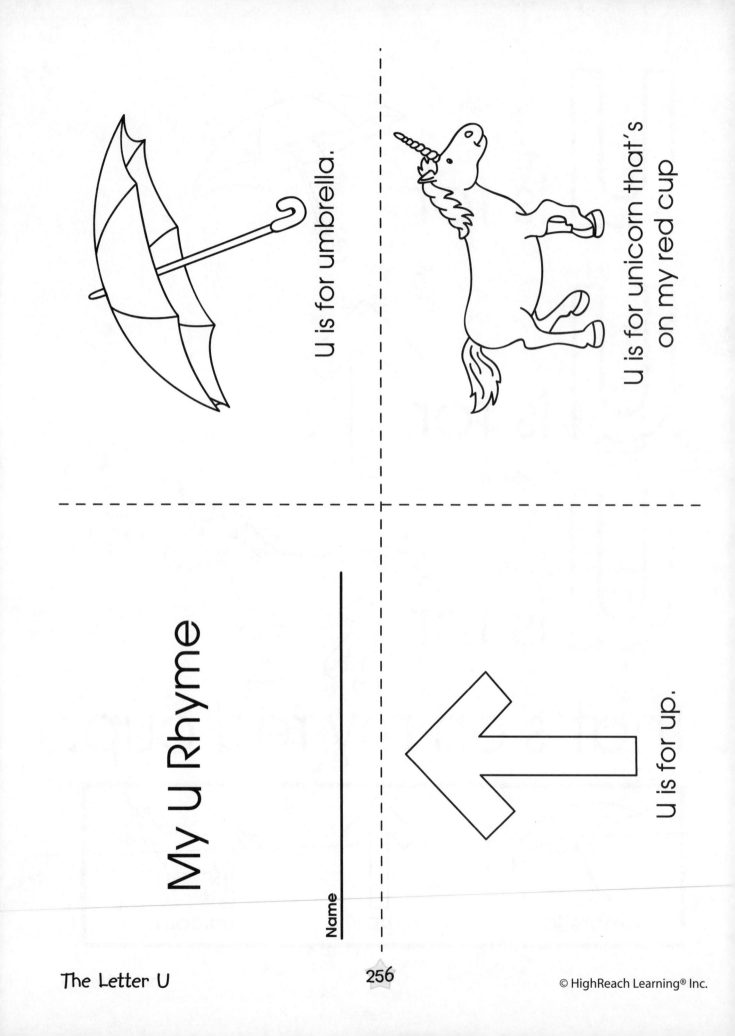

U is for umbrella.

U is for unicorn that's
on my red cup.

My U Rhyme

Name

U is for up.

© HighReach Learning® Inc.

© HighReach Learning® Inc.

The Letter V

Language Activities

Introduce Vinnie Vulture and the Letter V

Decorate a copy of the Letter V Display (page 257) as desired. Point to Vinnie Vulture on the display. Invite the children to guess what type of animal Vinnie is. If necessary explain that Vinnie is a vulture. You may wish to share the rhyme below several times and invite the children to join in.

VINNIE VULTURE

Vinnie Vulture wears a vest
As he ventures down the road.
Be very careful, Vinnie,
Or your volcano might explode.

Invite the children to discuss what they learned about Vinnie in the rhyme. Invite the children to name what Vinnie is pulling in the wagon. What do the children know about volcanoes? Would a real volcano fit in a wagon? Encourage the children to share their thoughts and ideas.

Point to both the capital V and the lowercase v on the display. Explain that these are both ways to write the letter. Explain that Vinnie likes the letter V best because it is the first letter of his name. Help the children decide if they know anyone whose name begins with V.

Talk About Letter V Words

Invite the children to talk about words they know that begin with the letter V. Write any suggestions down on sentence strips, a large sheet of paper, or chart paper. Attach the words to the wall at the children's eye level. Some familiar word suggestions are:

vanilla	violin	volcano	visor
vegetable	vine	volleyball	
vibration	vinegar	volume	

violin **vine** **volume**

vinegar **volleyball**

> ☆ *Learning Extension:* Invite the children to clap for the syllables of words that begin with the letter V (vine, vol-ca-no, vi-sor).

Discuss Vacations

Lead a discussion with the children about vacations. You may wish to share a recent experience with the children or talk to the children about a place that you would like to visit on a vacation. Invite the children to share their experiences with vacations, and mention that the word *vacation* begins with the letter V. Encourage the children to share details about their vacations, and expand the conversation based on what the children tell you.

> ☆ *Learning Extension:* If the children talk about or show special interest in a place they would like to visit, make it a point to provide information about that destination. Look for books, collect brochures, or search for information online about the destination. Share any information you gather with the children.

Language Activities

Share the Letter V Rebus Rhyme

Share the Letter V Rebus Rhyme (page 267) to develop a sense of rhythm and rhyme and to practice naming pictures. Show the display as you recite the rhyme several times. Afterwards, point to each picture on the chart and encourage the children to name it. Discuss each picture and invite the children to share times when they have seen similar items.

☆ **Learning Extension:** Talk about the letter V. Look at all of the words on the display. Help the children locate the letter V. Explain that the letter V can be written more than one way. Point to the capital V on the display and then point to the lowercase v. Help the children find all of the capital and lowercase letter V's on the display.

Create Letter V Rhyme Books

Give each child a copy of the Letter V Rhyme Book (page 268) and crayons or markers. Invite the children to point to the pictures as you read the text. Encourage the children to decorate the pictures as desired. Cut along the dotted lines and stack the pages in order. Staple the pages together. Invite the children to write their names on the rhyme books. Assist the children as needed.

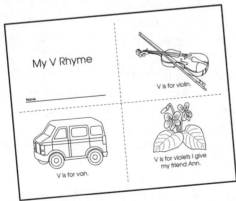

☆ **Learning Extension:** Invite a child to "read" his/her Letter V Rhyme Book to you. Encourage the child to point to the letter V in the book.

Talk About Volume of Voices

Show the children the volume control on a CD player and explain that it controls the volume of the music. When the volume is turned up, the music is loud. When the volume is turned down, the music is quiet. Play a song to demonstrate these concepts. As the music plays, move the volume control to vary the sound. When the music stops, ask the children to tell which volume of music they prefer. Explain to the children that sometimes we need to use a volume control for our voices. There are times when we need to use loud voices and times we need to use quiet voices. Help the children think of times when loud voices are appropriate, such as cheering at a ball game or calling out to a friend across the playground. Then help the children think of times when quiet voices are appropriate, such as when working in the classroom or during rest time. During the discussion, make sure to mention that the words *volume* and *voice* begin with the letter V.

The Letter V

260

© HighReach Learning® Inc.

Science Activities

Create a Vinegar Volcano

Help the children use a funnel to put some baking soda into a 20 ounce plastic soda bottle. Add a squirt of dishwashing liquid and several drops of red food coloring. Put the bottle in the center of a shallow pan and encourage the children to pack damp sand or dirt around it to form a volcano. (Be sure not to cover the opening of the bottle.) Invite the children to predict what will happen when you add vinegar to the volcano. Pour vinegar through the funnel into the bottle and encourage the children to observe what happens. (The mixture should foam out the top.) Make sure to mention that the words *vinegar* and *volcano* both begin with the letter V.

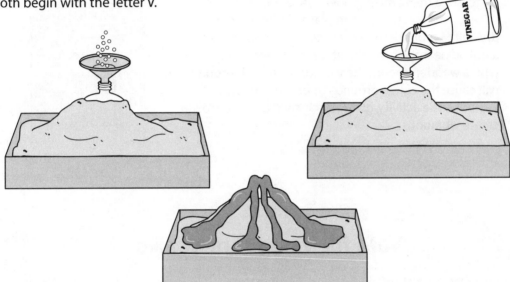

Explore Violets

Show the children some African violets. Provide unbreakable magnifying glasses for the children to use as they explore. Encourage the children to describe the flowers and share their discoveries. As the children explore, you may wish to mention that the word *violet* begins with the letter V.

Vote for Your Favorite Vegetables

Prepare samples of three different vegetables, such as carrots, celery, and bell peppers. Place the sets of samples on separate plates. Give each child a block, making sure that all the blocks are the same size. Invite each child to taste a vegetable sample from each plate, and then stack the block next to the plate for his/her favorite. Make sure to mention that the word *vegetable* begins with the letter V. When everyone has tasted the vegetables, have the children compare the stacks to see which vegetable was liked the best and which was liked the least.

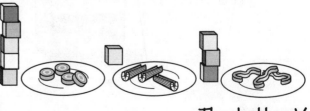

© HighReach Learning® Inc.

The Letter V

Science Activities

Explore Vibrations

Explain to the children that sound is made from vibrations that travel through the air, and mention that the word *vibration* begins with the letter V. Use the following demonstration to help the children understand this principle. Stretch plastic wrap tightly over the rim of a coffee can (without sharp edges) or a metal mixing bowl. Use a rubber band to secure the plastic wrap in place. Sprinkle a few dry coffee grounds in the center of the plastic. Hold a pot lid near the can and hit it rapidly and firmly with a wooden spoon. The vibrations from the sound will cause the coffee grounds to bounce around. Continue the activity, giving each child a chance to create vibrations.

Vote for Vinegar or Vanilla

Show the children a plastic bottle of vinegar and a plastic bottle of imitation vanilla extract. Name each liquid. You may want to have the children repeat each name and clap for the syllables (va-nil-la, vin-e-gar). You might also encourage the children to find the letter V or other familiar letters on the label of each bottle. Soak a cotton ball with each liquid and place each cotton ball in a separate cup. Place the cups on opposite ends of a table. Have each child in turn sniff each cup and vote for his/her favorite by standing behind the cup with the scent he/she prefers. Once all the children have chosen, lead the children in counting the number in each line. Help the children decide which scent had the most votes. You may want to mention that the words *vote, vinegar,* and *vanilla* all begin with the letter V.

The Letter V

262

© HighReach Learning® Inc.

Large Muscle Activities

Move Along a Vine

Create a vine with sidewalk chalk, masking tape, or a long jump rope outside. Show the children the vine, and help them realize that the word *vine* begins with the letter V. Encourage the children to move in assorted ways along the vine, such as crawling, walking, and hopping.

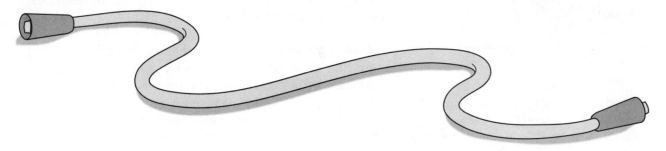

Play Volleyball

Set up a low net outside (if you do not have a net, make a line on the ground with chalk or tape). Divide the children into two groups, and encourage them to hit a volleyball back and forth to each other. They should try to hit the ball over the net. As the children play, mention that the word *volleyball* begins with the letter V.

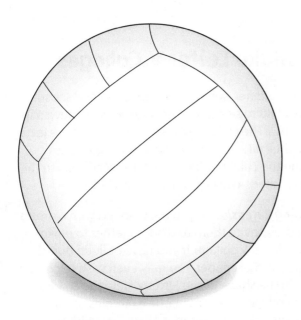

Move to Vivacious Violin Music

Play a recording of violin music and encourage the children to move to the music. If you have a real violin, show the children how the instrument is played. Invite the children to pretend to play the violin. You may wish to mention that the word *violin* begins with the letter V.

© HighReach Learning® Inc.

The Letter V

Art Activities

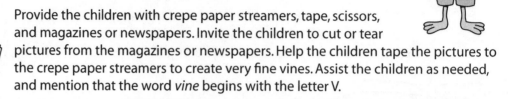

Create Very Fine Vines

Provide the children with crepe paper streamers, tape, scissors, and magazines or newspapers. Invite the children to cut or tear pictures from the magazines or newspapers. Help the children tape the pictures to the crepe paper streamers to create very fine vines. Assist the children as needed, and mention that the word *vine* begins with the letter V.

> ☆*Learning Extension:* After the children finish, write "V is for vine" on an index card for each child. Use a highlighter for each letter V and crayons for the other letters. Encourage the child to name each letter V, try to trace it, and then attach the card to his/her vine.

Make Visors

Cut paper plates into visor shapes as shown. Give each child a paper plate visor and help the child use a hole punch to make a hole on each end as shown. Invite the children to decorate the visors with crayons/markers. After the children finish, tie elastic string between the holes on the visors, and mention that the word *visor* begins with the letter V. Encourage the children to wear the visors, and give assistance if needed putting them on.

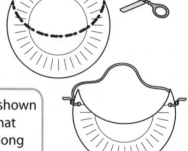

> ☆*Learning Extension:* Draw a cut line as shown on a large paper plate for the children that show readiness. Have the children cut along the line to make a visor.

Create Tactile Letter V's

Give each child a copy of the capital letter V (page 258), an old paintbrush, and a shallow dish of glue. Invite the children to trace the letter V with their fingers. Encourage the children to spread glue on their letter V's as desired. Provide the children with small bathroom cups filled with sand, salt, or rice. Invite the children to shake the sand, salt, or rice onto the glue. Set aside to dry. After the glue dries, invite the children to trace their tactile letter V's with their fingers. How does the V feel? Use descriptive words such as bumpy, rough, etc. as you interact with the child.

Make Letter V Collages

Give a child old newspapers or magazines and scissors. Invite the child to search for the letter V in the newspapers or magazines. The child may wish to tear or cut the letters out. Give the child a sheet of paper and a glue stick. Encourage the child to attach the letter V cutouts to the paper as desired. Assist the child as needed.

> ☆*Learning Extension:* If you are working with a group of children, invite them to work together to make one big letter V collage. If you have bulletin board, butcher, or chart paper, you may even wish to cut the paper in the shape of the letter V. Help the children locate and cut or tear out large examples of the letter from captions and headlines. Have the children glue all the letter cutouts to the paper.

The Letter V

264

© HighReach Learning® Inc.

Small Muscle Activities

Create a Village

Invite the children to use blocks to create a village with roads, houses, and stores. Explain that the word *village* means a small town. Provide toy cars and people for the children to place in their village. As they work, mention that the word *village* begins with the letter V.

> ☆ *Learning Extension:* Invite the children that show readiness to create a plan together for building their village. Encourage the children to discuss what types of buildings or other things they would like to use in their village. Write down exactly what the children say during the discussion. Then as the children work, encourage them to follow their plans.

Clean with Vinegar

Invite the children to help you make a simple cleaning solution. Show the children a plastic bottle of vinegar. You may want to encourage them to point to and name the letter V or other familiar letters on the bottle. Remove the top from a clean plastic spray bottle and place a funnel on top. Pour in one cup of water and one-fourth cup of vinegar. Replace the lid. Repeat to prepare several bottles. Show the children how to use the solution to clean windows or tabletops. They can spray on the vinegar mixture and then rub dry with paper towels or cleaning cloths.

Explore Letter V Lacing Cards

Draw several block letter V's on posterboard using the pattern on page 258 and cut out. Use a hole punch to make a series of holes around each letter cutout. Vary the number of holes so that some will be easier to lace than others. Tie a length of yarn to one hole and wrap the free end with tape. Be sure the yarn can wrap around the letter twice. Set out the letter V lacing cards. Assist the children as needed as they explore the lacing cards.

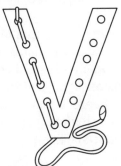

© HighReach Learning® Inc.

The Letter V

Cooking with Vinnie Vulture
Letter V Recipes

Vanilla Sandwiches

1 (3.4 oz.) package instant vanilla pudding mix
milk
1 (16 oz.) package vanilla wafer cookies

Encourage the children to help you prepare vanilla instant pudding according to directions on the package. Then invite the children to spread the pudding on the vanilla wafers to make little vanilla sandwiches.

Vegetable Soup

assorted canned vegetables
  (including diced tomatoes)
4 cans chicken broth

Invite each child to bring a can of vegetables from home. Encourage each child to pour his/her vegetables into a large soup pot. Add chicken broth and stir well. Heat until warm.

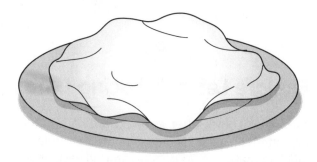

Frozen Velvet

ripe bananas (about 4 medium)
1½ cups buttermilk
1 cup sugar
1 tsp. vanilla
1 (8 oz.) container whipped topping

Peel and mash bananas with a fork. Measure 2 cups of bananas and put in a large bowl. Stir in the buttermilk, sugar, and vanilla. Freeze until mixture thickens slightly. Fold in whipped topping. Return to freezer until frozen. Remove from freezer for a few minutes to soften before serving. Serves about 8 children.

Very Berry Cobbler

2 cups berries, fresh or frozen (raspberries,
  cranberries, blueberries, strawberries, etc.)
1 cup milk
1 cup flour
1 cup sugar
1 stick butter, melted
vanilla ice cream (optional)

Preheat the oven to 350°. Pour butter on the bottom of a 9" x 9" baking dish and add berries. Beat together milk, sugar, and flour in a mixing bowl and pour onto berries. Bake for 35 to 40 minutes or until top is golden brown and firm. Serve warm with a scoop of vanilla ice cream if desired.

© HighReach Learning® Inc.

V is for  .

V is for .

V is for

I give my friend Ann.

violin **van** **violets**

© HighReach Learning® Inc.

The Letter V

My V Rhyme

Name _____

V is for violin.

V is for violets I give
my friend Ann.

V is for van.

© HighReach Learning® Inc.

W w

© HighReach Learning® Inc.

269

The Letter W

The Letter W

© HighReach Learning® Inc.

Language Activities
Introduce Wilbur Walrus and the Letter W

Decorate a copy of the Letter W Display (page 269) as desired. Point to Wilbur Walrus on the display. Invite the children to guess what type of animal Wilbur is. If necessary explain that Wilbur is a walrus. You may wish to share the rhyme below several times and invite the children to join in.

WILBUR WALRUS

Wilbur Walrus wanders
All around the town.
And if you want a waffle,
His wagon's where they're found.

Invite the children to discuss what they learned about Wilbur in the rhyme. Invite the children to name what Wilbur is pulling in the wagon. Have the children ever eaten waffles? Do they like or dislike waffles? Do walruses really eat waffles? What do the children think walruses eat? Encourage the children to share their thoughts and ideas.

Point to both the capital W and the lowercase w on the display. Explain that these are both ways to write the letter. Explain that Wilbur likes the letter W best because it is the first letter of his name. Help the children decide if they know anyone whose name begins with W.

Talk About Letter W Words

Invite the children to talk about words they know that begin with the letter W. Write any suggestions down on sentence strips, a large sheet of paper, or chart paper. Attach the words to the wall at the children's eye level. Some familiar word suggestions are:

wallpaper	watermelon	wind	worm
walrus	weather	wish	
water	wiggle	wood	

water **wallpaper**
wood **wiggle** **worm**

☆*Learning Extension:* Invite the children to clap for the syllables of words that begin with the letter W (wish, wal-rus, wa-ter-mel-on).

What's a Wish?

Encourage the children to share their thoughts and ideas about wishes. After the children finish, explain that a wish is something you would really like to have come true, and mention that the word *wish* begins with the letter W. Give the children examples of things you might like to wish for, such as a sunny day, a book, etc. Invite the children to close their eyes and think of a wish. Encourage each child to share his/her wish with the group.

Language Activities
Share the Letter W Rebus Rhyme

Share the Letter W Rebus Rhyme (page 279) to develop a sense of rhythm and rhyme and to practice naming pictures. Show the display as you recite the rhyme several times. Afterwards, point to each picture on the chart and encourage the children to name it. Discuss each picture and invite the children to share times when they have seen similar items.

☆ *Learning Extension:* Talk about the letter W. Look at all of the words on the display. Help the children locate the letter W. Explain that the letter W can be written more than one way. Point to the capital W on the display and then point to the lowercase w. Help the children find all of the capital and lowercase letter W's on the display.

Create Letter W Rhyme Books

Give each child a copy of the Letter W Rhyme Book (page 280) and crayons or markers. Invite the children to point to the pictures as you read the text. Encourage the children to decorate the pictures as desired. Cut along the dotted lines and stack the pages in order. Staple the pages together. Invite the children to write their names on the rhyme books. Assist the children as needed.

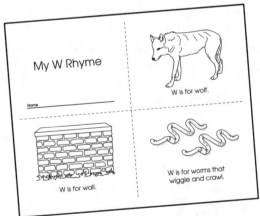

☆ *Learning Extension:* Invite a child to "read" his/her Letter W Rhyme Book to you. Encourage the child to point to the letter W in the book.

Talk About the Weather

Encourage the children to look outside and describe the weather to you. Is the sun shining? Is it cloudy? Is it hot or cold outside? Help the children realize that the word *weather* begins with the letter W. Share the song below and encourage the children to join in.

THE WEATHER SONG
(tune: "Twinkle, Twinkle, Little Star")

What's the weather like today?
Will we go outside to play?
Is it sunny? Is it wet?
Is it cold and snowy yet?
What's the weather like today?
Will we go outside to play?

☆ *Learning Extension:* Make a weather diary by stapling sheets of plain white paper between two sheets of construction paper. Base the number of pages on the time frame you think best for your group. Write the words "Today's Weather" on the cover. Each day, choose a child to observe the weather and draw a picture in the diary to record the day's conditions. Write exactly what the child says about the weather on the page. You may also want to print the date on each page.

The Letter W

© HighReach Learning® Inc.

Science Activities

Explore Wool Items

Provide the children with assorted wool items to explore. Explain that the items are made out of wool from sheep, and mention that the word *wool* begins with the letter W. Encourage the children to describe how the wool items feel. Provide unbreakable magnifying glasses and invite the children to look through them at the wool and describe what they see.

Talk About Wind

Encourage the children to explore the effects of wind. Explain to the children that they are going to pretend to be the wind, and mention that the word *wind* begins with the letter W. Sprinkle a spoonful of sugar on a small paper plate for each child. Distribute drinking straws and encourage the children to try to change the shape of the sugar by blowing through their straws. Encourage them to share their discoveries. What happens to the sugar when they blow through the straws? Why does the sugar change shape? What happens when the wind blows outside? Does it move things like the children move the sugar when they blow through the straws?

Weigh Water

Gather several small plastic containers of different shapes with lids. If possible, include some that hold the same volume but have different shapes. Place a small pitcher of water and the plastic containers in an empty water table or on a large tray with a rim to catch spills. Encourage the children to fill the containers with water and compare their weights using a balance scale. As the children explore, ask questions to encourage them to think. Some examples are listed below. Make sure to mention that the words *weigh* and *water* each begin with the letter W.

❖ Which of these two containers of water do you think will weigh more? How can we find out?
❖ Can you find two containers that weigh the same?
❖ One of these two containers weighs more than the other. How can we make them balance?
❖ Which of these two containers of water do you think will weigh less? How can we find out?

Wobble Eggs

Provide the children with plastic eggs and playdough or modeling clay. Encourage each child to press playdough or clay into one end of an egg, snap the halves together, and try to make the egg wobble on one end. Help the children experiment with the playdough or clay to discover the best way to make this work. As the children explore, ask questions to encourage them to think. Some examples are listed below.

❖ Does it work better to put the playdough in the big end or the small end?
❖ What happens if you fill both halves of the egg?
❖ Will the egg stand up when it is empty?
❖ What will happen if you add more playdough to the egg?
❖ What will happen if you take some of the playdough out?

© HighReach Learning® Inc.

273

The Letter W

Large Muscle Activities

Walk Like Walruses

Show the children how to walk like a walrus, and mention that the words *walk* and *walrus* both begin with the letter W. Begin by lying facedown on the floor. Place your palms flat against the floor and straighten your arms. Then move by walking with your hands, dragging your feet behind you. Encourage the children to imitate your actions.

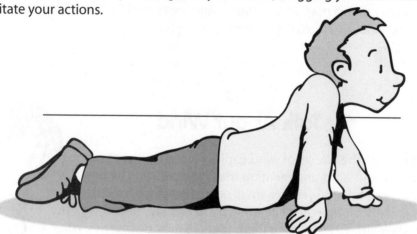

Wiggle All Around

Share the rhyme below and encourage the children to listen closely for the body parts to wiggle. Repeat the rhyme several times, and mention that the word *wiggle* begins with the letter W.

WIGGLE!

Wiggle your fingers and
    wiggle your toes.

Wiggle your shoulders and
    wiggle your nose.

Wiggle your elbows
    and wiggle your knees.

Wiggle your stomach now,
    if you please.

Wiggle all over from top to bottom.

Wiggles, wiggles, wiggles, we sure have got 'em!

Move to Waltz Music

Play a recording of waltz music and invite the children to move creatively. As they move to the music, mention that the word *waltz* begins with the letter W.

The Letter W

© HighReach Learning® Inc.

Art Activities

Create Tactile Letter W's

Give each child a copy of the capital letter W (page 270), an old paintbrush, and a shallow dish of glue. Invite the children to trace the letter W with their fingers. Encourage the children to spread glue on their letter W's as desired. Provide the children with small bathroom cups filled with sand, salt, or snips of wallpaper scraps. Invite the children to shake or press the sand, salt, or wallpaper onto the glue. As the children work, mention that the word wallpaper begins with the letter W. Set aside to dry. After the glue dries, invite the children to trace their tactile letter W's with their fingers. How does the W feel? Use descriptive words such as bumpy, rough, etc. as you interact with the child.

Make Wind Socks

Provide the children with large sheets of white construction paper. Encourage the children to use crayons or markers to decorate their papers. Encourage each child to tape several crepe paper streamers along one long side of the paper. Help the child curve the paper into a cylinder, taping the short ends together as shown. Attach a loop of yarn across the top of the cylinder. Encourage the children to take their wind socks outside. Challenge the children to discover ways to make the wind socks fly. If the day is breezy, they may be able to hold out the wind socks and catch the wind. Otherwise, they could hold the wind socks by the yarn and run. As they move, the wind socks will fly out behind them. As they fly their wind socks, mention that the term *wind sock* begins with the letter W.

Watercolor Paintings

Provide the children with paper, small cups of water, paintbrushes, and watercolor paints. Encourage the children to paint pictures using the watercolor paints, and mention that the word *watercolor* begins with the letter W.

☆*Learning Extension:* Encourage the children that show readiness to try to paint the letter W with the watercolor paints.

© HighReach Learning® Inc.

The Letter W

Art Activities
Make Letter W Collages

Give a child old newspapers or magazines and scissors. Invite the child to search for the letter W in the newspapers or magazines. The child may wish to tear or cut the letters out. Give the child a sheet of paper and a glue stick. Encourage the child to attach the letter W cutouts to the paper as desired. Assist the child as needed.

☆ *Learning Extension:* If you are working with a group of children, invite them to work together to make one big letter W collage. If you have bulletin board, butcher, or chart paper, you may even wish to cut the paper in the shape of the letter W. Help the children locate and cut or tear out large examples of the letter from captions and headlines. Have the children glue all the letter cutouts to the paper.

Create Wood Sculptures

Sand wood scraps to avoid splinters. Provide the children with the wood scraps and wood glue. Challenge the children to think about things they could create with the wood scraps. Encourage the children to share their ideas, and mention that the word *wood* begins with the letter W. Invite each child to use wood glue to attach several pieces of wood together. After they finish, encourage the children to describe their wood creations.

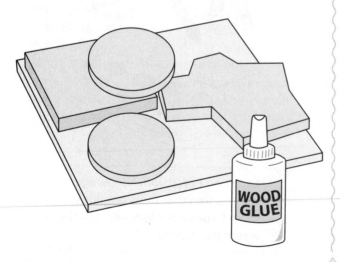

Paint on Wax Paper

Give each child a 12" x 12" sheet of wax paper. Invite the children to explore the wax paper. How does it feel in their hands? Does one side of the wax paper feel different from the other side? Help the children realize that the word *wax* begins with the letter W. Provide the children with assorted art materials, such as crayons, markers, paint, paintbrushes, etc. Invite the children to use the materials to decorate the wax paper as desired. Help the children notice what happens when they paint or color on the wax paper. How is it different from regular paper?

The Letter W

© HighReach Learning® Inc.

Small Muscle Activities

Play a Watermelon Seed Counting Game

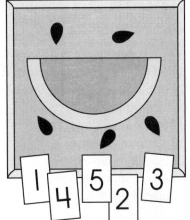

Make a felt watermelon slice and five felt seeds. To make the slice, cut a half circle of green felt that is 12" across. Cut a half circle of red or pink felt that is 10" across. Center the red or pink felt on top of the green felt with the flat sides touching and glue in place. Cut five watermelon seeds (about 1" long) from black felt. Place the watermelon slice on a felt board with the seeds around it. Number index cards 1–5, mix them up, and stack them facedown next to the felt board. Encourage the children to turn over the cards, name the numerals, and place the indicated number of seeds on the watermelon slice. Assist the children as needed.

☆ *Learning Extension:* Create felt seeds and index cards for the numerals 1–10 for the children that show readiness and an understanding of higher numbers.

Practice Weaving

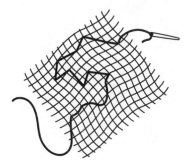

Cut a square of nylon netting for each child. Purchase some blunt plastic craft needles with large eyes. These are sold with children's craft supplies. Invite the children to weave yarn through the net. Help each child thread a blunt plastic craft needle with yarn. Encourage the children to weave the yarn in and out of the holes of the net to create designs. Help the children cut off the yarn, and thread the needles again as needed. As the children work, mention that the word *weave* begins with the letter W.

Create Worm Pictures

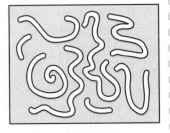

Cut corrugated cardboard boxes into pieces. Shortly before the activity, boil spaghetti. Drain the spaghetti, but don't rinse. Create designs with spaghetti worms. Give each child a piece of cardboard. Show the children the spaghetti and encourage them to pretend that the pieces of spaghetti are worms. Invite the children to arrange the worms on their cardboard as desired. As the children arrange the pieces of spaghetti on the cardboard, encourage them to describe what they are doing. Lay the spaghetti designs flat to dry. As the spaghetti dries, it will stick to the cardboard without glue.

Explore Letter W Lacing Cards

Draw several block letter W's on posterboard using the pattern on page 270 and cut out. Use a hole punch to make a series of holes around each letter cutout. Vary the number of holes so that some will be easier to lace than others. Tie a length of yarn to one hole and wrap the free end with tape. Be sure the yarn can wrap around the letter twice. Set out the letter W lacing cards. Assist the children as needed as they explore the lacing cards.

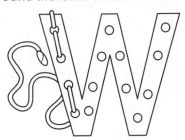

© HighReach Learning® Inc.

The Letter W

Cooking with Wilbur Walrus
Letter W Recipes

WALDORF SALAD

3 Granny Smith apples, cored
3 Red Delicious apples, cored
2 cups mayonnaise
¼ cup sugar
3 Tbsp. lemon juice, plus extra
3 Tbsp. orange juice
2 cups whipped topping
6 celery stalks, finely diced
1 cup golden raisins

Dice apples with skin still on and place in a bowl of water with a little lemon juice to keep them from turning brown. Whisk together mayonnaise, sugar, lemon juice, and orange juice in a large bowl. Fold in the whipped topping. Drain the apples and add to the mayonnaise mixture along with the celery and raisins. Stir until all of the ingredients are evenly coated. Chill.

WACKY WAFFLES

frozen waffles
whipped topping
chocolate chips
chocolate syrup
maraschino cherries

Heat frozen waffles according to the directions on the package. Give each child a waffle. Invite the children to create wacky waffles using the topics provided.

WATERMELON SHERBET

raspberry sherbet
lime sherbet
chocolate chips

Let sherbet sit out and thaw a little. Mix in chocolate chips with the raspberry sherbet. In large plastic or glass bowl, put a layer of lime sherbet about a ½ inch thick inside the bowl. This is the watermelon rind. Then add the mixed raspberry and chocolate chips, filling the bowl. Freeze until the sherbet is completely frozen. Turn out on a cutting board and slice like a real watermelon.

WONDERFUL WARM BANANAS

3 Tbsp. butter
6 ripe bananas, sliced
2 tsp. vanilla extract
1 cup sweetened flaked coconut
3½ Tbsp. powdered sugar
vanilla ice cream (optional)

Melt butter in a skillet over medium heat. Place the banana slices in the skillet, stir in the vanilla, and cook until the bananas are golden brown. Stir in the coconut, and top with powdered sugar. Serve warm, and if desired, over a scoop of vanilla ice cream.

The Letter W

278

© HighReach Learning® Inc.

W 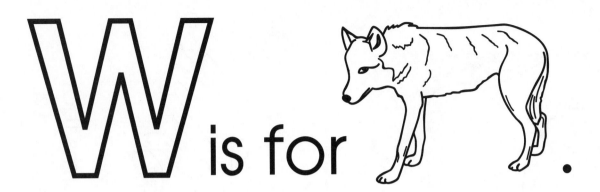 is for .

W  is for .

W 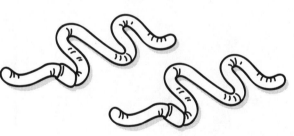 is for

That wiggle and crawl.

wolf   wall   worms

© HighReach Learning® Inc.

The Letter W

My W Rhyme

W is for wolf.

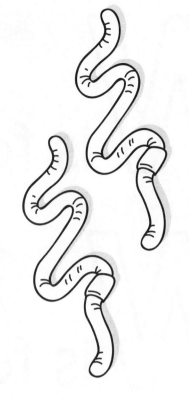

W is for worms that wiggle and crawl.

W is for wall.

Name

© HighReach Learning® Inc.

Xx

281

The Letter X

The Letter X

© HighReach Learning® Inc.

Language Activities

Introduce Xavier X-Ray Expert and the Letter X

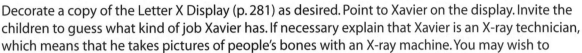

Decorate a copy of the Letter X Display (p. 281) as desired. Point to Xavier on the display. Invite the children to guess what kind of job Xavier has. If necessary explain that Xavier is an X-ray technician, which means that he takes pictures of people's bones with an X-ray machine. You may wish to share the rhyme below several times and invite the children to join in.

XAVIER X-RAY EXPERT

Xavier carries X-rays,
As he travels to and fro.
So if you break a bone,
You'll know just where to go!

Invite the children to discuss what they learned about Xavier in the rhyme. Invite the children to name what Xavier is pulling in the wagon. Lead a discussion with the children about X-rays. Have any of the children ever had to have an X-ray? Why? What happened? Where did they go to get the X-ray taken? Encourage the children to share their ideas and experiences.

Point to both the capital X and the lowercase x on the display. Explain that these are both ways to write the letter. Explain that Xavier likes the letter X best because it is the first letter of his name. Help the children decide if they know anyone whose name begins with X.

Talk About Letter X Words

Invite the children to talk about words they know that begin with or contain the letter X. Write any suggestions down on sentence strips, a large sheet of paper, or chart paper. Attach the words to the wall at the children's eye level. Some familiar word suggestions are:

ax	exit	fix	ox	X-ray
box	extra	fox	six	xylophone
exercise	extreme	mix	wax	

Explain that all of these words begin with or contain the letter X, but the letter X makes more than one sound. For example, in some words like *exit* and *X-ray*, it makes the /ks/ sound, and in other words like *Xavier* and *xylophone*, it makes the /z/ sound.

> ☆ **Learning Extension:** Invite the children to clap for the syllables of words that begin with or contain the letter X (X-ray, six, ex-er-cise).

Go on an X Hunt

Write several words containing the letter X and several words that do not on large index cards. While the children are not watching, hide all of the index cards around the room or outside. Invite the children to search for words with the letter X. Explain to the children that when you say "Go!" they should look for index cards with the letter X on them. When the children find the index cards, they should bring them to you. As you receive each card, point to and name the word on the card, and invite the children to point to the letter X.

Language Activities

Share the Letter X Rebus Rhyme

X is in [X-ray].
X is in [fox].
X is in [box] that
Holds my new socks.

X-ray   fox   box

Share the Letter X Rebus Rhyme (page 291) to develop a sense of rhythm and rhyme and to practice naming pictures. Show the display as you recite the rhyme several times. Afterwards, point to each picture on the chart and encourage the children to name it. Discuss each picture and invite the children to share times when they have seen similar items.

> ☆ *Learning Extension:* Talk about the letter X. Look at all of the words on the display. Help the children locate the letter X. Explain that the letter X can be written more than one way. Point to the capital X on the display and then point to the lowercase x. Help the children find all of the capital and lowercase letter X's on the display.

Create Letter X Rhyme Books

Give each child a copy of the Letter X Rhyme Book (page 292) and crayons or markers. Invite the children to point to the pictures as you read the text. Encourage the children to decorate the pictures as desired. Cut along the dotted lines and stack the pages in order. Staple the pages together. Invite the children to write their names on the rhyme books. Assist the children as needed.

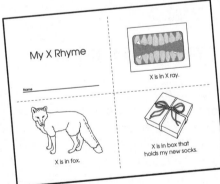

> ☆ *Learning Extension:* Invite a child to "read" his/her Letter X Rhyme Book to you. Encourage the child to point to the letter X in the book.

X Marks the Spot

Use a city map to locate each child's home address, and use a black marker to place an X on the home. Once each child's home has been marked, help the children count the X's. Does more that one person live on the same street? Does anyone live near the school?

> ☆ *Learning Extension:* Encourage the children that show readiness to dictate their addresses to you. Write each child's correct name and address on an index card. Invite the child to repeat his/her address after you.

The Letter X

© HighReach Learning® Inc.

Science Activities

Perform an Experiment with Milk

Explain to the children that you are going to perform an experiment with milk, and mention that the word *experiment* contains the letter X. Pour milk into a shallow dish. Drop several colors of food coloring onto the milk. Encourage the children to watch closely and discuss how the colors behave on the surface of the milk as they slowly spread. Use an eyedropper to squeeze a drop of dishwashing liquid onto each color. The colors will swirl explosively across the surface of the milk. Encourage the children to talk about why they think this happens, and explain that the reason is because the milk reacts to the dishwashing liquid in a way that causes the colors to swirl and spread.

☆ *Learning Extension:* Experiment with other liquids to see if the color behaves the same or differently. For example, try the same procedure in vegetable oil, water, or juice. Discuss the results with the children.

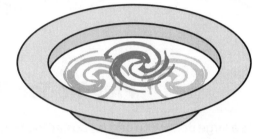

Examine Colors

Cut coffee filters into strips about an inch wide. Help each child balance a drinking straw on the rim of a large paper cup. Encourage each child to use a black marker to print a letter X near one end of a coffee filter strip, fold the other end of the strip over the straw, and secure with tape so that the X hangs a little above the bottom of the cup as shown. Assist the children as needed. Add a little water to each child's cup so that the end of the strip is in the water and the X is just above the water. Encourage the children to talk about what happens to their letter X's. As the strips soak up the water, the black ink on the X's should gradually separate into different colors.

Explore a Xylophone

Show the children a toy xylophone. Encourage the children to name the instrument if they can. Explain that this is a xylophone, and that the word *xylophone* begins with the letter X. Encourage the children to take turns playing the xylophone. What sounds does the instrument make? How do the mallets make different sounds? Is it easy or hard to play the xylophone?

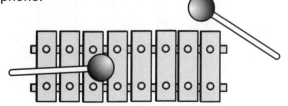

Examine X-Rays

Contact a local doctor's, dentist's, or veterinarian's office and ask if they would give you an old X-ray to share with the children. Tape the X-ray to a window or hang it near light. Point out the X-ray and explain that an X-ray is a picture that is taken of the inside of a person's body. A special machine takes the pictures to help doctors see if a bone is broken or if something else is wrong. Dentists also take X-rays to see if a cavity is forming. Encourage the children to share their experiences and ideas about X-rays. After the children respond, encourage them to examine the X-ray and talk about what they see.

© HighReach Learning® Inc.

The Letter X

Large Muscle Activities

Make the Letter X with Bodies

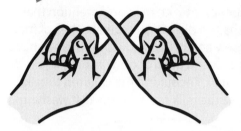

Challenge the children to think of ways that they can make the letter X using their bodies. Individually, they can cross two fingers to make an X, cross their forearms, or make the shape in other ways. Encourage them to try their ideas. Then help the children get into groups and work with their groups to make letter X's using their bodies. Encourage the children to talk about how hard or easy it is to make an X with their bodies.

Play Tic-Tac-Toe

Create a large tic-tac-toe grid on posterboard. Print X's on five index cards and O's on five index cards. Play tic-tac-toe with beanbags. Split the children into two teams. Give one team the X cards and one team the O cards. Have a child from the X team stand near the target, toss a beanbag onto the tic-tac-toe game board, and place an X card in the space where it lands. Then have a child from the O team stand near the target, toss a beanbag onto the board, and place an O card where it lands. If the beanbag lands where there is an X, the child replaces the X with an O and returns the X card to the X team. The first team to get three in a row wins. Repeat the game, having the children stand farther from the target. Talk about whether it is easier to toss the beanbag from a short distance or from a long way off.

Toss Balls in an X Box

Cover a large open-top box with white paper. Invite the children to help you decorate the box by using assorted colors of markers to draw X's on it. You may want to ask the children to name the letters on the box. Give each child a small ball to toss into the box. Encourage the children to help you count how many balls land in the box and how many miss.

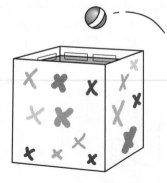

Do Sets of Exercises

Lead the children in performing different exercises such as jumping jacks, sit-ups, and toe touches. Encourage the children to discuss if they think the exercises are hard or easy, and mention that the word *exercise* contains the letter X.

The Letter X

286

© HighReach Learning® Inc.

Art Activities

Create X-Ray Pictures

As the children watch, use white chalk to print "X is for X-ray" on a sheet of black construction paper for each child. Read the caption aloud. Talk briefly about X-rays and help the children realize that the word *X-ray* begins with the letter X. If possible, show the children a real X-ray. Give the children the black construction paper and white chalk. Invite the children to create X-ray pictures of their hands. Suggest that each child use the white chalk to outline his/her hand. The children can then attempt to draw the bones of their hands to make the pictures resemble X-rays. Away from the children, lightly spray each paper with hair spray to keep the chalk from smearing.

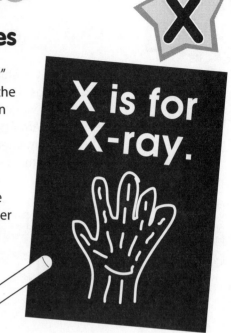

☆*Learning Extension:* Encourage the children that show readiness to use the white chalk to write a capital X and lowercase x on their papers.

Create the Letter X

Give the children glue, tape, craft sticks, straws, and other collage materials you would like to use. Challenge the children to use these materials to make letter X's on sheets of construction paper. You may need to demonstrate how to do this for the children. After the children finish, encourage them to talk about how they made the X's.

Create Tactile Letter X's

Give each child a copy of the capital letter X (page 282), an old paintbrush, and a shallow dish of glue. Invite the children to trace the letter X with their fingers. Encourage the children to spread glue on their letter X's as desired. Provide the children with small bathroom cups filled with sand, salt, or rice. Invite the children to shake the sand, salt, or rice onto the glue. Set aside to dry. After the glue dries, invite the children to trace their tactile letter X's with their fingers. How does the X feel? Use descriptive words such as bumpy, rough, etc. as you interact with the child.

Art Activities

Create a Box Structure

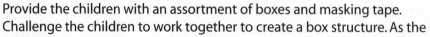

Provide the children with an assortment of boxes and masking tape. Challenge the children to work together to create a box structure. As the children work, mention that the word *box* contains the letter X. After they finish, provide the children with crayons, markers, or paint and invite them to decorate the structure as desired.

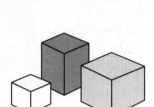

> ☆ *Learning Extension:* Invite the children to decorate their box structure with the letter X. They can use crayons, markers, paint, or tape to create the X's.

Create an X Butterfly

Draw a large black X on a sheet of construction paper for each child. Provide the children with crayons and markers. Invite the children to name the letters on their papers. Encourage the children to close in each side of the X to make butterfly wings. Invite the children to decorate the wings in any way they like. If the children wish, they can draw the butterfly's body or glue a craft stick to the center of the X to create one.

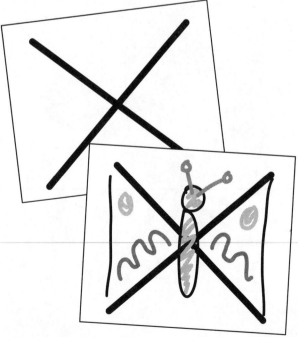

Make Letter X Collages

Give a child old newspapers or magazines and scissors. Invite the child to search for the letter X in the newspapers or magazines. The child may wish to tear or cut the letters out. Give the child a sheet of paper and a glue stick. Encourage the child to attach the letter X cutouts to the paper as desired. Assist the child as needed.

> ☆ *Learning Extension:* If you are working with a group of children, invite them to work together to make one big letter X collage. If you have bulletin board, butcher, or chart paper, you may even wish to cut the paper in the shape of the letter X. Help the children locate and cut or tear out large examples of the letter from captions and headlines. Have the children glue all the letter cutouts to the paper.

The Letter X

© HighReach Learning® Inc.

Small Muscle Activities

Create Exit Signs

As the children watch, use a highlighter to print large capital letters to spell the word *EXIT* on a sheet of construction paper for each child. Point to an EXIT sign if you have one in the room. Explain that the word *EXIT* means the way out. Invite the children to talk about other places they may have seen EXIT signs. After they share, encourage them to locate the letter X in the word. Encourage the children to squeeze glitter glue along each letter. When the glue dries, invite the children to feel the interesting texture.

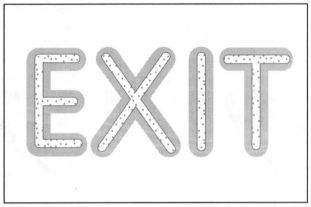

Build on the Letter X

Make a large masking tape X on the floor. Provide the children with an assortment of blocks. The children may wish to outline the X with blocks or build a structure on the letter X. As the children work, encourage them to describe their creations.

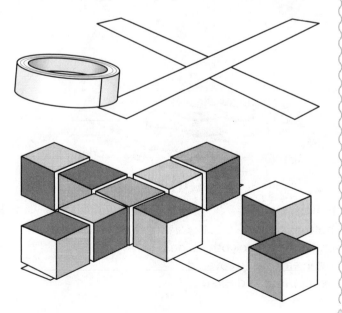

Explore Letter X Lacing Cards

Draw several block letter X's on posterboard using the pattern on page 282 and cut out. Use a hole punch to make a series of holes around each letter cutout. Vary the number of holes so that some will be easier to lace than others. Tie a length of yarn to one hole and wrap the free end with tape. Be sure the yarn can wrap around the letter twice. Set out the letter X lacing cards. Assist the children as needed as they explore the lacing cards.

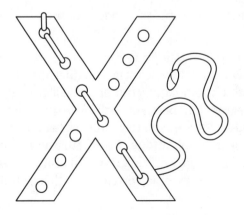

© HighReach Learning® Inc.

The Letter X

Cooking with Xavier
Letter X Recipes

X-CELLENT X'S

refrigerated breadstick dough
cinnamon sugar

Preheat the oven to 350°. Grease cookie sheets. Help each child arrange two strips of breadstick dough to form an X and sprinkle with cinnamon sugar. Bake for 10 minutes, or until golden brown.

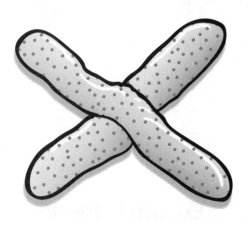

EXTRA CHEESY X TOAST

sliced bread
sliced cheese

Toast a slice of bread for each child. Give each child a piece of toast and a slice of cheese. Invite the children to tear or use plastic knives to cut the cheese into strips. Encourage the children to arrange the cheese slices like the letter X on the toast.

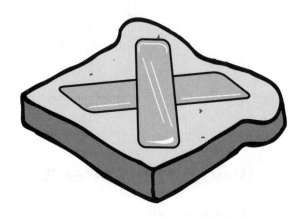

EXTREME CREPES

2 cups milk
¾ cup sugar
2 cups all-purpose flour
2 eggs
1 Tbsp. baking powder
1 tsp. vanilla extract
1 tsp. vegetable oil
jelly, fruit, or other toppings as desired

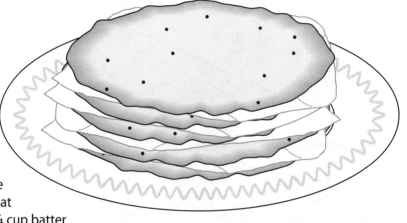

Place milk, sugar, flour, eggs, baking powder, vanilla, and oil in a blender; puree until smooth. Lightly butter a 6" skillet; heat over medium heat. For each crepe, pour ¼ cup batter into skillet; immediately rotate skillet until batter covers bottom. Cook until light brown. Run spatula around edge to loosen; turn and cook other side until light brown. Stack crepes, placing waxed paper between each; keep covered until ready to serve. Top crepes with jelly, fruit, or any other toppings as desired.

© HighReach Learning® Inc.

X  is in 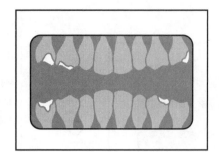 .

X is in  .

X is in  that

Holds my new socks.

X-ray   fox   box

© HighReach Learning® Inc. The Letter X

My X Rhyme

Name _____

X is in X ray.

X is in box that
holds my new socks.

X is in fox.

292

© HighReach Learning® Inc.

© HighReach Learning® Inc.

293

The Letter Y

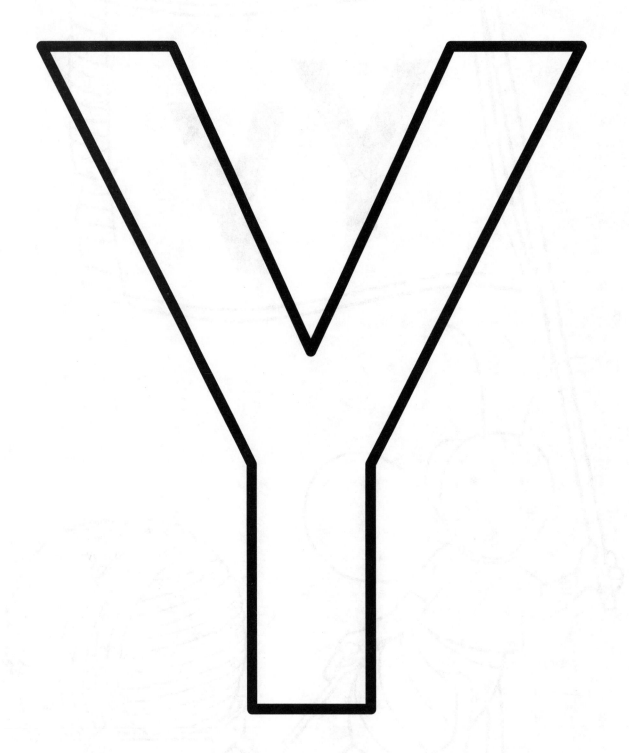

The Letter Y

294

© HighReach Learning® Inc.

Language Activities

Introduce Yorky Yellowjacket and the Letter Y

Decorate a copy of the Letter Y Display (page 293) as desired. Point to Yorky Yellowjacket on the display. Invite the children to guess what type of insect Yorky is. If necessary explain that Yorky is a yellowjacket, which is a type of wasp. You may wish to share the rhyme below several times and invite the children to join in.

YORKY YELLOWJACKET

Yorky the yellowjacket,
Is yellow and black with wings.
But please don't take his ball of yarn,
'Cause you might get a sting!

Invite the children to discuss what they learned about Yorky in the rhyme. Invite the children to name the item on the display that Yorky is pulling in the wagon. Have the children ever seen an insect like Yorky? What did the insect sound like? Do they think it would be okay to pet Yorky? Why or why not? Have the children ever used yarn to make anything? Encourage the children to share their thoughts and ideas.

Point to both the capital Y and the lowercase y on the display. Explain that these are both ways to write the letter. Explain that Yorky likes the letter Y best because it is the first letter of his name. Help the children decide if they know anyone whose name begins with Y.

Talk About Letter Y Words

Invite the children to talk about words they know that begin with the letter Y. Write any suggestions down on sentence strips, a large sheet of paper, or chart paper. Attach the words to the wall at the children's eye level. Some familiar word suggestions are:

yarn	yellow	yodel	yo-yo
yeast	yellowjacket	yoga	yucky
yell	yesterday	yogurt	yummy

☆ **Learning Extension:** Invite the children to clap for the syllables of words that begin with the letter Y (yes-ter-day, yeast, yo-gurt).

Yodel!

Play a recording of yodeling. As the children notice the music, they may respond by dancing. They may also decide to try to yodel! You may want to point out that the word *yodel* begins with the letter Y.

☆ **Learning Extension:** Invite the children to try to yodel their names. You may need to demonstrate how to do this with your own name.

Language Activities

Share the Letter Y Rebus Rhyme

Y is for 🧶.
Y is for YIELD.
Y is for the 🐂 that eats in the field.

yarn   yield   yak

Share the Letter Y Rebus Rhyme (page 303) to develop a sense of rhythm and rhyme and to practice naming pictures. Show the display as you recite the rhyme several times. Afterwards, point to each picture on the chart and encourage the children to name it. Discuss each picture and invite the children to share times when they have seen similar items.

> ☆ *Learning Extension:* Talk about the letter Y. Look at all of the words on the display. Help the children locate the letter Y. Explain that the letter Y can be written more than one way. Point to the capital Y on the display and then point to the lowercase y. Help the children find all of the capital and lowercase letter Y's on the display.

Create Letter Y Rhyme Books

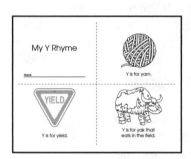

My Y Rhyme

Name

Y is for yarn.

YIELD

Y is for yield.

Y is for yak that eats in the field.

Give each child a copy of the Letter Y Rhyme Book (page 304) and crayons or markers. Invite the children to point to the pictures as you read the text. Encourage the children to decorate the pictures as desired. Cut along the dotted lines and stack the pages in order. Staple the pages together. Invite the children to write their names on the rhyme books. Assist the children as needed.

> ☆ *Learning Extension:* Invite a child to "read" his/her Letter Y Rhyme Book to you. Encourage the child to point to the letter Y in the book.

What Did You Do Yesterday?

As the children watch, print the word "Yesterday" at the top of a sheet of chart paper. Encourage the children to share their ideas about what the word *yesterday* means. Explain to the children that yesterday means the day before today, and mention that the word *yesterday* begins with the letter Y. Encourage the children to talk about something they did yesterday. Write each child's name and response on the chart paper. Afterwards, read all of the children's responses and then tell the children something that you did yesterday.

What's Yummy? What's Yucky?

As the children watch, title a sheet of chart paper "Yummy and Yucky." Invite the children to share their ideas about foods that taste yummy and foods that taste yucky. Write down the children's ideas as they talk about the different foods. Help the children notice that the words *yummy* and *yucky* both begin with the letter Y. After they finish, read the children's ideas back to them.

Yummy | Yucky

The Letter Y

296

© HighReach Learning® Inc.

Science Activities

Explore a Yardstick

Show the children a yardstick, and mention that the word *yardstick* begins with the letter Y. Invite the children to repeat the name and clap for the syllables (yard-stick). Pass the yardstick around and encourage the children to examine it. Some may notice and name some of the numerals on the yardstick. Explain that a yardstick is used for measuring. Encourage the children to look around the room and name some things they think are longer than a yardstick. Invite the children to take turns checking their predictions by holding the yardstick next to the items. Ask the children to name some things in the room they think are shorter than a yardstick. Encourage the children to check their predictions again. Challenge the children to look for something in the room that is exactly as long as a yardstick. Again, invite them check their predictions.

Make Yellowjackets Fly

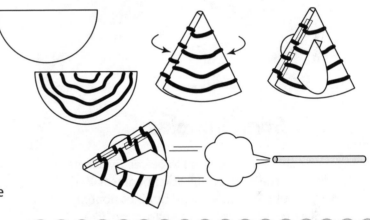

Cut assorted sizes of circles from yellow construction paper. Cut each circle in half. Make several of each size. Explain to the children that they are going to make yellowjackets and try to make them fly. Remind the children that yellowjackets are a type of wasp, and mention that the word *yellowjacket* begins with the letter Y. Invite the children to predict whether they think big yellowjackets or little yellowjackets will fly better. Encourage each child to choose a half circle of construction paper of the size he/she thinks will work best. Invite the children to use black crayons to draw stripes on the half circles. Help each child form the half circle into a cone as shown and secure with tape. Make sure the cone is completely sealed with tape except for the small hole at the end. Invite the children to cut wings from construction paper or tissue scraps and tape them to the yellowjackets. Once all the yellowjackets are ready, give each child a drinking straw. Have them insert the straws into the open ends of the cone shapes and blow as shown. Invite each child to try this several times. Afterwards, encourage the children to discuss which yellowjacket flew the highest and the farthest. Invite the children to suggest reasons for the results. You may also wish to encourage each child make another yellowjacket and see if it flies better than the first.

Graph Yogurt Preferences

Make a graph on chart paper with two columns and 15–20 rows. At the base of each column, draw a yogurt cup. Color one of the cups pink and the other cup blue. At the top of the graph print the question: Which yogurt is my favorite? Give each child two types of yogurt to taste, strawberry and blueberry. Show the children the graph and read the question at the top. Encourage the children to notice the letter Y in the word *yogurt*. Give each child a crayon or marker. Help the child put a mark in the column above the drawing of his/her favorite type of yogurt. The child may wish to write a letter, make a dot, or even write his/her name. When all of the children are finished, use the graph to help the children decide which type of yogurt they liked the best and which type they liked the least.

Which Yogurt is My Favorite?	
•	
•	
•	
•	•
•	•

Large Muscle Activities

Practice Doing Yoga

Locate a picture book about simple yoga exercises for children or look online for pictures of examples. Explain to the children that they are going to do some special exercises called yoga, and mention that the word *yoga* begins with the letter Y. Encourage the children to remove their shoes. Help the children try these exercises on exercise mats. Afterwards, encourage the children to talk about yoga. Did they like these exercises? Have they ever tried yoga before? When? Invite the children to share their experiences.

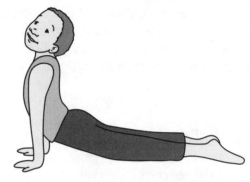

Sting Bubbles

Encourage the children to pretend to be yellowjackets, and mention that the word *yellowjacket* begins with the letter Y. Wave a bubble wand to send bubbles floating across the playground for the children to "sting" like yellowjackets with their fingers.

Move with Yellow

Invite each child to gather a yellow item from the classroom. Some examples may be blocks, toys, blankets, plush toys, etc. Invite the children to move their yellow items in different ways, such as the suggested directions listed below. Make sure to mention that the word *yellow* begins with the letter Y.

❖ Hold your yellow item behind your back
❖ Hold your yellow item over your head
❖ Put your yellow item under your foot

☆ *Learning Extension:* Use two-step directions such as those listed below for children that show readiness.

❖ Put your yellow item behind your back and then under your shirt
❖ Hold your yellow item in front of your nose and then put it on your head
❖ Hold your yellow item under your leg and then put it under your foot

The Letter Y
© HighReach Learning® Inc.

Art Activities

Make Yo-Yos

Show the children one or more toy yo-yos. Invite the children to explore the toys, and mention that the word *yo-yo* begins with the letter Y. Give each child two small paper plates. Invite the children to use crayons or markers to decorate the backs of the plates as they wish. You may want to mention that yo-yos come in many colors and styles, so not everyone's yo-yo will look the same. Encourage each child to glue or tape the plates together with the decorated sides showing and add a piece of yarn to the top.

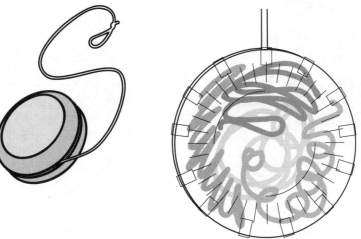

Make Letter Y Collages

Give a child old newspapers or magazines and scissors. Invite the child to search for the letter Y in the newspapers or magazines. The child may wish to tear or cut the letters out. Give the child a sheet of paper and a glue stick. Encourage the child to attach the letter Y cutouts to the paper as desired. Assist the child as needed.

☆ **Learning Extension:** If you are working with a group of children, invite them to work together to make one big letter Y collage. If you have bulletin board, butcher, or chart paper, you may even wish to cut the paper in the shape of the letter Y. Help the children locate and cut or tear out large examples of the letter from captions and headlines. Have the children glue all the letter cutouts to the paper.

Art Activities

Make Yummy Food Collages

Provide the children with large paper plates, food magazines, scissors, and glue. Encourage the children to find pictures of yummy foods, cut or tear them out, and glue them to their paper plates. As the children work, encourage them to talk about what they are creating, and mention that the word *yummy* begins with the letter Y.

Make Yellow Yarn Designs

Mix one part white school glue with one part water in a shallow dish. Give each child a piece of wax paper and a long piece of yellow yarn. Encourage the child to dip the yarn in the glue mixture and then arrange the wet yarn on the wax paper to create a design. Leave the yarn on the wax paper until the glue dries, and then peel it off. If desired, add an additional piece of yellow yarn to the creation for hanging. As the children work, mention that the words *yellow* and *yarn* both begin with the letter Y.

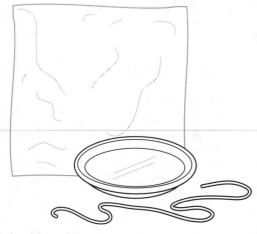

Create Tactile Letter Y's

Give each child a copy of the capital letter Y (p. 294), an old paintbrush, and a shallow dish of glue. Invite the children to trace the letter Y with their fingers. Encourage the children to spread glue on their letter Y's as desired. Provide the children with small bathroom cups filled with sand, salt, or snips of yarn. Invite the children to shake the sand, salt, or yarn snips onto the glue. As the children work, mention that the word yarn begins with the letter Y. Set aside to dry. After the glue dries, invite the children to trace their tactile letter Y's with their fingers. How does the Y feel? Use descriptive words such as bumpy, rough, etc. as you interact with the child.

The Letter Y

© HighReach Learning® Inc.

Small Muscle Activities

Homemade Yellow Playdough

Encourage the children to help you make homemade playdough using the recipe and directions listed below. As you make the yellow dough, help the children notice the color of the cornmeal, and mention that the word *yellow* begins with the letter Y.

1½ cups flour
1½ cups yellow cornmeal
1 cup salt
1 cup water
yellow food coloring

☆ *Learning Extension:*
Challenge the children to make letter Y's with their playdough. Encourage them to talk about how they might accomplish this task.

Mix all the dry ingredients in a bowl. Add yellow food coloring to the water and mix into the dry ingredients. Knead until pliable. Give each child some of the yellow playdough. Encourage the children to explore the dough and talk about their creations as they work.

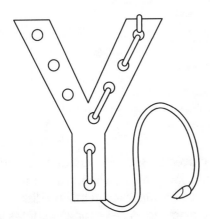

Explore Letter Y Lacing Cards

Draw several block letter Y's on posterboard using the pattern on page 294 and cut out. Use a hole punch to make a series of holes around each letter cutout. Vary the number of holes so that some will be easier to lace than others. Tie a length of yarn to one hole and wrap the free end with tape. Be sure the yarn can wrap around the letter twice. Set out the letter Y lacing cards. Assist the children as needed as they explore the lacing cards.

Explore Yo-Yos

Provide the children with a variety of yo-yos. Encourage them to try to yo-yo. You may have to demonstrate for them first. Be sure to provide close supervision as the children play, to prevent any accidents with the yo-yos. As the children play, mention that the word *yo-yo* begins with the letter Y.

© HighReach Learning® Inc.

The Letter Y

Cooking with Yorky Yellowjacket Letter Y Recipes

Yogurt Smoothies

1 (8 oz.) container plain yogurt
1 (6 oz.) can frozen orange juice concentrate, thawed
1 cup water
1½ tsp. vanilla
ice cubes

Place all ingredients except ice cubes in a blender. Process at high speed until smooth. Add enough ice cubes to raise the mixture to a 5-cup level. Process again until smooth. Makes 5 cups or ten small servings.

Yellow Cupcakes

1 cup flour
1 cup yellow cornmeal
2 Tbsp. sugar
4 tsp. baking powder
1 tsp. salt
1 cup milk
¼ cup oil
1 egg, beaten
butter

Preheat oven to 375°. Mix all of the ingredients except the butter together and fill cupcake tins. Bake for 20-25 minutes or until golden. Serve with butter spread on top.

Yellow Squash Casserole

4 cups sliced yellow squash
35 buttery round crackers, crushed
1 cup shredded cheddar cheese
2 eggs, beaten
¾ cup milk
¼ cup butter, melted
1 tsp. salt
2 Tbsp. butter

Preheat oven to 400°. Cook squash in a large skillet over medium heat with a small amount of water for about 5 minutes. Drain well and place in a large bowl. Mix together cracker crumbs and cheese in a separate bowl. Stir half of the cracker mix into the cooked squash. In another bowl, mix together eggs and milk, and then add to squash mixture. Stir in ¼ cup melted butter and add salt. Spread in a 9" x 13" baking dish. Sprinkle with remaining cracker mixture and dot with 2 tablespoons butter. Bake for 25 minutes or until lightly browned.

Yummy Yams

1 (40 oz.) can yams
1 (8 oz.) can crushed pineapple
marshmallows

Preheat oven to 350°. Encourage the children to mash the yams in a bowl, then add the pineapple with juice and stir. Place in baking dish and cover with marshmallows. Bake for 20 minutes and serve warm.

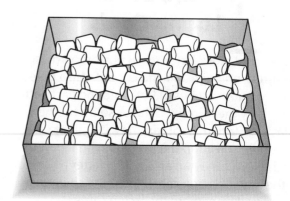

The Letter Y

302

© HighReach Learning® Inc.

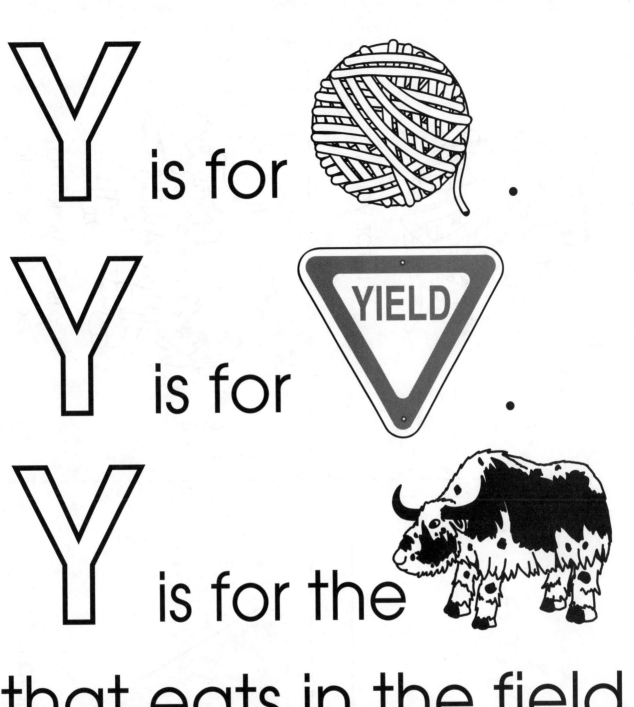

Y is for ⚪ .

Y is for YIELD .

Y is for the 🐃

that eats in the field.

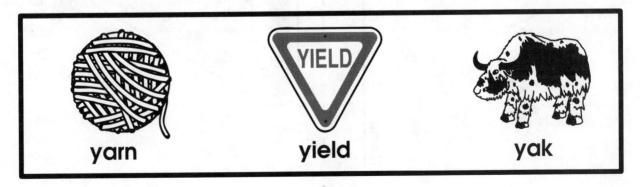

yarn   yield   yak

My Y Rhyme

Name _____

Y is for yarn.

Y is for yak that eats in the field.

Y is for yield.

The Letter Y

304

© HighReach Learning® Inc.

© HighReach Learning® Inc.

The Letter Z

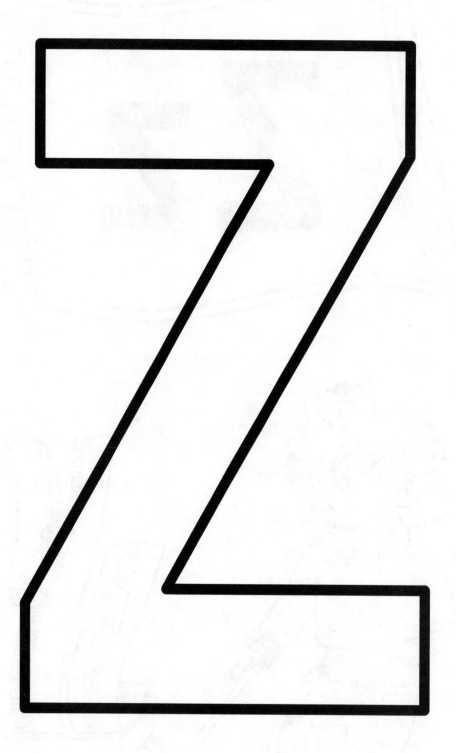

© HighReach Learning® Inc.

Language Activities
Introduce Zack Zebra and the Letter Z

Decorate a copy of the Letter Z Display (page 305) as desired. Point to Zack Zebra on the display. Invite the children to guess what type of animal Zack is. If necessary explain that Zack is a zebra. You may wish to share the rhyme below several times and invite the children to join in.

ZACK ZEBRA

Zack Zebra walks in zigzags
Everywhere he goes.
He likes to zip the zippers
In his wagon and on his clothes.

Invite the children to discuss what they learned about Zack in the rhyme. Invite the children to name what Zack is pulling in the wagon. Have the children ever seen a zebra before? Where? Do they know how to use zippers? Is it easy or hard to use zippers? Encourage the children to share their ideas and experiences.

Point to both the capital Z and the lowercase z on the display. Explain that these are both ways to write the letter. Explain that Zack likes the letter Z best because it is the first letter of his name. Help the children decide if they know anyone whose name begins with Z.

Talk About Letter Z Words

Invite the children to talk about words they know that begin with the letter Z. Write any suggestions down on sentence strips, a large sheet of paper, or chart paper. Attach the words to the wall at the children's eye level. Some familiar word suggestions are:

zebra	zither	zoom
zigzag	zipper	zucchini
zinnia	zoo	

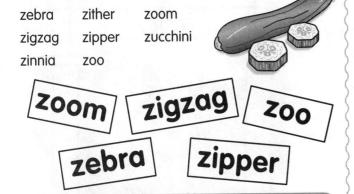

> ☆ **Learning Extension:** Invite the children to clap for the syllables of words that begin with the letter Z (zith-er, zoom, zuc-chi-ni).

Play a Zany Name Game

Explain to the children that you are going to play a name game. Say your name, but replace the first letter of your name with the letter Z. For example, if your name is Heather, your zany name would be Zeather. Recite the rhyme below and help each child decide how his/her name would sound if it began with Z. For example, a child named Jim would be Zim and a child named Kayla would be Zayla! Continue saying the rhyme until each child knows his/her zany letter Z name!

If your name began with Z,
How would it sound to you and me?

Language Activities

Share the Letter Z Rebus Rhyme

Share the Letter Z Rebus Rhyme (page 315) to develop a sense of rhythm and rhyme and to practice naming pictures. Show the display as you recite the rhyme several times. Afterwards, point to each picture on the chart and encourage the children to name it. Discuss each picture and invite the children to share times when they have seen similar items.

☆ *Learning Extension:* Talk about the letter Z. Look at all of the words on the display. Help the children locate the letter Z. Explain that the letter Z can be written more than one way. Point to the capital Z on the display and then point to the lowercase z. Help the children find all of the capital and lowercase letter Z's on the display.

Create Letter Z Rhyme Books

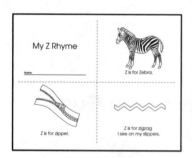

Give each child a copy of the Letter Z Rhyme Book (page 316) and crayons or markers. Invite the children to point to the pictures as you read the text. Encourage the children to decorate the pictures as desired. Cut along the dotted lines and stack the pages in order. Staple the pages together. Invite the children to write their names on the rhyme books. Assist the children as needed.

☆ *Learning Extension:* Invite a child to "read" his/her Letter Z Rhyme Book to you. Encourage the child to point to the letter Z in the book.

Who Lives at the Zoo?

Read the children a nonfiction book about the zoo. Encourage the children to share their ideas and any experiences they have had with the zoo. Make sure to expand the conversation based on what the children tell you and try to answer any questions they may have. Invite the children to talk about what types of animals live at the zoo. Help the children notice that the word *zoo* begins with the letter Z. Brainstorm a list of animals that live at the zoo and write down exactly what the children say. You may need to give suggestions such as zebras, lions, bears, tigers, seals, birds, snakes, etc. Some of the children may be familiar with the word *zebra*. You may wish to share that zebras are animals that sometimes live at the zoo, and mention that the word *zebra* begins with the letter Z.

The Letter Z

308

© HighReach Learning® Inc.

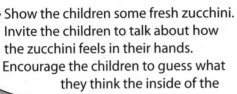

Science Activities

Explore Fresh Zucchini

Show the children some fresh zucchini. Invite the children to talk about how the zucchini feels in their hands. Encourage the children to guess what they think the inside of the zucchini looks like. Have any of the children ever tasted zucchini? Invite them to share their experiences. Away from the children, cut open the zucchini. Show the children the inside of the zucchini. What color is the inside? What does it look like? Are there seeds inside? Expand the conversation based on what the children tell you. During your discussion, you may wish to mention that the word *zucchini* begins with the letter Z.

☆ *Learning Extension:* Provide the children with a balance scale and a few different sizes of zucchini. Invite the children to explore the zucchini and the balance scale. Interact with the children as they explore. You may wish to ask questions such as the following examples. Which zucchini weighs the most? How can you tell? Can you find two that weigh the same? How do you know? Assist the children in discovering the answers to the questions as needed.

Make String Zingers

Use the tip of a knife (away from the children) to make a small slit in the bottom of a large plastic picnic cup for each child. Tie a paper clip to the end of a string, push the paper clip through the slit, and turn it so that it lies flat against the inside of the bottom of the cup. Secure the clip with masking tape. Wet the string with water. Hold the cup in one hand and firmly grasp the wet string between the thumb and forefinger of the other hand, starting just below the bottom of the cup. Pull your fingers down the string. What happens? The string zingers should make some very interesting sounds!

Who Has a Zipper?

Who has a zipper? Encourage the children to look at their clothing and see whether or not they are wearing zippers. Help the children notice that the word *zipper* begins with the letter Z. Invite all the children who have zippers to form one line and all the children without zippers to form another line. Help the children to decide if there are more children with zippers or without. Encourage the children to suggest strategies to find out. For example, the children might suggest counting the number in each line and comparing. The children may also decide to bring the lines side by side, pair off, and see which line has children left.

☆ *Learning Extension:* Encourage the children to use two different types of string, such as thread and yarn, to make the zingers. Invite the children to compare the sounds each type of string makes. Do they sound different or alike?

© HighReach Learning® Inc.

The Letter Z

Large Muscle Activities

Walk Along a Zigzag Path

Make a zigzag path around the playground or classroom. Mark the path with chalk or masking tape. Encourage the children to zoom along the zigzag path. As the children move along the path, mention that the words *zoom* and *zigzag* both begin with the letter Z.

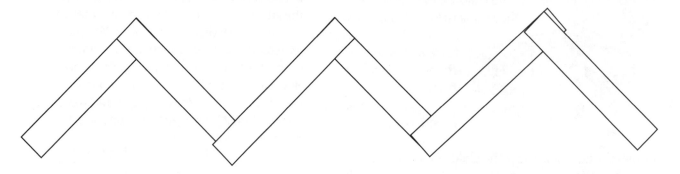

Play the Zebra Says

Explain to the children that you are going to pretend to be a zebra and give directions on how to move in different ways. Some examples are galloping, or even zipping or zooming. After the children understand the concept of the game, invite one child at a time to be the zebra and lead the group in different movements. As the children play, mention that the word *zebra* begins with the letter Z.

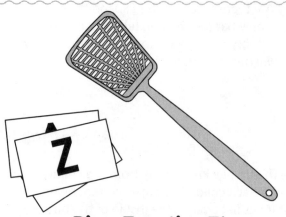

Play Zap the Z!

Print the letters A–Z on index cards. Encourage the children to sit in a circle. Spread out the letter cards faceup in the center of the circle. Sing the traditional alphabet song and pass a clean, unused flyswatter around the circle. When the children reach the letter Z in the song, the child holding the flyswatter should stand up, find the letter Z index card, and zap it by swatting it with the flyswatter. Repeat the game several times, rearranging the cards so that the letter Z is in a new location each time a new round is played.

☆*Learning Extension:* As you play the game, invite the children to zap the letter Z and then find and zap the first letter in their names.

The Letter Z

310

© HighReach Learning® Inc.

Art Activities

Create Tactile Letter Z's

Give each child a copy of the capital letter Z (page 306), an old paintbrush, and a shallow dish of glue. Invite the children to trace the letter Z with their fingers. Encourage the children to spread glue on their letter Z's as desired. Provide the children with small bathroom cups filled with sand, salt, or rice. Invite the children to shake the sand, salt, or rice onto the glue. Set aside to dry. After the glue dries, invite the children to trace their tactile letter Z's with their fingers. How does the Z feel? Use descriptive words such as bumpy, rough, etc. as you interact with the child.

Make Zipper Rubbings

Collect a variety of old zippers. A good source would be a thrift shop. You can often find used garments there for less than the cost of a new zipper. Simply cut the zippers from the garments. Show the children several zippers, and mention that the word *zipper* begins with the letter Z. Encourage the children to explore the zippers. Explain to the children that they can use the zippers to make rubbings. Give each child a sheet of plain white paper. Show the children how to lay the paper on top of a zipper and rub over it with an unwrapped crayon. Invite the children to try the same technique. The children may choose to unzip the zippers part of the way or all the way, and others may decide to have the zippers zipped. Encourage the children to be creative.

Zigzag Pictures

If the children are unfamiliar with the term *zigzag*, draw a few zigzag lines on a sheet of paper to demonstrate. Provide the children with crayons, markers, paper, and masking tape. Help the children tear off pieces off masking tape to create zigzag lines on their papers. After they finish, encourage them to decorate their zigzags with the crayons or markers as desired.

© HighReach Learning® Inc.

The Letter Z

Art Activities

Create Zinnias

Explain to the children that there is a pretty flower called a zinnia, and mention that the word *zinnia* begins with the letter Z. If possible, show the children a picture of a zinnia or a real plant. Provide the children with white paper, crayons or markers, glue, and assorted colors of art tissue. Encourage the children to create colorful zinnias using the materials. Assist the children as needed, and encourage them to talk about their pictures as they create.

☆ *Learning Extension:* After the children finish, write "Z is for zinnia" on an index card for each child. Use a highlighter for each letter Z and crayons for the other letters. Encourage the child to name each letter Z, try to trace it, and then attach the card to the back of his/her picture.

Make Zebra Masks

Prepare a paper plate mask for each child from a heavy-duty paper plate. Cut eyeholes and trim the sides as shown to make the shape resemble a zebra's face. Provide the children with the prepared paper plates. Encourage each child to cut or tear two ears from white construction paper and glue them to the mask. Help each child glue some snips of black yarn to the mask for the mane. Provide cotton swabs and black paint and encourage the children to paint stripes on the masks. When the paint dries, help each child tape a wide craft stick to the back of the bottom edge of the mask to create a handle. Invite the children to hold their masks in front of their faces as they pretend to be zebras.

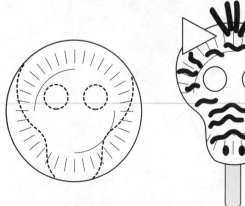

Make Letter Z Collages

Give a child old newspapers or magazines and scissors. Invite the child to search for the letter Z in the newspapers or magazines. The child may wish to tear or cut the letters out. Give the child a sheet of paper and a glue stick. Encourage the child to attach the letter Z cutouts to the paper as desired. Assist the child as needed.

☆ *Learning Extension:* If you are working with a group of children, invite them to work together to make one big letter Z collage. If you have bulletin board, butcher, or chart paper, you may even wish to cut the paper in the shape of the letter Z. Help the children locate and cut or tear out large examples of the letter from captions and headlines. Have the children glue all the letter cutouts to the paper.

The Letter Z

© HighReach Learning® Inc.

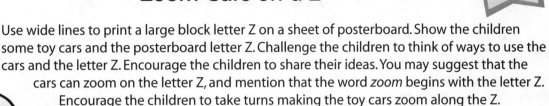

Small Muscle Activities

Zoom Cars on a Z

Use wide lines to print a large block letter Z on a sheet of posterboard. Show the children some toy cars and the posterboard letter Z. Challenge the children to think of ways to use the cars and the letter Z. Encourage the children to share their ideas. You may suggest that the cars can zoom on the letter Z, and mention that the word *zoom* begins with the letter Z. Encourage the children to take turns making the toy cars zoom along the Z.

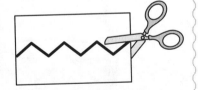

Explore Letter Z Lacing Cards

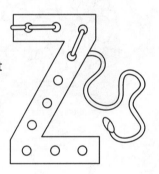

Draw several block letter Z's on posterboard using the pattern on page 306 and cut out. Use a hole punch to make a series of holes around each letter cutout. Vary the number of holes so that some will be easier to lace than others. Tie a length of yarn to one hole and wrap the free end with tape. Be sure the yarn can wrap around the letter twice. Set out the letter Z lacing cards. Assist the children as needed as they explore the lacing cards.

Cut Along Zigzag Lines

Draw bold zigzag lines on several index cards. Provide the children with the zigzag index cards and scissors. Invite the children to practice cutting the zigzag lines, and give assistance as needed. As the children work, mention that they are cutting zigzag lines, and that the word *zigzag* begins with the letter Z.

☆ *Learning Extension:* Invite the children to draw their own zigzag lines on construction paper. Challenge the children to cut along their zigzags!

Make a Zither

Explain to the children that a zither is a musical instrument that has strings, and it is played by plucking the strings with your fingers. To help the children become familiar with this concept, make a pretend zither from a shoe box. Slip several rubber bands over the box and have the children pluck the rubber bands with their fingers. As they explore, mention that the word *zither* begins with the letter Z.

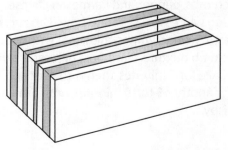

Cooking with Zack Zebra
Letter Z Recipes

ZESTY POPCORN

¼ cup butter, melted
1 bag microwave popcorn
1 envelope powdered ranch dressing mix

In a large bowl, have children drizzle butter over hot popped popcorn. Sprinkle powdered ranch salad dressing mix over popcorn and toss. Serve in individual cups or bowls.

ZEBRA CAKE

1 (9 oz.) package chocolate wafers
2 cups whipped topping

Dab ½ teaspoon of whipped topping on each wafer. Stack wafers together on a serving plate to make a log about 14 inches long. Frost the log with the remaining whipped topping and roll in plastic wrap. Freeze for 4 to 6 hours. Let thaw for one hour before serving. Cut the log at a 45 degree angle to see the zebra stripes.

BAKED ZUCCHINI CHIPS

2 medium zucchini, cut into ¼ inch slices
½ cup seasoned dry breadcrumbs
⅛ tsp. ground black pepper
2 Tbsp. grated Parmesan cheese
2 egg whites

Preheat oven to 475°. Stir together the breadcrumbs, pepper, and Parmesan cheese. Place egg whites in a separate bowl. Dip zucchini slices into the egg whites, then coat with the breadcrumb mixture. Place on a greased baking sheet. Bake for 5 minutes, then turn over and bake for another 5 to 10 minutes, until browned and crispy.

Z

Z is for 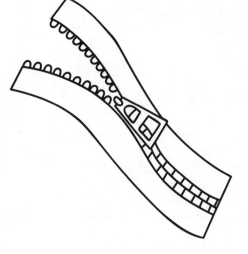.

Z is for .

Z is for ⟋⟍⟋⟍⟋⟍I

See on my slippers.

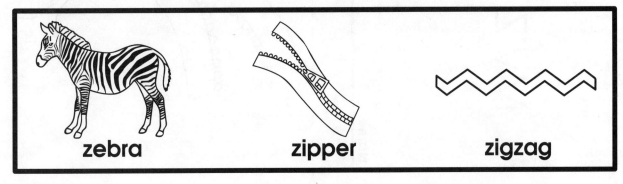

zebra   zipper   zigzag

© HighReach Learning® Inc.

The Letter Z

My Z Rhyme

Name

Z is for Zebra.

Z is for zigzag
I see on my slippers.

Z is for zipper.

© HighReach Learning® Inc.

Anytime Alphabet Activities

Classroom Alphabet Parade

Invite the children to make flags to carry in a parade by using the reproducible displays for each letter located throughout this resource book. Invite the children to choose the letter displays they would like to decorate. After they decorate the letter displays, help the children attach the letter displays to sheets of construction paper. Then help the children roll newspaper tightly and secure with masking tape to make a handle. Tape the construction paper to the handle. Invite a child holding the letter A to pull a wagon and lead the parade. The others can follow in alphabetical order, holding their flags. As they march, they can sing the song below, substituting the appropriate letter name and Alphabet Friend for A and Alvin.

THE ALPHABET PARADE
(tune: "Old MacDonald")

Here comes the alphabet parade.
Everybody march!
Here comes the alphabet parade.
Everybody march!
Here's the letter A,
Here's the letter A.
Letter A, letter A,
Alvin likes the letter A.
Here comes the alphabet parade.
Everybody march!

Sensory Letters

Fill several large zipper-top bags with sand, flour, or shaving cream. Fold the tops over and secure with packing tape. Encourage the children to practice writing letters on the outside of the bag with their fingers. Each material offers a unique sensory experience and a "no mistakes" way to practice writing skills.

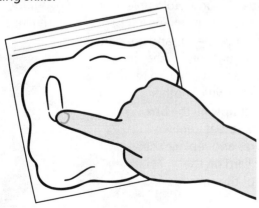

Letter Rubbings

Cut large block-style letters from sandpaper using the reproducible patterns from this resource book and glue each on a sheet of paper. Encourage a child to choose a letter and clip it to a clipboard. Help the child clip a plain sheet of white paper over the sandpaper letter and rub over it with the side of an unwrapped crayon. The letter will be revealed on the child's paper. Repeat with assorted letters, or for as long as the child shows interest.

© HighReach Learning® Inc.

Alphabet Review

Anytime Alphabet Activities

Playdough Letters

Encourage the children to shape letters with playdough. You may need to demonstrate how to do this, and assist the children as needed. Once they get really good at this, they may even want to make their full names with playdough letters!

☆ *Learning Extension:* Provide the children with alphabet cookie cutters, toy rolling pins, and playdough. Encourage the children that show readiness to try to find the letters in their names.

Alphabet Books

Alphabet books are available with a wide variety of themes. Whenever you begin a new theme, be sure to check out one or more alphabet books related to the topics you will discuss. Share the books often and encourage the children to try to name the first letters of words throughout the books.

Alphabet Caterpillar

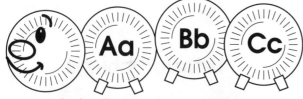

Gather 27 small paper plates. Decorate one to make a caterpillar head. Label each of the other plates with a capital and lowercase letter pair (Aa–Zz). Attach construction paper legs to the base of each plate. Encourage the children to line up the plates in order on the floor to make a big caterpillar.

Beep for Beginning Sounds

Draw and color a side view of a car on posterboard, cover with clear contact paper, and attach to the side of a box. Print any capital and lowercase letter pair on an index card and attach it with a loop of tape to the door of the car. Place items or pictures of items that begin with the letter in the box. Add a few that do not begin with the letter. Locate a small bicycle horn or similar horn that beeps. Work with one child at a time to practice identifying beginning sounds of words. Hold up each item. Encourage the child to name it, decide if it begins with the letter on the door of the car, and beep the horn if it does. If not, then he/she must keep the horn quiet. To repeat the game with another letter, simply fill the box with different items or pictures and replace the letter card on the door of the car.

Alphabet Review

318

© HighReach Learning® Inc.

Anytime Alphabet Activities

Letter Walk

Take the children on a walk around the neighborhood. Be sure to have plenty of adult supervision. As you walk together, encourage the children to find and name letters on street signs, mailboxes, storefronts, and other places.

Looking at Logos

Collect several logos from fast food restaurants, stores, and other local businesses that are attractive to the children in your group. Place the logos in a photo album with self-adhesive pages. Often some of the first letters children recognize are the letters found on logos for their favorite restaurants or stores. Look at the logos with the children and encourage them to identify each. Name the letters in each logo. As the children become familiar with the letters, encourage them to point out letters they recognize.

Mystery Letters

When you are focusing on a particular letter, use white crayons to write examples of the letter on several sheets of white paper. Provide the children with the prepared papers along with watercolor paints. As the children paint on the papers, encourage them to describe what happens! What letters appear on their papers?

Alphabet Magnets

Encourage the children to explore alphabet magnets on a magnet board or other magnetic surface, such as a refrigerator or file cabinet. They may want to sort the letters in different ways, arrange them to make their names, or use them in other ways. If you do not have magnetic letters available, you can make your own set of capital and lowercase letters by following the directions below.

1. Mix together 4 cups flour, 1 cup salt, and 2 cups water.
2. Roll out mixture on a smooth floured surface with a rolling pin.
3. Cut out 52 equal circles using a film canister, two-liter bottle cap, or another small round cutter.
4. Bake for one hour at 350°.
5. Allow to cool. Paint 26 a light color and 26 using a different light color.
6. Allow to dry. Use a nontoxic black permanent marker to print capital letters A–Z on one color.
7. Use the marker to print lowercase letters a–z on the other color.
8. To make the letters shiny, coat each with white school glue and let dry.
9. Attach a small magnet or strip of self-adhesive magnetic tape to the back of each letter.

© HighReach Learning® Inc.

Alphabet Review

I Know the Alphabet!

_____

(name)

© HighReach Learning® Inc.